The Sands of Oxus

Sadriddin Aini in 1925

Bibliotheca Iranica
Literature Series No. 6

The Sands of Oxus

Boyhood Reminiscences of Sadriddin Aini

CঙৎD

Translated from the Tajik Persian
with an introduction and notes
by

John R. Perry and Rachel Lehr

MAZDA PUBLISHERS
1998

For a list of volumes published in this series, see page 277

Mazda Publishers
Academic Publishers Since 1980
P.O. Box 2603
Costa Mesa, California 92626 U.S.A.
www.mazdapub.com

Library of Congress Cataloging-in-Publication Data
Aĭnī, Sadriddin, 1878-1954.
[Ёddoshtho. Qismi 1. English]
The Sands of Oxus: Boyhood Reminiscences of Saddriddin Aĭnī/
Translated from the Tajik Persian with an introduction
and notes by John R. Perry and Rachel Lehr
Translation of Ёddoshtho, pt. 1.
p.cm.—(Bibliotheca Iranica: Literature Series; No. 6)
Includes bibliographical references.

ISBN:1-56859-078-4
(alk. paper)

1. Aĭnī, Sadriddin, 1878-1954—Childhood and youth. 2. Authors,
Tajik—20th Century—Biography.
I. Perry, John R. II. Lehr, Rachel, 1945-   . III. Title. IV. Series
PK6978.9.A36Z464213 1998
891'.578—dc21
98-39882
CIP

Contents

Illustrations

Acknowledgements

The main body of this translation was completed with the help of a grant from the National Endowment for the Humanities, awarded to John Perry during 1984-85. He would like to thank the various friends and colleagues whose subsequent input helped to improve the translation or its presentation, in particular Edward Allworth, Jeffrey Brooks, Michael Christiana,, Adeeb Khalid and Ranjana Patnaik.

Rachel Lehr wishes to thank Kim Mueser for initiating her part of the project, and Dodojon Tojiev of the Tajikistan State University for helping her understand Tajik traditions. She would also like to acknowledge grants she received from IREX and Fulbright-Hays to study in Tajikistan in 1981-82, without which she would not have begun this translation.

We are grateful to Dr. Kamoliddin Aini and the Aini International Foundation in Dushanbe for permission to reproduce unique photographs (frontispiece and figs. 1-4, 7-10) from his *Kornomayi Aini* (*Book of the Life of Sadriddin Aini,* Dushanbe 1978); and to David King for kindly providing a photograph from the King Collection (fig. 5).

This year marks the 120th anniversary of the birth of Sadriddin Aini. To all our Tajik and other Turkestani friends who, wittingly or unwittingly, have contributed to our appreciation of their culture, we wish long life, peace and prosperity.

July 1998

Introduction

The sands of Oxus, toilsome though they be,
Beneath my feet were soft as silk to me . . .

Rudaki

The autobiography of Sadriddin Aini is a modern classic of Tajik literature. During most of the period in which the Soviet Union was the only viable matrix for the cultural expression of its "captive nations," Aini's oeuvre—written in the traditional Perso-Arabic script of his homeland, but published in the Russian Cyrillic alphabet adapted to his variety of Central Asian Persian—was classifiable only among the fringe phenomena of twentieth-century Russian literature, and known abroad only through indirect translations from the Russian. With the devolution of the USSR, it can take its rightful place among the monuments of modern Persian literature, which looks back on a thousand years' heritage and beyond the frontiers of Iran, Afghanistan, India and Central Asia to a growing diaspora in Europe and America.

Aini (1878-1954), trained amid the medieval cloisters of a Bukhara madrasa (religious college), used his talents in the service of reform and revolution, fictionalizing his youthful memories for critical and didactic effect even before he recorded them in factual form. They thus evoke aspects of Maxim Gorky and Mark Twain, reflecting both the realities of a traditional society under imperial Russian rule on the eve of the Revolution and the moral awakening of an intelligent boy whose adoptive brother is the son of a slave. In the Soviet Union of yesterday, Aini had attained the status of an exemplary hero among the Soviet nationalities, the founder of modern Tajik literature and one of the leaders of the cultural revolution in Uzbekistan and Central Asia at large. A part of his autobiography (our Appendix II) was incorporated in translation in the Russian school curriculum, and the whole of this heroic success-story inspired a generation of Central Asian writers

to adapt Gorky's exemplification of Socialist Realism to the needs
of their own nascent literatures. Criticized by the Stalinist establishment in 1938 and later, he was nevertheless spared the full
force of the purges that effectively silenced so many of his
contemporaries; and despite a flurry of revisionist writing in the
wake of Tajikistan's independence (1992), he has remained
secure on his pedestal.

Sadriddin was born on 15 April 1878 in Soktaré, a village to
the north-east of Bukhara, in what is now the republic of Uzbekistan. It was then a part of the emirate of Bukhara, reduced to
vassalage by imperial Russia only a decade before. He was the son
of a small farmer and part-time carpenter, Sayid-Murod Khoja,
who had studied briefly at a madrasa in Bukhara city, and taught
his son to read and write. From the age of twelve Sadriddin
himself moved to Bukhara to study, and for the next sixteen years
(1890 to 1906) worked his way through several of the madrasas,
acquiring a traditional education in the Arabic and Persian classics
and the Islamic sciences. In 1894 his first poems appeared in
lithographed editions, and in 1895, in accordance with the usage
of classical Persian poets, he adopted the pseudonym Aini (*'aynî*:
"original, genuine," amongst other meanings), which became in
effect his surname.

Disillusioned with the trite, traditional curriculum and the hy-
pocrisy of many of his clerical colleagues, Aini taught himself
about the modern world by reading secular books and liberal
imported newspapers—an activity forbidden by the emir
—together with a group of like-minded fellow students. With the
turn of the century, Aini's poetry began to desert the conventional
lyrical-mystical vein of Classical Persian verse for themes of social
protest. From 1907 he taught at one of the New Method (*usull-i
jadid*) schools introduced in Central Asia by Tatar reformists and
joined a reformist movement of liberal Uzbek and Tajik intellectuals, the Young Bukharans (*Yosh Bukhorlilar*).[1]

In 1917, revolution and civil war swept through Russia and her
Central Asian possessions. The emir, with the support of his
imperial overlords, closed the Jadid schools and had Aini and
several of his associates imprisoned and flogged. Rescued by a
band of Russian revolutionary troops, he fled to Samarkand in
Russian Turkestan and turned to journalism, helping to orchestrate

[1] See Bečka, *Sadriddin Aini, Father of Modern Tajik Culture*, pp. 17-19;
Medlin *et al.*, p. 48ff., esp. the New Method madrasa syllabus on p. 51.

the propaganda campaign mounted by the Communist Party against the emir's regime. In 1920 the emir was toppled; Aini married and settled in Samarkand, was elected a member of the Central Executive Committee of the Bukhara People's Soviet Republic in 1923, and from the next year devoted himself full-time to literary activities. From 1926 to 1933, as adviser to the Tajik Publishing House in Samarkand, he endorsed the change from the Arabic to the Latin alphabet, helped establish a new written style of Central Asian Persian ("modern literary Tajik") both in theory and by the precept of his own prose output, and generally supervised the early stages of Soviet Tajik writing and translation. His own oeuvre includes four novels (the first of their genre in Tajik), a half-dozen shorter fictional and quasi-historical works, a Tajik dictionary, the first Uzbek children's book, and numerous poems, scholarly monographs and articles, journalistic and propaganda essays, editions, translations, and anthologies.[2]

Honors and political responsibilities barely kept pace with his productivity. He became a member of the Central Executive Committee of the Tajik SSR (established in 1929), was awarded the Red Flag of Labor in 1931 and a Republic annuity in 1933. In 1934 he was elected president of the newly established Writers' Union of Tajikistan, and in 1951 became the first president of the Tajikistan Academy of Sciences. In the Soviet Union at large, Leningrad State University conferred upon him an honorary doctorate in 1948, and in 1949 he was decorated with the Order of Lenin. In the same year he began work on his autobiography, receiving a Stalin Prize for the first two parts in 1950. In spring of 1954, already ill, he moved from Samarkand to Dushanbe, capital of the Tajik Republic, where he died on 15 July, aged eighty-six.

* * *

Such in superficial outline is the career of a culture-hero of our time.[3] In subjecting it to a closer examination and attempting to

---

[2] See the Bibliography, and the Introductions to Appendixes I and II. An extensive bibliography is to be found in Bečka, *Sadriddin Ayni*, pp. 106-8; Aini's collected works in Tajik (*Kulliyot*) run into 13 volumes.

[3] Aini's own concise autobiography (*Mukhtasari tarjimai holi khudam*, "Pages From My Own Story"), his daughter Kholida's *Zhizn' Sadriddina Aini* and Bečka's *Sadriddin Aini* are the main sources for this summary.

establish a critical yet sympathetic assessment of Aini's life and works, we run a number of clear risks. Ideologies and attitudes on all sides of the conventional barriers to understanding, be they East or West, Left or Right, have run the gamut of conceivable variation during this short and bitter century, to end up every bit as barbed and bigoted as before. Just how "original" or "genuine" was Aini? And how do we know?

The most obvious area of obfuscation is the chameleon-like Soviet culture in which Aini came of age and by which his achievements were celebrated. Even the casual reader will have noticed that Soviet-era photographs were routinely, and openly, "touched up" by hand—a practice that was not solely necessitated by the poor technical quality of Russian equipment, and one that continues even in post-Soviet publications, long after it has been abandoned in the rest of the world. Soviet writing was likewise "improved" with the heavy outlines and bold colors of decreed propaganda: not only the official puffery of anonymous Party hacks, but every published statement of "personal" experience or opinion (since there were ideally no private persons, only units of the communist collective) had to apply this cosmetic layer, or submit to its application. A Czech scholar (and, incidentally, biographer of Aini), speaking of the new cultural revolution in Tajikistan at a conference in western Germany, after the debacle of the USSR, feels thus constrained to excuse any embarrassing contradictions in his earlier publications: "You must understand that at that time I was writing in an isolated country ruled by a patently unpleasant ideology, about the literature of a country even worse off in this respect."[4]

Compounding the effects of Sovietization is the rose-tinted Orientalist or Sovietologist view of the pre-modern principalities of Muslim Central Asia, tending as it did to focus on the culturally brilliant and relatively enlightened High Timurid period from Ulugh Beg to Husayn Baiqara (1447-1506), ignoring the savagery of Timur's campaigns that preceded it and the decadent tyrannies that followed it. Aini's account of the cynical theft of the peasants' livestock by the Uzbek emir and his clerical underlings (Chapter 14) is perhaps selected and exaggerated in accordance with his socialist consciousness; but a Western scholar's picture of enlightened Uzbek courtiers, masters of three literary languages,

---

[4] Jiří Bečka, "Zentralasien im Umbruch: aktuelle kulturelle Entwicklungen in Tadschikistan," *Archív Orientální* 62/3 (1994), p. 153.

poetry, philosophy and music (a generalization from the case of one personality explicitly described by Aini as the exception, not the rule)[5] is similarly one-sided, the obverse of the Soviet cliché of contented peasants singing in the cotton-fields. The balance of truth undoubtedly lies somewhere in between. With the fall of the Soviet empire, however, and the rise of ethnic and ideological antagonisms, truths have increased in quantity and polarization: Turkic chauvinism and Tajik irredentism, neo-Communism and Islamic extremism now compete to rewrite the history of Aini's world. It is time for him to tell it again.

If he is to tell it to English readers through the medium of English, his words should not be further filtered through Russian. Existing English translations of Aini's reminiscences—all at second hand, from Russian translations—are not only selective and abridged, but often jarringly distorted by the translators' slavish reproduction of the inadequate Russian transcription of Tajik names, misunderstanding of the Russian orientalists' notes, and ignorance of Tajik culture. Thus every khoja is turned into a hajji (as Ibrohim Khoja becomes "Hadji Ibragim"), Sayyid into Sa'îd ("Saïd"), wooden mill-wheels into millstones.

At the personal level of the autobiography, we are confronted by a traditional and rigidly-ordained society, especially in the realm of the family and the private life of the individual. This has fostered a reticence behind the public persona that poses difficulties for both biography and translation. Before the advent of Soviet socialism, Central Asian women were segregated in public and secluded at home from the male domain of the house, the *mehmonkhona*, where interaction with outsiders took place. The family was a hierarchy: family members usually addressed each other, and referred to each other, not by name but by kinship term, and while the senior members used the familiar forms of address, children addressed their parents and younger siblings addressed older ones with the formal pronouns and verb forms. These features were—and are—typical of traditional Asiatic societies, whether Muslim or not. After Communism altered much of the external character of society, the attitudes born of this were still slow to change, even among intellectuals and self-proclaimed revolutionaries. Thus Aini himself, in his concise (but chronologically complete) autobiography, tells us nothing about his own wife and children.

---

[5] Allworth, *Central Asia*, pp. 351, 354-5.

Figure 1. Aini in the hospital at Kagan after his release
from the emir's prison in 1917

Nevertheless, let us risk a sympathetic expansion of the unvarnished biodata presented above, bearing in mind these critical caveats—but not to the degree that they paralyze all common sense.

Aini was born in a rural backwater of a land where material standards of living had not changed appreciably in more than a thousand years, and where most aspects of cultural life had declined since the last great efflorescence of Irano-Islamic art, literature, and science under the Timurids four centuries before. He not only taught himself to take advantage of whatever traditional lore had survived, but transcended what for many another like him had become a mere sinecure. Not content to become a village mullah and batten on the superstitions of his people (cf. Author's Introduction, last page), or even to remain a respected scholar and teacher in Bukhara, he chose the unpopular and dangerous course of Tatar-inspired educational reform and, ultimately, of Russian-imported socialist revolution. The long-overdue political and socioeconomic upheaval would certainly have happened without him; but the resurgence of a national Persian literature in the land whence it had first sprung, and the sometimes strange new courses in which not only Tajik but also the Turkic literatures of Central Asia now flow, are in large part due to Aini's transitional influence as the *mirob* of the written word in the Pamirs and the Oxus basin.

Aini's life is in itself an allegory of the dizzyingly rapid changes that in a single generation have swept many regions of Muslim Asia (not only within the Soviet realm) from the Middle Ages into the twentieth century. Like other seminal writers of his generation elsewhere in the region (such as Taha Husayn in Egypt, or Muhammad-Ali Jamalzadeh in Iran), Aini was conscious of this opportunity and freely exploited his childhood memoirs to illustrate the social attitudes, moral convictions, and literary predilections of his maturity. Such idealization by hindsight is perhaps an inevitable concomitant of autobiography: in life, the child may be father of the man, but the man who sets out to record this process risks fathering more on the child than it could have conceived at the time. Dramatic satisfaction and a virtually seamless integration into the narrative generally serve to justify the set pieces and contrived dialogues which punctuate Aini's memoirs. Such are the episode where, at the age of no more than ten, he puts to shame a much older but poorly-educated madrasa student who has beaten all comers at the Nawruz wrestling match (end of Appendix II), and his artisan uncle's defense of a simple but honest laborer against the disdain of a village aristocrat and teacher (Chapter 12). This didactic embellishment of life and legend lies firmly within traditions of Persian literature that antedate Islam and are to be seen at their most sophisticated in the works of the thirteenth century poet and moralist Sa'di, whose homiletics Aini admired from early childhood.

Yet the greater part of Aini's earlier memoirs is artless description and unforced narrative that unconsciously tells us much about the man behind the teacher and the unchanging, unchangeable aspects of the land and society in which he grew up. Earlier and more fundamental than the Tajiks' role in the intellectual and literary life of the region was their contribution (strictly, that of their predecessors, including the Sogdians) to its material culture, notably the elaborate systems of irrigation without which the oases of the arid Oxus basin could not have supported an extensive civilization. Aini the boy farmer is at his most lyrical when surveying the spring greenery and animal vitality of his home village of Soktaré, sited on an arterial canal fed by the Zarafshon river (beginning of Appendix I), and at his most poignant in describing the devastation of crops and homes wrought by the encroaching desert sands near his winter residence of Mahallai Bolo (Chapters 4-5). Aini the nascent socialist is most scathing in his depiction of man's inhumanities where injustice involves the land and the water (Chapters 13-14, 28).

By the nineteenth century the originally nomadic, pastoral Turks of the Oxus Basin had largely become sedentary farmers, · competing with and to a great extent supplanting their Tajik subjects. Their ruling families, notably the emirs of Bukhara (who, like the Ottoman sultans, styled themselves *pâdshâh* in the manner of Persian monarchs), were naturally the biggest landowners, not only deriving a large part of their revenues from rents on crown lands (*amlok*) and taxes on all other properties, but extorting free labor for their residences and girls for their harems from among their tenants (Chapters 14, 28). They formed the top of a feudal pyramid, at the bottom of which labored landless sharecroppers and journeyman artisans who were often tied to their employers by self-renewing "loans." Aini describes the lot of the sharecropper both indirectly, by means of a folktale (Chapter 7), and as contemporary history (Chapter 28); and that of the artisans ironically, in the words of their "benefactor" (Chapter 19).

*   *   *

Such extracts from Aini's reminiscences as have hitherto been translated into western languages (indirectly, from Russian) have focussed on his student days in Bukhara city. These afford more extensive insights into the cultural life of urban Central Asia and more dramatic episodes as the young Aini's social conscience is jolted awake. But it is to his boyhood in the countryside that we owe an account of the earliest formative influences on his character and a picture of the day-to-day existence of the farmers and rural artisans who made up the majority of the emir's subjects.

The odds against Aini's physical survival and intellectual growth were weighted against him from the outset. As late as 1928 a Russian doctor in Bukhara estimated that only forty percent of children lived to be fifteen, and only 4.3 percent to be sixty.[6] In 1889 when he was eleven, both Aini's parents died in a cholera epidemic (he survived a bout himself in Bukhara four years later). Virtually single-handedly he nursed his three sick brothers back to health, harvested and sold their produce, and finally their house, to pay off debts incurred by the funerals and support his surviving family (Chapters 25-27, 29); for this he resigned himself to forgoing his dream of following his elder brother to study at a madrasa in Bukhara, of which he had sampled briefly (Chapter 22). For meanwhile, encouraged by his father, he had acquired a taste for learning, and especially for poetry. His misadventures at the village boys' school (*maktab*) and subsequently at the girls' school and under the tuition of his snobbish cousin Sayid-Akbar Khoja (Chapters 15-17 and Appendix II) only increased his determination to pursue higher studies. Salvation came in a chance encounter with an enlightened young Bukhara intellectual, Sharifjon Makhdum; impressed with the boy's precocious poetic talent, he persuaded Aini's elder brother and the latter's teacher to help send him to Bukhara (Chapter 29).

The madrasas, some thirty of which are mentioned in Aini's reminiscences, were the proud relics of those centers of Islamic learning that had reached their zenith in Nishapur and Baghdad during the twelfth century and to which the medieval European university is arguably indebted. They in turn may have evolved out of the north Indian *vihara*, the Buddhist seminary, exemplars of which flourished in pre-Islamic Bukhara and from which the

---

[6] Bečka, *Sadriddin Aini*, p. 14.

city may have derived its name.[7] Formerly a vigorous corporate intellectual endeavor, the madrasa had by this time degenerated into little more than a factory for government functionaries of the emirate, most of whom—in Aini's estimation—regarded the prose and poetry of secular humanism (of which Persian was the primary vehicle) with suspicion, and all ideas outside their own narrow definition of the realm of Sunni Islam with overt hostility.[8]

The saving grace of traditional Islamic education, even in decline, was its egalitarian nature: a brilliant boy (not, normally, a girl) who survived the *maktab* would find no social barriers to his entering a madrasa. Aini persevered, working as a servant in various madrasas and in the home of Sharifjon Makhdum, known by his pen-name of Sadri Ziyo, who in 1898 bought him a cell in the Qukaltosh madrasa—cramped, windowless, and with a door so low that he had to stoop to enter or leave.[9]

By this time Aini had gained recognition as a poet. This brought with it a new kind of threat that, in subtly different forms, was to hang over him for the rest of his life. Creative writing was, and was to remain, inseparable from political patronage. The emir Abdul-Ahad, who fancied himself as a Maecenas, claimed first

---

[7] See Frye, esp. pp. 8-9, 132; Bečka, "Traditional Schools II," p. 130. This word also surfaces in the Persian phrase *bahâr-e chin*, generally translated as "Chinese temple"—a byword for beauty and tranquility.

[8] Aini gives examples in the second part of his Reminiscences, where madrasa teachers and students regard studying Russian, or even wearing "Russian" (actually, Tatar) shoes to be heretical, and madrasa teachers are depicted as hating their colleague Ahmad Donish for his scientific study of astronomy (*Bukhara*, pp. 27-37). For a generally more sanguine view of the state of traditional learning in the Bukhara emirate during the late nineteenth century, see Allworth, *Central Asia*, pp. 349-56.

[9] The Qukaltosh madrasa, built in 1578 by a younger brother of the ruler Abdullah Khan Shaybani, was one of the largest and best in Bukhara: it boasted 160 residential cells and a rich library. This period of Aini's life, including the episode described below, is recounted in the third part of his Reminiscences. As Sirjani points out in his introduction to the Persian recension of *Yoddoshtho* (xxix-xxx), Aini does not acknowledge his benefactor by name; since Sharifjon had been appointed chief kadi of Bukhara shortly before the emir's fall, he was in Soviet eyes tarred with the same brush as his predecessors, and Aini did not judge it politic to praise him. (See also Sadri Ziyo in the Glossary.)

right to any new talent in his domains: Aini was summoned by the *rais* and "invited" to compose a eulogy of the *pâdshâh* and deliver it at the court in Karmana, some seventy miles north-east of Bukhara. He steadfastly refused, pleading sickness. Finally one of his former teachers brought from the chief kadi a direct threat of imprisonment if he refused, and he compromised to the extent of sending the emir a suitable eulogy every week or two. But instead of frequenting the best Bukhara circles, as absentee courtiers were supposed to, he sought out the society of bazaar carters, and after six months was quietly dropped from the roster of court poets.

Aini's verses up to about the turn of the century were in the traditional lyrical style, derivative of Hafiz, Sa'di, and Bedil. But from about the time of his interview with the *rais* notes of social and political criticism could be heard: his poem *Dahyak* (Ten percent) of 1903 excoriates the loan shark, a figure Aini was to treat at length in his novella *Margi suldkhuir* (Death of the Moneylender, 1939); his celebrated *Zaminro boyad nafurulshed* (You must not sell your land) of 1909, on a similar theme, is no longer merely cynically descriptive but rebelliously prescriptive, particularly since it was first published at the end of his school textbook (see below).[10]

Aini was absorbing several new influences and channeling them into his writing. In Bukhara itself there was the polymath Ahmad Donish, whose autobiographical *Navodir ul-vaqoye'* (Remarkable Events; ca. 1880) included an appreciation of his experiences in the Russian capital and a criticism of the methods of madrasa teaching—by implication an indictment of the emir's regime and the whole social and political order it upheld. From outside the emirate came the fictional travelogue *Siyâhatnâma-yi Ibrâhîm Beg* by Zayn ul-'Âbidîn Marâgha'î (three volumes, ca. 1902-1909), similarly castigating the backwardness of Qajar Iran, and various liberal newspapers and magazines in Persian and Turkish that were published in Calcutta, Istanbul and Bagh-chesaray in the Crimea, and circulated clandestinely in Iran and the Central Asian khanates.[11]

---

[10] Aini's poetry is to be found in Vol. 8 of his collected works (*Kulliyot*; Dushanbe, 1981).

[11] See Bennigsen and Lemercier-Quelquejay, esp. pp. 168-9, 272. Bukhara's first newspaper was *Bukhoroyi Sharif* (Bukhara the Noble, a conventional epithet of the city; from 1912). Aini's first newspaper articles were

In 1907 Aini found an active outlet for his inchoate reform-
ism. Within the preceding decade, groups of Tatar intellectuals,
determined to train an educated bourgeoisie of their own in order
to compete with Russia and the rest of the Christian west, had set
up schools at which secular subjects such as mathematics, geogra-
phy, bookkeeping, hygiene, and foreign languages were taught
with western methods of pedagogy. This movement, known as the
usûl-i jadîd ("New Method"), was regarded by the conservative
clergy as a challenge to the madrasa and an affront to Islam.
Nevertheless, it found ready converts in Central Asia, even among
some liberal mullahs. Working at the Jadid school as a Tajik
interpreter, Aini was enabled to learn at first hand the new curriculum and teaching methods. Together with his boyhood friend
Abdul-Vohid Munzim (Chapter 29) he soon founded his own
school, to which poor parents could send their sons free of charge.
In 1909 he compiled the first Tajik primary school textbook and
reader to include secular subjects, *Tahzib us-sibyon* (Cultivation of
the Young). He was to remain active in the Jadid movement and
the Young Bukharans society until the outbreak of the First World
War, when the Russians, seeing the Jadids as an arm of the Pan-
Islamic and Pan-Turkish pretensions of their Ottoman enemy,
turned a blind eye as the emir and his clerical establishment closed
down all Jadid schools.

In 1915 Aini left Bukhara for a time and worked at a cotton-
ginning plant in Russian Turkestan; this experience provided him
with material for his first novel, *Odina* (1926), subtitled "The
Fortunes of a Poor Tajik." In 1916, when he was thirty-eight and
a figure of some consequence in literary and educational circles,
the emir sought to muzzle him with an appointment as a professor
(*mudarris*) at one of the most prestigious Bukhara madrasas; Aini
diplomatically accepted the post *pro forma*, but did not take up
office—to the satisfaction of his colleagues, who divided his salary
among themselves.

In August 1918, after Aini's escape to Samarkand, the emir
rounded up several suspected revolutionaries, including Sadriddin's younger brother, Sirojiddin, who died in the same dungeon
from which his elder brother had barely escaped. Aini's grief was
expressed in a *marsiya*, a traditional poetic elegy; but in content

---

published in the socialist weekly *Shu'lai inqilob* (Flame of the Revolution;
from 1919) of Samarkand, which became the organ of the Communist Party
of Samarkand and may be considered the precursor of the Soviet Tajik press.

this was an unrestrained indictment of the Bukhara regime. Sentenced to death in absentia by the Bukharan clergy, Aini was also shunned by the mullahs of Samarkand.

In the same month the Communist Party of Turkestan was formed, and began to fund, staff, coordinate, and finally to control the several secret organizations working to overthrow the emir. Early in 1919 a nervous breakdown forced Aini to give up his teaching at the Jadid school in Samarkand; he immediately plunged into journalism, contributing to both Tajik and Uzbek revolutionary journals which were now organs of the Communist Party, and spent a month in Tashkent preparing speeches and other propaganda to be used in the Bukhara campaign. In 1920 Bukhara was secured when the leftist faction of the Young Bukharans gained control of the movement and called on the help of the Red Army under Frunze; the emir fled to Tajikistan and subsequently took refuge in Afghanistan.[12] Two years later the last member of Aini's family — his elder brother, Muhyiddin — was killed by a band of Basmachis.

* * *

Any of the personal injuries Aini suffered — the murders of his brothers, and his own near death at the hands of the "butchers of Bukhara" (as he called the emir's overworked executioners in his *Jallodoni Bukhoro* of 1922) — would have been sufficient cause for him to join the avenging ranks of the Bolsheviks. More likely, sober observation that the Muslim masses were politically inert, and the conviction that a minority of liberal reformists alone was powerless against the unenlightened self-interest of the emir's regime, persuaded him to desert the waning fortunes of the Jadids. Tragically, there was now no middle ground. The Muslim masses, fearful for their religion and traditions, joined the conservative élite, anxious to preserve their privileges, in a resistance that lasted until 1926 in the form of guerrilla raids by the Basmachis. Liberal educated Muslims like Aini either cooperated with the Russian revolutionaries, and were thus damned in popular eyes, or temporized too long and were retrospectively damned in the eyes of the Soviets.[13] But there were also cultural reasons why Aini — as a Tajik, and a Muslim, who had still not joined the Party in

---

[12] See Rakowska-Harmstone, pp. 22-3.

[13] Ibid., pp. 21-2; and cf. note 9 above, concerning Sharifjon Makhdum.

1931—judged at this stage that the Communists were the most sensible option for himself and for the future of Central Asia.

The Jadid experiment was a cultural outgrowth of a broader political movement, pan-Turkism, centered at Kazan and Istanbul. For a Tajik writer the threat of being swamped in a homogenized Turkish ocean—or even beached by a recrudescent Uzbek nationalism riding in the wake of pan-Turkist imperialism—was not to be ignored, any more than the obvious political threat could be ignored by the infant Soviet state. Sure enough, by 1927 Jadidism, which had earlier been hailed by the Bolsheviks as a progressive movement, was deemed reactionary, and Aini was criticized for his sympathetic portrayal of the Young Bukharans in his Uzbek-language *Materials for the History of Bukhara*, published in 1926.[14] In his 1930 novel *Dokhunda* (The Highlander) he put into his hero's mouth a contemptuous dismissal of the Jadids' cautious educational reforms as providing unwitting support for a revitalized emirate, and later formally renounced his Jadidist past.

In one field, however—that of Tajik national and cultural identity --he refused to compromise. Extremists among his Uzbek nationalist colleagues dismissed Tajiks as either originally Turks, who had been Persianized by the madrasa-reared élite of the emirate, or Iranians who had been Uzbekized so thoroughly that they should now hold their peace. His answer was the literary history and anthology *Namunai adabiyoti tojik* (Representative Sample of Tajik Literature), written in 1925, which linked contemporary Tajik language, literature and culture to its thousand-year-old roots in the Classical Persian of Samanid times. Tajikistan was still merely an autonomous republic within the Uzbek SSR; the book was actually banned by the Party in Uzbekistan, and only published a year later, in Moscow, after the intercession of Russian orientalists.[15] Nevertheless, Aini never became a mere Tajik chauvinist: he remained an Uzbek writer as well, careful to stress the cultural interdependence of the two peoples. His novel *Qullar* (Slaves, 1934) was first published in Uzbek, a year before the Tajik version, *Ghulomon*. He assisted in the rehabilitation of the fifteenth-century Chaghatay poet Navâ'i (a victim of the discredited nationalists' adulation) with a monograph in 1948.[16]

---

[14] Allworth, *Uzbek Literary Politics*, pp. 59-60.

[15] Bečka, *Sadriddin Aini*, pp. 26, 39.

[16] See Allworth, *Uzbek Literary Politics*, pp. 81-2, 85.

The next in the series of threats to Aini's artistic and personal survival came, indirectly, from his most famous contemporary. Also a member of an Asiatic ethnic minority of the Russian empire, who likewise had his early training in a theological seminary and graduated to journalism, who was born twenty months after Aini and died one year before him, this was Joseph Jugashvili, known as Stalin, the "Man of Steel." Dushanbe, the capital of Tajikistan, was renamed Stalinabad between 1929 and 1961, and both the political and the cultural tentacles of his dictatorship reached into Central Asia in the 1930s. As the Tajik representative, Aini in 1932 helped organize the first congress of the Union of Soviet Writers; two years later he attended this meeting in Moscow, where he was elected to the board and met Maxim Gorky, the father of socialist realism. This philosophy was officially ordained for all Soviet artists; enforced in Central Asia by means of "Bolshevik criticism," it served to identify victims for the purge of 1937-38. Like many another, Aini survived by joining in the chorus of stereotyped vituperation against "enemies of the people . . . traitors to their country . . . spies of capitalist governments . . . fascist hirelings;"[17] though he did not stoop either to individual denunciation of colleagues or personal panegyric to the new *pâdshâh*.

Aini himself was declared an "enemy of the people" during 1937-38, and his works were removed from some library catalogues.[18] As late as 1952 he was accused of a serious ideological error for his edition of a work attributed to the Indo-Persian poet Amir Khusrau, the *Chahor darvesh* (Four Dervishes; in Vol. 11 (1951) of Aini's collected works), which he called in his introduction "one of the most appealing and important national monuments." The Party criticized it as depicting religious fanaticism and debauchery.

Aini was what today would be called a workoholic: despite being elected to and appointed to offices in writer's unions, academies, committees, city soviets, the Supreme Soviet—all of which he took seriously—he wrote regularly for up to twelve

---

[17] Ibid., pp. 79-80 and note 1, 133; cf. Bečka, *Sadriddin Aini*, pp. 39-40, 42.

[18] Examples of diatribes against Aini and other Tajik writers in the press during 1937-38 are given in Kamâl al-din 'Aini, *"To ahl-e dânesh o fazli, hamin gonâhat bas," Central Asia and the Caucasus Review* Vol. 4, No. 11 (Fall 1995/1374), pp. 143-4.

hours a day, with pen and inkpot. When he fell ill in 1952, he complained at having to cut down his writing schedule to eight hours a day. At the same time, he was no recluse; visitors were welcome wherever he lived. In October 1920 he married Salohat-Begim, the daughter of the late Domullo Mahmud, a madrasa teacher of Samarkand. He was still too poor to afford his own house, and lived for over two years in the home of his mother-in-law; this lady liked him especially because he wore the traditional robes and turban of a madrasa mullah. He had two children, a son, Kamoliddin, and a daughter, Kholida, both of whom followed in his footsteps as academics.

Despite his being an oasis Tajik, foreign to Dushanbe, Aini was apparently genuinely liked and respected as president of the Tajikistan Academy of Sciences, a post he held from 1951 until his death. His status protected not only him, but probably many of his colleagues accused of deviations during Stalin's reign, from more than verbal criticism.[19] An even more solid knot in this safety-net was the historian Bobojon Ghafurov, who somehow managed to stay in Stalin's good books throughout his tenure as First Secretary of the Party of Tajikistan (1946-56; he served subsequently as director of the Oriental Studies Institute until his death in 1977). He and Aini, more than any other Tajik scholars and writers, succeeded by a judicious combination of steadfastness and compliance in preserving a sense of national and cultural identity during the most restrictive and destructive years of Stalinism. Aini did not live to see the rehabilitation of the nationalists in 1956.

*   *   *

Aini's dedication to the Tajik cause, and at the same time his aptitude for creative compromise, are shown in his contribution to the Tajik language and its study. Before evaluating this, we should briefly broach a question that is not so straightforward as it seems: What is the Tajik language?

From at least the sixteenth century, Persian speakers of Iran, Afghanistan and Central Asia—as distinct from speakers of Turkish—were often referred to as *Tâjîk*, a word probably derived from *Tâzî*, the earlier Persian term for "Arab" and originally connoting "Muslim." This epithet was then applied especially to

---

[19] Rakowska-Harmstone, pp. 264-5.

the Persians of northeastern Afghanistan and the Oxus basin, where they were most intermingled with Turks. First the southward expansion of Turks (Uzbeks and Turkmen), then the stabilization of national frontiers, drove a wedge between the Persians of the Iranian plateau and those of the northeast. With the dialect continuum broken, spoken Persian of Samarkand, Bukhara and (to a lesser extent) southern Tajikistan developed quite separately from that of Iran, incorporating some Uzbek vocabulary and idioms. The written Persian of the east, however (as used not only by Tajiks but by the Uzbek and Indian Mugal élite in administration and serious literature, especially poetry) remained essentially identical with that of Iran for much longer. The spoken dialects, though increasingly divergent from the written norm, were nevertheless included under the blanket term "Persian" (*pârsî, fârsî*). There was no such language as "Tajik" before about 1925.

By 1925, the Bolsheviks had determined that Central Asia was to be divided up into national republics named for the dominant ethnos and presumably speaking the corresponding ethnic language (since such was then the simplistic, Eurocentric definition of a nation). These languages, moreover, were to be the tools of the Soviet proletariat, not of the vanquished élite: Uzbek, Tajik, Kirghiz, etc. were to be stripped of their Arabic vocabulary and Classical Persian idioms—and the alphabet that went with these—and enriched by means of Russian borrowings and calques. This would facilitate the education of a native proletariat and administrative cadres. Only then would these tongues of a backward, feudal culture become vehicles of modern Soviet socialist literature. Local intellectuals—including Aini—who were drafted into codifying and promoting the decreed language, having no simple designation other than "Persian," referred to it first as "the language of the Tajiks" (*zabân-i tâjîk*), a phrase which is still used; only gradually did they take the small morphological step which is a considerable semantic leap, to the optional *zabân-i tâjîkî* (or, in the "Tajik" orthography, *zaboni tojikī*) "the Tajik language; Tajik." Aini himself coined the terms *zaboni forsu-tojik* and *forsii-tojikī* "Tajik Persian," underlining his belief that the national language still did, and should, belong to the Persian linguistic and literary community.

In a series of articles published in the journal *Ovozi tojik* (The Tajik Voice) in 1926-27, Aini contrasted the current state of Iranian Persian, which by his calculation contained 60-70 percent

Arabic loanwords in its lexicon, with the "simpler and purer" Tajik. The comparison is of course unfair: literary Persian bureaucratese and journalese before the language reform of the late 1930s and 1940s was indeed syntactically convoluted and highly Arabicized, but so was the Persian prose of Ahmad Donish and the emir's secretariat. What Aini meant by "Tajik" was the spoken tongue and the written reflexes of this, polished lightly with madrasa Persian, in which he and his immediate colleagues sought to educate and arouse the newly literate—an embryonic literary language. On a practical level, Aini in his own writings both preserved old Tajik terms in use among traditional artisans and farmers (many appear in the Glossary) and coined new ones for items and concepts introduced in the twentieth century (e.g., *zarfi garmukhunuk-nigohdoranda*, lit. "hot-and-cold-keeping flask," since replaced by the prosaic *termos*). Stylistically he is still considered a model, and works of his both in Tajik and in Uzbek are subjects of linguistic research for a new generation of Tajik scholars.

The cultural dilemma of early Soviet Tajik writers was stated in political terms: should they adopt the Persian of Iran (the major literary dialect) and fulfill their international revolutionary obligation to spread Lenin's word abroad, or should they work to adapt the speech of their own people as a literary language, the better to teach and reform at home? The answer was never in doubt, and was not so much an anticipation of Stalin's policy of "socialism in one country" as a life-or-death necessity for Tajik identity: the Uzbek ultranationalist wing was ever ready to abolish this pocket of Persian culture.

In the preface to his pioneering Tajik dictionary, compiled in 1936-38 and published as Volume 12 (1976) of his Collected Works, Aini the pragmatist expressed the conviction that the new Tajik, with its roots in Persian but already owing much to Uzbek, would also borrow increasingly from Russia—a prediction that has since been proved correct. He did not, however, include any Russian vocabulary in the body of the work, despite the urgings of his Russian orientalist friend Y. E. Bertel's that he "touch up" the work for appearance's sake; as a result, his dictionary languished unpublished for thirty-eight years.[20] At the first Tajik language conference, held at Dushanbe on 22 August 1930, Aini was a staunch advocate of the modified Latin alphabet that in 1927 had

---

[20] Kamâl al-din 'Aini, *"To ahl-e dânesh o fazli,"* pp. 139-42.

been proposed for the languages of Soviet Muslim Asia and was to be used for the next decade. At a language planning conference in 1938, however, he objected strongly (and successfully) to the proposal to abolish from literary Tajik the postposition *-ro* (Persian *-râ*; used to mark the direct object, among other functions).

In 1939 a decree from Moscow replaced the Latin orthography of Tajik with a modified Russian alphabet, ostensibly to facilitate the learning of Russian. In the wake of the recent purges of "bourgeois nationalists," what little discussion there was of this sudden change took the form of praise for Stalin's genius and an endorsement of the alleged petitions of the workers for the new alphabet.[21] Aini's reaction is not recorded. He was now too old to learn Russian well, and continued to use Arabic script for Tajik and Uzbek to the end of his life.

To return to our initial question: What is Tajik—or rather, what was the Tajik of this contradictory scholar, poet and storyteller who was so devoted to it? For it must be noted that Tajik has been changing dramatically in the last decade. Gorbachev's *perestroika* and *glasnost'* unleashed a wave of language legislation throughout the USSR, an attempt to secure official status for the titular republic languages against Russian (which had come to dominate in all public domains) before the impending breakup of the union. Tajikistan was the first Soviet republic in Central Asia to pass a language law in 1989, which was redrafted as that of an independent country in 1992. By the terms of this, the government is committed to replacing Russian (and Russianisms in Tajik) for all official use, and to reverting to Perso-Arabic script in due course. Despite the slow rate of these changes (due to financial difficulties and conservative foot-dragging), the language is in fact changing before our eyes, if not yet in our ears.[22] A short sample of vernacular Tajik as incorporated by Aini in "The Village School" is appended to this introduction.

*   *   *

Yoddosht'ho is a many-faceted work, not easily categorized. There are antecedents in eastern Islamic literature for the autobiographi-

---

[21] *Gazetai muallimon* (Stalinabad, weekly) 1939, 18 April, p. 4; 14 July, p. 5; 2 Oct., p. 4.

[22] See Perry, "From Persian to Tajik to Persian."

cal *Bildungsroman*, or narrative of personal experience and growth: Avicenna (d. 1037) and al-Ghazâli (d. 1111) each left an *apologia pro vita sua* in Arabic. From Central Asia comes the Persian *Badoye' ul-vaqoye'* of the sixteenth-century writer Vosifi (Vâsefi), which Aini abstracted and edited (Vol. 13 of his Collected Works), and the similarly-titled work of Ahmad Donish. But these works take little or no note of the author's childhood experiences, and Aini himself acknowledges only Maxim Gorky (1868-1936) as an inspiration for his own Reminiscences, as well as for much else in his literary evolution: specifically, his simplicity of style, heroic characters, and use of folklore (cf. Chapters 6-7 and 23).[23]

The importance of the first volume of *Yoddosht'ho* as a document of the socioeconomic background and recent history of Central Asia can be seen in many of the chapter references given above. It is a valuable record not only for the Western student of traditional Muslim Asian society but for his counterpart in the Middle East and especially in modern Central Asia, which has seen much of what Aini describes here swept away or transformed in the course of a single generation. Its additional merits as a story, a repository of folk literature and lore, and an intellectual odyssey, will emerge from the text itself.

As the last of Aini's oeuvre, *Yoddosht'ho* is written in his most mature style and in a language that, while it can be elegantly archaic for effect, is consciously Tajik and no longer merely a vernacularizing of madrasa Persian. One lexical index of this is the change in form of the frequently-occurring word for "story": usually *hikoyat* (as in literary Persian) in Aini's earlier works, it is most often realized as *hikoya* (the vernacular, and now standard, Tajik form) in his Reminiscences. One syntactic index is Aini's invariably preposing reported speech before the verb of speaking (cf. the paragraph from *Maktabi kuÌhna* above), a feature of Uzbek Turkish assimilated by Tajik that is entirely contrary to literary Persian usage.

Considering that he had first to invent a viable language, Aini's range of expression, no less than his range of genres, is impressive. Never a mere propagandist, he contrives to involve the reader in his indignation, grief, joy, or mockery. Even in his early "Butchers of Bukhara" (1922) his deadpan, clinical description

[23] *"Omūzishi man az Maksim Gor'kii,"* in *Aknun navbati qalamast*, Vol. 1, pp. 308-9.

of the efforts of the emir's executioners to fulfill their quota more efficiently during the pogrom against the Jadids—from slitting throats as the victims are laid with their heads protruding over the edge of a trench, to garrotting them against the gallows pulley (ironically described as the "New Method" of executing Jadids)—anticipates Solzhenytsin's *Gulag Archipelago*.

Aini's avowed debt to Gorky, whose childhood memoirs he discovered soon after writing the "Butchers of Bukhara," may well be the lip-service of a dutiful Soviet writer. However, it is bolstered by a remarkable coincidence of life and art. Each is an orphan, a potential victim of his society, who glories in overcoming the barbarity of his milieu and acquiring the skills and sensibility of a writer. Gorky's three books of reminiscences take him from the age of five (ca. 1873) into his thirties (ca. 1901); the first opens with a dramatic triple rite of passage—the death of his father and, on the same day, the birth and death of his brother. Aini's four books, stretching from his sixth to his twenty-sixth year (1884-1905), begin with the sharply-etched memory of his own rite of passage, his circumcision. Each is a self-conscious (not to say self-righteous) autodidact: Gorky's third book, "My Universities," ironically alludes to the fact that he was denied entrance to the tsarist university of Kazan, while Aini—in Chapters 15-17, in "The Village School" and throughout the account of his madrasa years—points out with grim humor, and ill-concealed professional indignation, the shortcomings of an antiquated schooling.

Each, however, puts his own psychological and stylistic stamp on his boyhood reminiscences. Aini, though like Gorky more concerned with the world about him than with his personal progress, is less reticent about his emotions and relationships. Where Gorky's irony is outspokenly bitter (the better to accord with his pseudonym), Aini's—in the Persian tradition—is often sugared with humor.

Each was one of the few established writers of pre-revolutionary Russia to survive and flourish into the Soviet period, and each produced as his magnum opus a panoramic, multi-volume novel (*Klim Samgin*; *Ghulomon*) of social conditions in the last decades of the Russian empire. Each found by 1930 that fame had its price—an uncomplaining support for Stalin's orthodoxies—and paid. In Aini's case, and that of many another intellectual from the Asiatic backwaters of the Russian empire, the new regime was infinitely better in promise and initial achievement than anything he or his forefathers had ever experienced. The nationalities policy, with its cultural bureaucracy for each ethnic enclave, was an instant gratification of both personal and national aspirations. When the Russian soldier flung open the gate of the emir's dungeon in 1917 and called, in a mixture of Russian and Uzbek, "Come out! The Russian Revolution has freed you!"[24] nothing on earth could have induced Aini to stay.

The one person who stands out as the first and most forceful influence on his life and thought is, not unnaturally, his father, whose stern didactic tone punctuates the fun and games of his earliest recollections. Sayid-Murod's proprieties, however, are not those of conventional religious observance and class consciousness, but of practical sympathy and tough-minded social conscience, coupled with an angry anti-clericalism and anti-authoritarianism. Brusque and outspoken, incapable of dissimulation, he was temperamentally more suited to the role of revolutionary than his son. Though the child's conscience was molded by his uncompromising father (Chapter 21), a more practical role model for his later years seems to have been his equally open-minded and sympathetic (but more tactful and diplomatic) uncle, Usto Amak (Chapter 11). His good-humored irony is the tone most often adopted by Aini in his attempts to make sense of a society that he had always suspected was badly skewed. A more remote figure whom Aini clearly emulated is the classical Persian poet Sa'di. Likewise an orphan, later a refugee, always a shrewd observer and sly satirist of the human comedy of medieval Islam, "Shaykh" Sa'di was the subject of two of Aini's scholarly publications, and his verses are appealed to at several crucial points in our narrative (e.g., in Chapter 9 and Appendix I). Sa'di was a firm believer that, in this imperfect world, white lies and prudent dissimulation did not necessarily compromise true goodness and integrity.

*   *   *

The body of this translation comprises the first part of Aini's unfinished four-part autobiography, *Yoddosht'ho* (Reminiscences), subtitled "In the Country," which describes his boyhood spent in two villages near Bukhara up until his twelfth year. Appendix I, a fictionalized presentation of materials that would

---

[24] Aini, *Mukhtasari tarjimai holi khudam*, p. 84.

later appear in Chapter 9 of his Reminiscences, is an account of the young Aini's encounter with, and conquest of, local superstition and popular magic; it includes an episode from his later adolescence as a student in Bukhara. Appendix II, similarly presaging Chapters 15-17, is a description of his primary education, set chiefly in a traditional village Koran school (*maktab*). Chapter numbers have been supplied in Reminiscences; section numbers in the Appendixes are original (with two extra added to "The Village School"). Aini's original footnotes are distinguished by the addition of "—A." We have not supplied running page references to the originals, since pagination differs in the various editions of Aini's works, and in any case most sections are fairly short.

Aini takes the house as his opening metaphor in the quatrain with which he introduces *Yoddosht'ho*. His own houses in Samarkand and Dushanbe, where he spent his last years, were turned into museums; the work he wrote in them is also a museum, not only of Sadriddin Aini's life and works but of the land and the era that formed him. It is, moreover, a declaration of personal and communal revolution for a traditional Muslim, even a writer, to open up his walled and segregated home to the public, and a rare privilege for the reader to be invited into the inner courtyard.

*   *   *

In order to demonstrate the basic characteristics of Tajik—the Cyrillic writing system with six extra letters modified by a hook, slash or superscript, the sound patterns and grammatical structure and, for Persian speakers, the ways in which it differs from the Persian of Iran—we append here an analysis of a short paragraph of Aini's prose taken from Appendix II, "The Village School." The "prayers" referred to are written as charms on scraps of paper, to be dissolved in water and drunk as a cure. Aini is reproducing the direct speech of an uneducated village woman, so this is not to be seen as fully representative of his general narrative style (though it is quite close). The reader will notice immediately how speech precedes the verb of saying, and how adverbials are frequently expressed by "serial verbs" such as *burda dodan* "carry-give," i.e., "take for/deliver to" someone.

A. Modern Tajik Text

1. Ман аз роҳи дур, аз Обкена омадам,-гуфт он зан.-маро
2. ҳамсояамон Шарофбой, ки занаш зоида натавониста
3. дарди сахт кашида истодааст, як танга дода барои дуои
4. кушоиш фиристоданӣ шуд, занҳои ҳамсоягони дигар
5. ҳам ки ҳар кадом дардманд будаанд, барои дардҳои худ
6. дуо фармуданд ва «ҳар вақт пул ёбем назри домуллоро
7. медиҳем, бурда медиҳӣ» гуфтанд. Ман ҳам аз барои
8. савоб ба ин қадар роҳ пои пиёда хеста омадам...-Кадоми
9. ин дуоҳо ба кадом дард аст?-гуфта он зан пурсид.

B. Phonemic Transcription

1. *man az rohi dur, az obkena omadam, guft on zan. maro*
2. *hamsoya-amon šarofboy, ki zanaš zoyida natavonista,*
3. *dardi saxt kašida istoda-ast, yak tanga doda baroyi duoyi*
4. *kušoyiš firistodaní šud, zanhoyi hamsoyagoni digar*
5. *ham ki har kadom dardmand buda-and, baroyi dardhoyi xud*
6. *duo farmudand va har vaqt pul yobem nazri domulloro*
7. *medihem, burda medihí guftand. man ham az baroyi*
8. *savob ba in qadar roh poyi piyoda xesta omadam...–kadomi*
9. *in duoho ba kadom dard ast? gufta on zan pursid.*

C. Word-for-Word Gloss

1. I from way-far, from Âbgina came, said that woman. Me-to
2. neighbor-our Sharâfbây who wife-his borne not-been-able
3. pain-severe drawn has-stood, one *tanga* given for prayer-of
4. solution about-to-send he-became, women-neighbor-other
5. too who each-which suffering they-have-been, for pains-of self
6. prayer they-ordered and "Any time money we-find alms-of
master
7. we-give, taken you-give," they-said. I also from-for [spiritual]
8. reward by this much way on-foot risen I-came. . .—Which-of
9. this prayers to which pain is? having-said that woman she-
asked.

D. Persian Transcription

١. ‏من از جای دور، از اَبَگینه اَمدم ـ گفت اَن زن. مرا

٢. ‏همسایه مان شراف بای که زنش زائیده نتوانسته

٣. ‏درد سخت کشیده ایستاده است یك تنگه داده برای دعای

٤. ‏کشایش فرستادنی شد، زنهای همسایگان دیگر

٥. ‏هم که هر کدام دردمند بوده اند برای دردهای خود

٦. ‏دعا فرمودند و "هر وقت پول یابیم نذر داملارا

٧. ‏میدهیم، برده میدهی" گفتند. من از برای

٨. ‏ثواب باین قدر راه پای پیاده خیسته اَمدم. . . ـکدام

٩. ‏این دعاها بکدام درد است؟ ـ گفته اَن زن پرسید.

E. Idiomatic Translation

"I've come all the way from Âbgina," the woman said. "My neighbor, Sharof-boi's wife, can't deliver her baby and is in great pain. He gave me a *tanga* and sent me for a childbirth prayer. My other neighbors' wives all have various pains and asked me to bring back prayers for them too, and said they'd send you the money as soon as they could. I've come all this way on foot to do a good deed . . . –Which prayer is for which pain?" she asked.

NOTES: Cyrillic **o** represents a Tajik vowel more rounded than the Persian /â/, closer to Russian **o**. The letter **и** after a vowel has the value /yi/, but in most other positions is equivalent to simple /i/; stressed final **й** (as a part of the word) is distinguished by the macron from unstressed final **и** (as used for the *ezâfeh* syllable). The letter **e** is pronounced /ye/ initially, but after a consonant represents /e/ in Tajik; **ё** is always /yo/, e.g., **ёбем** /yobem/. Other Cyrillic characters supplemented by hooks or slashes to represent Tajik sounds not found in Russian are: **х** /h/, **қ** /q/ (exemplified here), and **ғ** /gh/, **ӯ** /ū/, **ҷ** /j/ (not occurring here). For pronunciation, see the introduction to the Glossary.

Figure 2. Aini (front row, center) at the first Tajik language conference, Dushanbe, 1930

Reminiscences

Book I

Ин хона зи хишти кӯҳна андохтаам,
Дар вай ҷашне зи рафтагон сохтаам,
То аҳли замони мо бидонанд, ки ман-
Як умри ҷавонӣ ба чи раҳ бохтаам.

Муаллиф

In khona zi khishti kūhna andokhtaam,
Dar vay jashne zi raftagon sokhtaam,
To ahli zamoni mo bidonand, ki man -
Yak umri javonī ba chi rah bokhtaam.

Muallif

این خانه ز خشت کهنه انداخته‌ام

در وی جشنی ز رفتگان ساخته‌ام

تا اهل زمان ما بدانند که من

یک عمر جوانی بچه ره باخته‌ام

مؤلف

I built this house from bricks of ancient clay,
To honor in it those who've passed away,
And tell the story of my long-lost youth,
To edify the people of today.

The Author

Author's Foreword

Ever since I took pen in hand and joined the ranks of Soviet writers, I have been meaning to record my reminiscences and offer them to my readers, especially my younger readers. Since my memories have already served as raw materials for a good many of my novels, novellas, essays, and historical tales, they may provide much that is beneficial to young readers in their own right. Autobiography always seemed to me more difficult than writing fiction, so I put it off until such time as I was more experienced. Because, just as no-one can fully appreciate life today—Soviet socialist life—unless he has actually experienced the old days, so too no-one who has not truly experienced life under the Soviet socialist system—especially literary life—and made this lifestyle truly his own, can realistically describe life as it was under out-and-out feudalism. Granted, whatever one's profession, he becomes fully experienced only at the end of his life, and granted, too, no-one knows for certain when the end of his life will be. Yet since I am now over seventy, my limbs are growing weaker day by day, and my capacity for work is diminishing, I feel the time has come to complete this task that I consider so important. So I shall seize this slim chance offered by whatever remains of my life, and begin.

My reminiscences will be recorded in the following approximate order. Part One—my childhood in the country; Part Two—my youth in the city, which will include an account of my schooldays at the madrasa in Bukhara and its curriculum, the various social classes of the city and their occupations; then my experiences in the movement against the emir's regime, my flight to Samarkand, and events from the February to the October revolutions of 1917 and beyond.[1]

---

[1] Aini did not carry his project for Part Two beyond 1905, i.e., before his active involvement with reformist or revolutionary groups; instead, the account of his student days extended into a further two volumes, published as Part Three and Part Four, still under the heading "In the City."

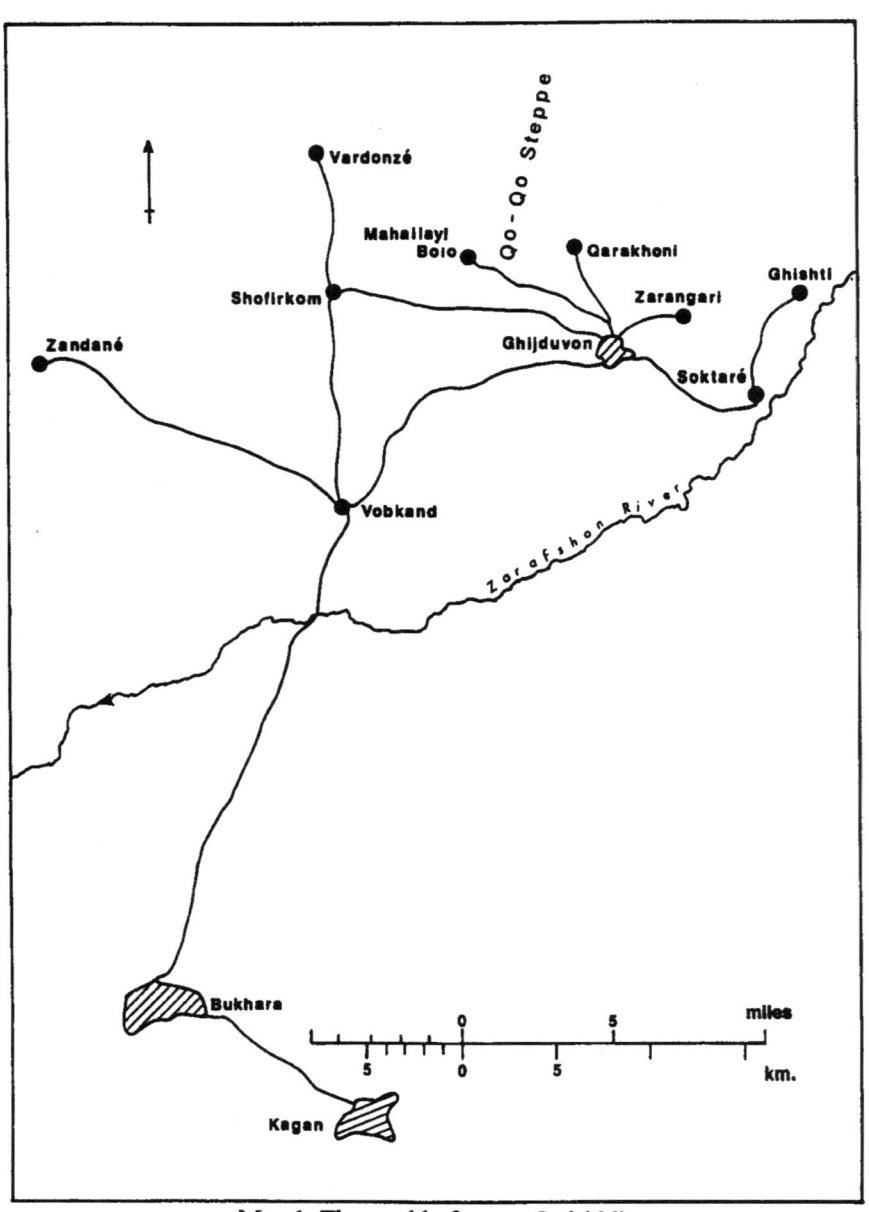

Map 1. The world of young Sadriddin

Author's Introduction

Since my childhood was spent in the country—to be exact, in two villages some distance apart and differing from one another in agriculture and culture—1 should begin by providing some geographical, ethnographical and biographical information so that my reader may better appreciate the background to these memoirs.

The village of Soktaré was in the province[2] of Ghijduvon, one *farsakh* (five miles) east of the town of that name, on the banks of the Zarafshon river. Because of its site, and since it also had a fair-sized canal, the Mazrangon, running through it, Soktaré was fertile and productive, and most of its houses boasted walled gardens with plenty of fruit trees. The fields around this village were rich and produced a varied crop, including rice and vegetables, which require a great deal of water.

The populace was made up of four ethnic groups: Tajiks, Arabs, Urgenchis, and Khojas. The Khojas in turn constituted four clans: Mirakoni, Sayid-Atoyi, Ghijduvoni, and Soktaregi. The original inhabitants of the village were Tajiks and Soktaregi Khojas; the Urgenchis had come from Urgench,[3] the Mirakonis from Mashhad,[4] the Ghijduvonis from Castle Ghijduvon, the Sayid-Atoyis from a village called Sayid-Ato in Shofirkom province, and the Arabs were reputedly the remnants of the early Arab settlers.[5] The language of the inhabitants was for the most part

---

[2] Aini generally uses the modern Soviet term *raion* for administrative subdivisions. One of the earlier terms was *tuman*, a word of Mongol origin referring to a regiment of 10,000 mounted men and hence the area of pasturage that would support them.

[3] Formerly Gurganj, a city south of the Aral Sea, on the upper reaches of the Amu Darya delta. It was at this time an important commercial center in the khanate of Khiva.

[4] Mashhad is a city in northeastern Iran, the site of a major Shi'i shrine and a center of religious learning since the sixteenth century. Mirakon is a village southwest of Bukhara.

[5] The Muslim Arab armies conquered Bukhara in 709 C.E. and ruled Central Asia as part of the caliphate until the rise of independent Iranian dynasties during the ninth century.

Tajik, though the Sayid-Atoi Khojas spoke Uzbek, and the local Arabs, unlike those elsewhere, habitually used Uzbek.

The basic occupation of the inhabitants was farming, most of them being smallholders or landless peasants. Most of the larger properties were owned by two Mirakoni families who were known locally as Qozibacha ("kadi's sons") and Mutavalli ("superintendants"). The smallholders and landless engaged in sharecropping (*choryak-kori*), seasonal and maintenance labor, or other odd jobs. Most of the Tajiks worked on the Emir's estates, and the Urgenchis were mostly retail grocers.

The Khojas, especially the Mirakonis and Ghijduvonis, also had a sideline in prayer healing: the sick and crazed were brought from everywhere around to their houses, where they recited prayers over them in order to cure them. Every morning in the mosque, after the dawn prayer, the older Khojas used to chant aloud a prayer with its own peculiar cadence called the *avrodi fathiya*;[1] the sick and the not-so-well from outlying villages would gather here every morning in hopes of being cured merely by hearing this prayer.

This village had an elementary school (*maktab*) attached to the mosque which functioned summer and winter alike, and even a small madrasa where elementary courses in religious studies were offered. On this account Soktaré was the best-educated and most advanced village in the whole region. The spiritual direction of the village was in the hands of the Mutavallis, who were the biggest landlords among the Mirakonis. Temporal and governmental administration was in the hands of the Tajiks, and it was from among their biggest landlords that local officials such as village headmen (*arbob*, *oq-saqol*) were "elected," i.e. appointed.

My father and grandfather were among the Soktaregi Khojas of the village.

The other village, Mahallayi Bolo ("Upper Mahalla"), lay some five miles to the northwest of Castle Ghijduvon, in the province of Shofirkom, one of a group of settlements called collectively Dehnavi Abdullojon, situated on the edge of the shifting sands that formed part of the Kizil Kum desert. Because of the low water level this village was poorly irrigated; and after the Shofirkom canal to the north of it was inundated by sand and wiped out, and then the new watercourse was dug on the southern side (which was at a lower elevation than the village), Mahallayi

---

[1] A concatenation of short chapters of the Koran, including Sura 110 (in which the word *fath*, "victory," occurs prominently).

Bolo could be described as utterly without water.[2] Thus there were no fruit trees to speak of, apart from a sort of sour apple called "hoji-khon" that grew here and there on the banks between the fields, and no orchards as such. The only fruit that was plentiful were grapes, since vines flourished among the sand dunes.

Most of the land around Mahallayi Bolo belonged to the emir; part of it was additionally designated as *vaqf* for the Miri Arab madrasa, to support which one tenth of its revenues was earmarked. Because of the dryness of the soil, the crops were mostly wheat, barley, millet and beans. No vegetables were grown, and though some native cotton was cultivated for local needs, most of it was not watered and on every bush could be seen only one or two unopened bolls.

This village was thus extremely poor. Most of the houses were of mud brick. There were one or two rich landlords (*boi*) and a few farmers of middling means, but everybody else lived from hand to mouth. Though agriculture was the basic means of livelihood, it was not sufficient for the general run of the inhabitants, who farmed at a loss and had to make up for it by other activities. The *bois*, who in addition to their commercial activities had amassed a good deal of land, paid little or no government taxes on their crops; they were on good terms with the governors and tax-assessors and were thus able to dump their tax burdens onto the shoulders of the poorer peasants, which contributed to the general impoverishment (a situation I described in the novel *Ghulomon*, "Slaves").

Hardly any handicrafts were practiced in Mahallayi Bolo; the only artisans were the cobblers who ministered to barefoot wretches like themselves. In the center of Dehnavi Abdullojon there were boot-repairers, who fixed new uppers or soles on worn-out boots, but the market was controlled by the second-hand dealers, who took all the profit (this topic, too, is treated in *Ghulomon*).

Some of the inhabitants of Mahallayi Bolo worked as shepherds, or gathered firewood, or performed seasonal or casual labor for the *bois*. The chief winter work for everybody was cotton-processing. Middlemen provided the bolls of native cotton, which was then extracted by hand, carded, cleaned, and handed over to the landlord—together with the seeds—in exchange for a pittance: the payment was in fact the husks of the cotton bolls for the

---

[2] For these events see Chapters 5, 13 and 14.

workers to use as fuel in their braziers and hearths (see also in *Ghulomon*).

My maternal grandfather and uncles were from this village.

Soktaré and Mahallayi Bolo were situated some ten miles apart, and each was twenty-five miles from Bukhara—Mahallayi Bolo lay due north of the city, and Soktaré a little to the north-east.

*   *   *

According to my father Sayid-Murod Khoja, his father, Sayid-Umar Khoja, could read and write and was skilled in weaving and carpentry; he was particularly known for his carpentry. Once, the mosque of Mahallayi Bolo collapsed, and the villagers cast about for a master carpenter to repair it; someone recommended my paternal grandfather, Sayid-Umar Khoja, and he was brought to Mahallayi Bolo. He repaired the mosque beautifully, and on one of the pillars carved in his own hand the words "The work of Sayid-Umar Khoja Soktaregi."

The villagers, none of whom could read and who did not even have a *maktab* attached to the mosque, were amazed that a carpenter should be literate as well. They asked him on behalf of the whole community to take on the post of imam of the mosque that he had repaired, hoping that the good fortune he had so far brought would continue and enable the village to produce a few literate people. (Their previous imam had been illiterate, having only a few chapters of the Koran and one or two prayers by heart.) He would also be able to ply his trade of carpentry, for which there was considerable local demand.

My grandfather accepted. In Soktaré, for all his skill, he had not been able to profit fully from his carpentry, since even among his own relatives there were already several skilled carpenters. Here there were no other woodworkers except makers of spinning wheels and cotton-combs. Moreover, in the nearby village of Boloyi Rūd, and in two other local villages, Sarvaré and Tabari-yon, were several flour mills, but nowhere was there a mill-wheel maker. My grandfather was a master wheelwright, too, and reckoned this would be a source of extra income if he moved here, on top of his imam's emoluments.

Bearing all this in mind, my grandfather was glad to take the offer. To start off with, they lodged him with one Hamroh Khon by name, whose house was next to the mosque. My grandfather lived here, in the men's quarters, for several years, and in the evening when he had finished his day's carpentry he would teach his landlord's eldest son, Dehqon, to read. During that time his own eldest son—my father—was studying in Bukhara, while his younger son, his widowed sisters and their children, and his wife lived in Soktaré. At last the loneliness and the repeated lengthy traveling were too much for my grandfather. He bought a plot of land at the western extremity of Mahallayi Bolo and built himself a walled house. In the yard he planted apricot saplings, which do not need much watering, and when all was finished he moved his whole family from Soktaré to settle here.

After a few years, however, my grandfather saw that the house and garden he still owned in Soktaré were going to wrack and ruin and his land there was lying uncultivated. So, since he was now too old to work as hard as he used to, he was obliged to take my father out of school and put him in charge of the house there. When he announced this to the villagers of Mahallayi Bolo, they immediately cast about for a suitable wife for my father, and decided on one of Hamroh Khon's daughters—his third eldest child, by the name of Zevaroy. Since Hamroh Khon was a man of modest means with no aristocratic pretensions, the wedding was not too expensive and the marriage settlement agreed on was my grandfather's smallholding by the house in Soktaré.[3]

When my father told me this part of his story, he would add: "I was very fond of studying, and had no wish to become head of the household and give up the madrasa. But I realized that my parents had grown old and couldn't manage easily without my help, so I had to comply. In the summer I stayed with your mother in Soktaré, working the land and picking the fruit, and in the winter I lived with my father in Mahallayi Bolo, making mill wheels and weaving. But I never lost my love of learning, and—in the hope that they would succeed where I had failed—I taught your maternal uncle, Mullo Dehqon, and a few of the village boys the rudiments of reading, took them all to Bukhara and installed them in a madrasa. Your uncle continued with his lessons, but the others all came back after a few years at the madrasa, set them-

---

[3] Marriage settlement (*mahr*): in accordance with the *shari'at*, the amount of this is agreed upon by both families and a written contract is drawn up and witnessed by a mullah. *Mahr* consists in theory of two parts: a sum (or its equivalent in kind) paid by the groom to the bride before the wedding, and an undertaking to indemnify her with a further sum in the event of a divorce. In practice it often amounts to a bride-price paid by the groom or his parents to the father or other male guardian of the bride (cf. Chapter 7).

selves up as village mullahs and lived off people's gullibility. My efforts had been wasted."

One day, four of my father's former pupils—Mullo Bobojon, Mullo Hamroh, Mullo Abdulvohid and Mullo Sobit—came to our house to see him. Mullo Bobojon had become imam of the village of Rūbaho, to the south of Mahallayi Bolo. Addressing him, and pointing to the others, my father said: "These were the sons of well-to-do men, and couldn't keep up with the rigors of a madrasa education. You, on the other hand, came from a poor family and spent your childhood in hardship, but you had obvious talent. I had hopes that you would fight ycur way through the hardships of madrasa life and prove yourself a lion; alas, you turned out to be a leader of foxes."[4]

Mullo Bobojon laughed, then indicated his companions and asked, "In that case, what have *they* turned out to be?"

Fixing them with a half-angry, half-mocking look, my father replied: "They were wolf cubs, and have turned out in the end to be wolves, as the poet said."[5]

My father's purpose was obvious: not so much to criticize Mullo Bobojon, who because of his poverty had not the means to persevere at the madrasa, but to lash out at the others, who despite their having the means had thrown away their chance of an education in order to become village mullahs (Mullo Sobit was the son of Abdurahim-Boi, who features in my novel *Ghulomon*).

It was not long before first my father's mother and then, two years later, his father died. But even then my father did not give up his double residence: the summer he would spend in Soktaré, farming and weaving, and the winter at Mahallayi Bolo, making mill wheels and weaving. He wove only to furnish clothing, blankets, cushions and so on, for the family, but the mill wheels he made for sale.

Thus it came about that I was born in the village of Soktaré, in Ghijduvon *raion*, and spent my preschool childhood at Soktaré in the summer and at Mahallayi Bolo in the winter.

---

[4] *Kaloni rūbaho*, a barbed pun: the name of the village, Rūbaho, can also mean "foxes."

[5] An allusion to a couplet in Sa'di's *Gulistan*, Book 1, Story No. 4 (see, e.g., Rehatsek's translation, pp. 789-80): "Though hand-reared among humans, there's no help--He'll turn out wolf, who once was the wolf's whelp."

1. The Celebration

The house had a fairly large yard enclosed by a high mud-brick wall, except on the south side, where there was an orchard and kitchen garden separated from the neighboring fields by a lower wall. The east side of the wall adjoined the neighbors' house, the west side was next to the fields, and the north side, in which was the entrance gate, ran alongside the main street of the village. Inside and adjoining the entrance porch was a mud-brick barn, and next to it a stable. Opposite these stood the men's living quarters-cum-guestroom (*mehmonkhona*), a raised building of unbaked brick with a porch and a *sufa*. At the base of the porch stood a weaving shed, and adjoining the south wall of the guestroom was an alcove under which stood a carpenter's workbench and lathe for making mill wheels. The front of this alcove and the south face of the guestroom were shaded in summer by the apricot trees in the orchard. To the north of the guestroom stretched a summer *sufa*, served by a large Balkh mulberry tree, which provided both fruit and shade. Between the guestroom *sufa* and the stable was a shallow pit in which was collected rubbish from the yard.

This area was called the outer yard, and was connected to the inner yard by means of a passageway leading from the side of the barn. Here, behind the barn and stable, were two wooden buildings facing each other, each with four doors, two to the north and two to the south. The south doors of the south building opened onto the kitchen garden, and the north doors of the north building onto the high wall overlooking the street. Between these buildings lay the inner yard; the remaining doors opened into this yard, which was shaded by two large apricot trees. At the east end of the inner yard were two porches which served as a combined kitchen and bakery, one for the south and one for the north building; the one attached to the north building also had another carpenter's workbench set up next to the hearth. The south building did not have an anteroom, and people left their shoes by the doorway; the north building had an anteroom where shoes were left upon entering, and where additionally another loom had been installed. At the west end of the inner yard, behind the barn and stable and adjoining them, was a long *sufa* where the family would sit outside on summer evenings.

*   *   *

The first memory I have of this yard was on a day when the south building and *sufa* were full of men and the north building was full of women. In the middle of the courtyard, between the two kitchens, a large copper pot of pilau was cooking; young men were serving pilau on earthenware plates to the male guests and bringing the empty plates back to the cook. In the women's quarters an old woman—whom some addressed as if she were a servant, and others as if she were in charge—was serving the pilau, helped by a few other old women wearing *jomachas*.

My father and uncle, my grandfather and uncles on my mother's side and other male relatives were welcoming the men, while my mother, grandmother, and the wives of my uncles were seeing to the women. At one corner of the *sufa* a drummer, a *surnay* player, and two tambourine players were seated playing, and the tambourine-players sang together and in turns. Across from the musicians at the end of the *sufa* a tall young man, his tunic tucked up into his waistband, was clapping to the music with a pair of whetstones in each hand as he danced.

I was standing with the other boys in front of the musicians, watching and listening to them. I felt doubly happy because I was wearing such fine new clothes as I had never worn before: a smooth white tunic and matching pants, and over this an embroidered *joma*, as well as a new cap, which my mother had embroidered with flowers. These new clothes, especially my bright white tunic, not only pleased me enormously but also attracted the attention of the other boys. One of them felt a part of my tunic between his fingers and called another older boy over to examine it.

"What's it made of?" he asked.

The other boy looked at my tunic and made a face. "Linen! This tunic is made of linen! My father had a *silk* tunic made for *me* for my celebration!" Then he added, "Ergash is wearing a linen tunic and pants today, too—and his father was my father's slave."[6]

---

[6] Ergash is portrayed as a hero in *Ghulomon*; the supercilious boy here is the son of Abdurahim-Boi, a slave-owner and cotton merchant depicted as a villain in the novel. -- A.

Ergash, though not a blood-relation, was "milk-brother" to Aini's elder brother Muhiddin, i.e., suckled at the same breast; Aini's father therefore

"This fellow's father," explained the first boy, pointing at me, "made that outfit for Ergash, too."

I did not know the difference between linen and silk at that time, but I knew that my father wove a very soft and white material compared to other fabrics. So instead of spoiling my pleasure, the insult made me hate this supercilious boy even more, for he had bullied me several times in the past.

When the musicians had gathered their instruments and were preparing to leave I discovered that all the guests had gone, and only relatives remained in the yard. My father paid the musicians, and as he was seeing them out I asked him to let them stay because I liked them so much. One of the musicians told me, "We're off to another celebration now, but we'll stop here on our way back."

They mounted their donkeys and began to leave.

"In that case, I'm going with you to that celebration," I said, running after the musicians. But my father suddenly grabbed my arms and held me back as I kicked my feet in the air, crying and shouting, "I'm going, I'm going!" Meanwhile, the other boys were running ahead of the drummer, hoping to go to the other celebration, and beckoning me to join them.

My grandfather approached us and said, "You don't have to go, we'll make our own music. You can play the drum, and I'll play the *surnay*."

I liked this suggestion so much that I stopped crying. Playing the drum would be much more fun than just listening to it. But on second thoughts, I wondered where my grandfather could find a drum for me and said, "You're trying to trick me—where are you going to find a drum?"

---

treated him on a par with his own sons in providing him with a circumcision feast and new clothes.

Slavery was of long standing in Central Asia, and Khiva and Bukhara in particular had thriving slave markets from the 16th to the early 19th centuries. Slaves were mainly foreign captives, e.g. (Buddhist) Kalmuks from the eastern steppes and Iranians kidnaped in Khurasan by Turkman raiders; fellow Muslims were not supposed to be enslaved, but such Shi'i "heretics" were accounted fair game. Under pressure from Russia (where slavery had been officially abolished in 1725) the emir undertook in 1868 to abolish the practice, but it continued clandestinely up until the 1920 revolution.

He took hold of his long white beard, which came down over his chest, and looked at it. "With a white beard like this, would I pull a trick on a little boy like you?"

He went off to the women's quarters and returned with a small bronze plate; then he went to the kitchen and brought the tube that my mother used for blowing up the fire. He broke off two twigs from a branch of the apricot tree, and brought all of these things over to the *sufa*. He turned the plate over and sat me in front of it, then put the sticks in my hands, sat across from me and put the tube to his mouth. I beat the plate with the sticks, rat-tat-tat, and he whistled as though playing the *surnay* . . .

Meanwhile, my father and the others were running all over the place looking for my older brother and Ergash, and this commotion distracted me from my playing. I thought that the two of them had gone off with the musicians, leaving me behind, and I was jealous. Someone said that they were hiding in an apricot tree in the orchard. Relieved, I jumped up and ran with the others to see the truants up the tree.

Father scolded my brother; "Shame on you, Muhyiddin, a big boy like you being afraid and running away! Look at your little brother, who is eight years younger than you, happily playing his drum. Get down from there!"

Muhyiddin retorted, "My little brother doesn't know what's going on yet!" Then, bursting into tears, "I'm not coming down!"

My uncle Qurbon-Niyoz, who was young and strong, climbed straight up the tree, pried first my brother and then Ergash from the branches, and handed them down to the others, who stood them on the ground, but would not let them escape, and took them straight to the south building.

My father's praise of my drumming made me so proud that I ran right back to the *sufa* to pick up where I had left off. My grandfather was still there, and encouraged me: "Come, the *surnay* can't play without the drum." So I picked up my sticks and started playing my drum again. My father did not go to the south building with the others, but came over to us and sat by the edge of the *sufa* to listen to my drumming. My father's attention made me even prouder, and I beat the drum ever harder. . .

After a while, Uncle Qurbon-Niyoz came out and invited us to come and play inside.

"But there isn't a *sufa* inside," I protested.

"We've made you a very nice *sufa* out of quilts," he said.

I looked to my "partner," my grandfather, for advice.

"Fine, let's go," said Grandfather, "Your brothers will admire your talent."

Grandfather's logic appealed to me, so I picked up my sticks and drums and ran off to the house, eager to impress them, while my grandfather and uncle followed. My father, however, remained at the edge of the *sufa*.

Inside the house were three beds made of piled-up quilts: on two of them sat Muhyiddin and Ergash, and it was obvious that the third bed was my "drumming *sufa*." When I trotted over toward the bed my eyes met my brother's: he was no longer crying, and gave me a forced, embarrassed smile. In reply I merely pouted haughtily; I had not understood anything of what they had been up to, since I was entirely preoccupied with my drumming—my pride and joy—and had expected my elder brothers to be impressed by it.

I went straight to my playing *sufa*, but Grandfather came over and told me, "The drum won't sound right placed on a soft quilt. You lie on your back with your sticks and I'll hold the plate in front of you so you can play. Then you'll be able to make such a racket that not even the bells on Abdurahim-Boy's camels can match it." So I resumed playing, fancying that the music I made was like the bells of a camel caravan.

Suddenly, strong hands grabbed my legs, forced them apart, and pressed them hard against the floor. I tried to stand up, but my grandfather held me down by placing my own "drum" against my chest so that I could not move. Then I felt such a searing pain between my legs that I could not breathe. When I recovered my breath, in my rage my puny fingers became as strong as a rooster's spurs, and I scratched my grandfather's face and pulled his beard with all my might, screaming, "So you *did* trick me for all this beard of yours!"

The house filled with uproarious laughter. Although I was crying with pain, inside I was laughing too. My grandfather's lacerated face and beard hurt him so much that despite his great age tears welled up in his eyes and he bawled like a baby.

Such were the events of my circumcision feast.[7] It is the earliest of my recollections. Though I was very young at the time, the

---

[7] *Tūyi khatna*: the Uzbek word *tūy*, which Aini has used up to this point – deliberately vaguely!--without the qualifying *khatna* "circumcision," denotes any communal celebration of a rite of passage, particularly a wedding. Circumcision of boys is "recommended" in Islam, and in practice is universally performed as marking acceptance into the Muslim community. In

memory of this episode stayed with me, perhaps because the experience was so extremely painful, the music so exhilarating, and the taste of revenge so sweet—and all of these sensations for the first time took hold of me all at once.

The house described above was in the village of Mahallayi Bolo, and had been built by my paternal grandfather for himself and his family. The loom and carpenter's bench in the outer yard were my father's. The south building was our home, and the north one was my paternal uncle's. The loom in the anteroom of the south building and the workbench under the kitchen alcove also belonged to my uncle.

2. After the Celebration

It seems that after the circumcision our family's financial situation became very tight. I did not feel the squeeze directly, but I suspected from their gloomy late-night conversations that the circumcision feast had had some unpleasant consequences for my parents.

One evening my father was telling my mother about the numerous debts he had incurred on account of the *tūy*. "Fortunately, I didn't take any loans from money-lenders," he said; " I didn't take the Qozibachas' advice to mortgage our land in Soktaré to them, because if I did we would end up without a home there and would be left as refugees in this barren hamlet."

"Do you mean the loans you took were interest-free?" my mother asked in surprise.

"Of course!" my father answered, and explained. "I took small loans from everyone, ranging from twenty to thirty *tangas*. My largest debt was fifty *tangas* from your father, which he had saved for his own funeral expenses. He told me, 'You can pay back this debt any time before I die, but don't let my younger brother Ali-khon know about it.' And," added my father, "Don't you tell anyone, either."

"All the money was lent without interest?" my mother asked incredulously.

Central Asia it was performed at the age of about seven, by the barber, and accompanied by communal feasting and entertainment at the parents' expense.

Figure 3. Aini with his children, Samarkand, 5 May, 1929

"Yes, of course, I didn't borrow any money from strangers or moneylenders. All of my loans were from relatives who live in Soktaré and close relatives. Even when I asked them for a loan, they insisted on giving me the money: 'Don't think of this small sum as a loan, consider it a circumcision gift,' they told me. I thanked them and answered that their giving me an interest-free loan at such a time was gift enough, especially since they are no better off than I am."

"As I see it, the feast would have cost less if we had held it in Soktaré," my mother said regretfully. "Our village is a hungry one, and even if you cooked a hundred pots of rice here the people would still not be satisfied."

Father disagreed. "In the first place," he said, "the wealth of the guests, not their appetite, determines the expense of the celebration: if you offer a poor man something to eat he will gladly accept it, but if you don't offer him anything, he won't ask, no matter how hungry he is. On the other hand, you have to offer a rich man not one but three plates of food, whether he's hungry or not, and if you don't he will go off in a huff because you haven't shown him sufficient respect. I think that if we had held the feast in Soktaré it would have cost us three times as much, and even then we wouldn't have satisfied the important people there, especially the Mirakoni Khojas. In that kind of place a big fuss is made at a feast: a great deal of food is served, and at the end everyone is given a *joma*, or if they can't afford that, at least they give out sugar loaves. There is no way we could have met those standards."

My father paused, then continued more calmly, "In the second place, since I got married I've hardly been to any celebration in Soktaré except for those of my relatives, because I haven't spent winters there and weddings and circumcisions usually take place in the winter. But here I've been invited to the house of every poor person, the hungry ones as you call them, at least once or twice. So I had to give a party for these people, and relatives and friends from Soktaré could come if they wanted—which they did."

"It's been a year now since the circumcision. How many of the loans have you paid back?" my mother asked.

"Not many; but first I paid your father back, and then a couple of small loans, to those who needed the money."

"You needn't have rushed to pay my father back," my mother said. "He said you could repay him any time before he died. Why him before anyone?"

"First of all," replied my father, "who knows whether he or I will die first? Second, money is more dear to an older person than a young one. I wouldn't be surprised if he worried about the loan every night from the time I took it to the time I paid him back. So I knew that I had to put the old man at ease before all the other debts were settled." After a little reflection my father continued, "My point in discussing these financial matters is not to add up our debts or to worry you, but only to let you know that things are going to be tight: let's not buy meat at the bazaar and let's eat a little less, but please don't be upset. We can make do with milk and curds for a little while. We can buy rice from the bazaar sometimes, so that on market nights, or if guests come, we can make *shir-birinj*."

"We don't need to buy rice either," my mother said.

"How so?" asked my father. "After all, milk without rice isn't food."

"Because we have rice."

"Where?" my father asked in surprise, half-rising from his seat. My mother answered, "When you bought rice for the feast I filled a bag with it and hid it in a trunk, thinking it might come in useful during hard times. Now that our first priority is to pay off our debts, we can certainly use that rice."

"Good for you!" exclaimed my father. "It's true what they say: 'a thrifty cook is wealthier than an Indian merchant.'"

My brother and I slept together, and as I was listening carefully to the conversation I thought that he was fast asleep. Then I noticed that he was crying under the quilt. My parents heard his weeping and came right over.

"What happened? Why are you crying?" they asked.

"Now how can I go to Bukhara to study? Couldn't we have done without a circumcision feast?" he asked, weeping.

"How can you go? When the time comes I'll take you there myself," my father answered. "There's no need to cry."

"You don't have any money, so how can I study in the city without money?" he asked in a faltering tone.

"Don't be upset, son," said Father. "You're not going to Bukhara for another two years, and by then I will have paid back the loans and we'll have money for your studies."

*   *   *

The following morning, a Sunday, I helped my mother make hard halva. First she browned some flour in butter in an iron pot, then stirred in a cup of mulberry syrup that we had brought from Sok-taré. Into this mixture she stirred in more flour, and kneaded it until it was the consistency of dough. Next she sprinkled flour onto a tray, spread out the dough over it, and when it had cooled and hardened she cut me a piece. The rest she cut up into squares, sprinkled with flour, and put away in a tin.

Nibbling on the piece of halva, I went out to the street and ran into my brother coming from the village. When he saw me he said, "That isn't halva, it's fried bread! Real halva is soft and buttery."

"Where have you eaten buttery halva?"

"At Grandfather's house. Uncle Qurbon-Niyoz had bought it, and he gave me some too. It was *really* delicious," my brother said, then asked, "Would you like some too? If I find some for you, will you eat it?"

"Of course!"

"Then go and beg Father for some!"

"Don't you want some too?"

"Sure, I want some too!"

"Then why don't you ask Father yourself?"

"Because I'm afraid that he'll charge it to my account and put off sending me to Bukhara."

"But I want to go to Bukhara too."

"You're still young! By the time you're supposed to go to Bukhara, Father will have found plenty of money and he'll have forgotten the halva."

"Well, all right, I'll ask him," I said.

We went to my father's weaving shed. Munching on my piece of hard halva, I told my father, "I want some butter-halva!"

Without lifting his eyes from the loom my father asked me, "That halva in your hand has butter in it; what more do you want?"

"I want butter-halva that is *really* delicious and that I've never tasted before. That's what I want!"

"If you've never tasted it, then how do you know it's so good?"

"Because my brother told me."

Frightened, Muhyiddin ran out. It was obvious from my careless answer that he had inveigled me into asking for the halva. My father laughed and told me, "Go tell your mother to bring Muhyiddin to me."

I went to my mother and told her. Brother was there and he reproached me: "Why did you have to repeat what I said to Father?"

I knew my brother was right to scold me, but I was too proud to admit to being in the wrong, so I replied, "All right, if you had been in my shoes, what would you have said?"

My brother had no answer for this, and turned beet red. Admittedly, under the circumstances, no other answer had been possible; my mistake was that I had sung the praises of butter-halva to my father without ever having tasted it myself. But my brother did not realize this.

Mother dragged my unwilling brother over to my father's loom. We assumed that Father was going to reprimand him for putting me up to it. But instead, when we stood before his loom, he laughed and took off his glasses, and as he was cleaning them he asked my brother, "Muhyiddin, do you know the village of Boloyi Rūd?"

"Yessir!"

"There, at the edge of the river, is a mill stream. When we went to see the mill I pointed it out to you, right?"

"Uh-huh!"

"You know it?"

Yes, I know it."

My father looked at my mother and said, "These two boys decided that I would get them some butter-halva today. Well, today is bazaar day, and this will be their bazaar night. There's no need to cook anything else. Instead, you can start spinning more thread for my bobbins—they're almost used up. I was afraid that, if Muhyiddin didn't know where Boloyi Rūd was, I'd have to go there for halva myself. Since he evidently does know, he needn't take me from my work!"

My father took out one *tanga* (15 kopeks) from his pocket, gave it to my brother, and said, "After you pass the mill stream you will come to the bridge over the river, and when you cross the bridge you'll see a large house with a gate right in front of the bridge. This is the house of Master Barot the halva-maker. Inside his yard is a large building where the halva is made. Go into that building and greet whoever you meet there, tell them I sent you, give them the *tanga* and ask for a *qabza* of halva. He'll give you a piece wrapped in paper to bring home."

"How much is a *qabza* of halva?" I asked my father.

"Two handfuls."

"Who gets to eat it, me or my brother?" I asked.

Father stopped weaving and cupped his hands together to show me, and explained, "One *qabza* is this much. A big piece like that will be enough for all of us."

My brother got ready to go and I was allowed to go with him. Off we set for Boloyi Rūd on our halva-buying expedition.

The village of Boloyi Rūd was less than a mile north of Mahallayi Bolo. From our yard, which was at the edge of the village and bordered the plain, its trees and buildings could clearly be seen. We slipped and slid across the fields, which were iced over, and were having so much fun that we did not even notice when we had arrived at the canal.

Boloyi Rūd is located on the north bank of the old Shofirkom canal. That is why the village is called Boloyi Rūd (above the river, or canal). From the south bank of the canal ran a stream which turned a mill wheel when the water was high enough. When we reached that point there was no running water in the stream, only frozen patches. I asked my brother to show me the mill, which was twenty yards down from the stream crossing. My brother agreed and we went to see the mill.

3. The Halva Factory

We took a quick look inside the mill and came back out. Since there was no water in the canal we did not use the bridge, but crossed over on the chunks of ice, pelting each other with snowballs, then climbed up onto the north bank by the bridge and went in through the gate facing it. In the courtyard was a tall mud-brick building about four times as big as an ordinary nine-beam house. On the south side of this building were two doors, both of them closed. We opened the nearer one, and went inside.

At the far end of the building was a line of cooking fires, and on each fire sat a cooking pot, tilted forward. Syrup was boiling in some of these pots, and in others soapwort was being whipped into a foam with a handful of twigs bound together, called a *chelchub*. At the end of the row of cooking-fires was a level pot in which oil was boiling. One man was pouring flour that had been browned, a little at a time, into one of the large tilted pots, and two others were mixing this syrup with wooden paddles. As the flour blended in they kept on shoveling up the resulting batter, turning it over, and slamming it back down. A tall, dark, middle-aged man with a long beard was giving orders to everybody and showing them what to do.

At the other end of the building was a broad, high *sufa* and on it was a large wooden tray, a good two yards across, surrounded by a layer of sheepskins. At the edge of the *sufa* by the tray was a bin of flour.

The halva-maker scooped out some flour with a large metal shovel and spread it out on the tray. Then he went back to the pot where flour and syrup were being mixed and checked to see how it was going. When the flour had blended in and the mixture looked like bread dough, the master told his workers, "That's enough, bring it out!"

The workers began shoveling out the syrupy dough onto the wooden tray.

The master, evidently free of his most demanding work, looked at us and asked, "What do you want?"

My brother greeted him and handed over the *tanga*. "Father sent us for a *qabza* of halva."

"Fine," the master said, "but we've already sent the halva we made this morning to the bazaar. So just watch for a while and we'll give you some fresh halva when it's ready."

The syrupy dough was spread out over the flat tray. All the men working at the pots washed their hands up to the elbows and squatted down on the skins around the tray. The master also sat down at their head. One young worker remained standing by the flour bin with a big metal shovel. The halva-makers took the dough in their hands and kneaded it into a long snake, joining the ends to form a ring; then, bending over the tray, they kneaded the ring into a broad, flat layer that reached right up to the edge. Then the young man with the shovel sprinkled flour on it, and the kneaders folded the halva in half to make two layers. Then they kneaded it again until it covered the tray as it had the first time, the young man spread more flour on it, and the kneaders folded it in half again to make a compact mass of four layers.

The halva-makers continued in this fashion, so that the third time there were eight layers, the fourth time sixteen, the fifth time thirty-two, the sixth time sixty-four, the seventh time one hundred and twenty-eight, the eighth time two hundred and fifty-six, the ninth time five hundred and twelve, the tenth time one thousand and twenty-four, and so on until twenty-five folds had been completed and the layers of the cake, seen end-on, were as thin as threads in a skein. "That's enough," the master told his workers.

He picked up a large knife and cut up this cake into pieces about a hand's breadth square. He took one of these pieces and weighed it on a scale in the corner of the *sufa*. It was a bit light.

He broke off a bit from a second lump and added it to the scale. Then he wrapped the bigger piece in paper and gave it to my brother. "Take this to your father," he said. He divided the smaller piece into two equal portions and gave it to us, saying, "Eat this on the way home."

We set off homeward at a run, for it was already very late.

4. The Shifting Sands

It was spring. The apricot trees in our forecourt were in bloom, brightening up the whole garden. The villagers of Mahallayi Bolo were busy tilling the fields, digging irrigation ditches, and pruning the tangled vines. The village boys were grazing their cows and sheep, or those of their landlords, on the newly green canal banks or unplowed fields. On one such day I grew bored with the blossoms and greenery in our yard, and decided to go out and explore the fields and meadows. I told my elder brother of my intention and asked him to come with me; he agreed, but left the onus of getting parental permission on my shoulders.

First I went to my mother and asked her permission for my venture. "Ask your father," she replied. "If he lets you go out, it's all right with me." So I went to my father.

He was sitting on the porch, busy carving a mill wheel, his glasses on his nose, painstakingly working on the slots for the blades. After chiseling for some time, he measured the cavity with a stick that was covered with black markings. Then, using a steel spike with a blade narrower than the chisel, he punched through the hole, turned to me, and said, "Well, what can I do for you?"

"I've come to ask if I can go out for a walk."

"Who with?"

"My big brother, Muhyiddin."

"Your big brother isn't going anywhere. He still hasn't learned his school lessons for the past week. Until he has them by heart and has repeated them to me, I'm not letting him out to play or go for a walk anywhere. You can go where you like."

"Then you take me for a walk!"

"Take yourself! The wolf won't eat you, the fields are full of boys; your foster brother Ergash should be down by the canal—he usually grazes his flock thereabouts."

I went outside. The open country was broader and sweeter than our front yard; a light breeze blew, bringing to the nostrils a delicate fragrance. The young stalks of wheat and barley sown in autumn covered the black earth with fresh green. The young grass, clover,and other wild plants on the river bank glistened with a dazzling intensity. The air was neither cold not hot, just perfect. The village boys had been out loading manure into paniers on their donkeys' backs and scattering it over the fields that were to be sown, and on their way back they mounted their unburdened donkeys and drove them at a gallop.

I went straight to the waters' edge, to where I could see the trees standing when I looked from our house. On this side, the south bank of the canal, there was no-one in sight; only swallows and sparrows in the branches of the newly-budding willows, singing a song which—like the weather—was sheer delight.

On the other side—the north bank of the canal—on top of a low sand dune, the shepherd boys were wrestling. Ergash was with them. I sat on the nearer bank to watch them; even though the water was low, I was scared to cross. Suddenly Ergash caught sight of me and ran down to the water's edge, calling, "Come on, come on over! The water's no more than ankle-deep!"

I hitched up my trouser-legs and waded into the stream. It really was barely ankle-deep. I crossed over and joined Ergash and the other boys. The boys then left off wrestling and started to play "catch": one would run away and another would catch up with him and grab him. If he couldn't hold onto him, he was "it."

But the fine red sand, as soft and powdery as sifted flour, gave way beneath the boys' feet and one after the other they sank or stumbled and fell over. This game soon tired them out. Some of them stretched out on the soft sand to bask in the spring sunshine, others ran after their straying flocks.

The boys were less adroit, it seemed to me, than their lambs and kids, which skipped across the sand with confidence and ease. The young goats butted and wrestled, chased and caught each other, just like the boys, while the lambs that had wandered off to graze far from their mothers would run bleating after the flock—and none of them ever stumbled.

Ergash asked me: "Why don't you take a present for your mother and father?"

I was surprised. "What kind of present can I get from a sand-bank?"

Ergash persisted. "Have you ever eaten mushrooms?"

"No, not so far as I remember."

"Well, with all the rain we had yesterday, there's enough mushrooms sprung up in the sand to gather by the sackful! I've already picked a bag to take home; if you like, I'll pick some for you too."

"Fine," I agreed. Ergash took up his shepherd's staff and we set off across two of the low dunes toward a third. Here, wherever he saw a tuft of grass, Ergash scraped it away with his staff and there, beneath the flimsy veil of sand, the mushrooms came to light. I set to work picking them, and had just about filled my shirt lap when Ergash said, "Open your lap and let me see what you've got." I did so, and he took a look at my mushrooms. "Pour them on the ground," he said. I let them drop, and he sorted the scattered mushrooms into two piles. One pile consisted of very big mushrooms with short stalks, while the others had long thin stalks and heads like broad, thin fish-scales. Ergash pointed out the big ones, which were very few, and said, "These ones are edible, and very tasty." Then he pointed out the ones with thin stalks: "These are bitter and poisonous; you mustn't eat them."

We walked over a few more dunes and collected a kerchief-ful of edible mushrooms. Meanwhile the wind had risen and a storm was threatening. By the time we reached the canal it was gusting strongly and the air was thick with swirling dust. The animals grew restive, and the boys shouted warnings to each other and ran to prevent them scattering. Ergash too herded his charges together and drove them to the water's edge, below the level of the sand dunes. A boy on the top of one of the dunes yelled excitedly: "The sand is shifting!"

Ergash raced up to the top of the dune with me close behind him. The wind was coming from the northeast; I kept my back to it and forced my way up the dune. The sand, like a stretch of water whipped into waves by the wind, was slowly washing forward: layers of sand from the surface of the dune were already pouring onto the bank, and the underlying layers were forming moving waves behind them.

Meanwhile the wind was blowing stronger and the air was growing darker with the dust. The boys drove their flocks toward the village, the animals running and bleating wildly as if pursued by wolves. For my part, I clutched the kerchief full of mushrooms to my chest and headed for home. The plowed fields afforded a firmer footing than the sands, and the wind was now at my back, so the journey home was not so difficult. But there was no trace now, either on the ground or in the air, of that spring freshness that had greeted the start of my trip: the young grass and budding leaves had faded beneath a layer of dust and sand.

When I reached home my father was still busy cutting the holes in his mill wheel—so busy that he never even asked where I had been and what I had done. After watching him at work for a while I went to my mother and gave her the mushrooms, asking her to hurry up and cook them, as I was very hungry.

Mother looked at the mushrooms and exclaimed, "Oh, what a lot! There's enough for all of us." My brother Muhyiddin, doing his homework in the hallway, called, "Watch out that he hasn't gone and picked poisonous toadstools!"

"I know how to tell good mushrooms from poisonous ones!" I answered him haughtily.

"They're all good edible ones," my mother confirmed, and took them over to the stove in order to clean and fry them.

My father worked on the mill wheel for as long as he could see, but that day dusk fell earlier than usual. The wind rose and it rained sand, just like a rainstorm, and in no time the earth was carpeted with sand. We closed the doors as tight as we could and lit the lamps, but the sand continued to invade the house through chinks in the door. After a meal of fried mushrooms, in preparing which I had played my part for the first time, I went to bed early. I was so tired from the exertions of that day that I plunged into a deep sleep and did not wake up until after first light, when I heard my father talking to my mother in agitated tones. It appeared that the sandstorm had swept over many villages and had obliterated field after field, including my grandfather's vineyard.

"Hurry with the tea," my father told her. "I must go and help them, to save a part of your father's vines and to prevent this kind of catastrophe happening again."

I got up and went outside. The weather was calm and clear, with a light breeze, but the walls of the house and the yard had come to resemble a sandbank. Sand lay ankle-deep in the forecourt, the apricot blossoms looked like dead bees, all trace of grass and leaves was lost to view beneath the sand. The garden which yesterday had gladdened the heart with its fresh shoots and blossoms was today sad and listless, like that of a house in mourning. I washed my hands and face and came back inside, and sat down next to my father. We drank tea with fresh cream together. My elder brother went to his corner to continue his homework. My father told my mother to collect the ax, mattock, handsaw and pruning shears, while he put on his work clothes and got ready to go and help my grandfather. "I'm coming too," I told Father.

"As you like," he replied. "Yesterday you went out and saw newly green fields, today you'll see a parched sand desert. One must see each of these in his lifetime."

So, father and son, we left the house and went off to Grandfather's. There, Qurbon-Niyoz, Ravshan-Niyoz and Niyoz-Khon, Grandfather's sons —my uncles—were ready to start work. Grandfather's fifth son Ali-Khon, however, had loaded his capacious saddlebags on his horse and was preparing to set off for the bazaar; he was a tea-seller who made the rounds of four market towns. My father asked him, "Why don't you give the bazaar a miss today and help out in this time of common disaster?"

"I need no orchards or fields—the bazaar is enough for me. It doesn't worry me if the world ends in flood or fire," Ali-Khon replied.

"Miserable blackguard," my father muttered to himself. Grandfather's voice was heard from the house: "Don't talk to him, he's not one of us, he's a pig!" Evidently father and son were at loggerheads quite apart from the matter of the crop damage wrought by the sandstorm.

My uncles put the mattock, ax, shears and other implements in their satchels and moved off. Grandfather packed the bread, teakettle and other things into *khurjins* and mounted a donkey; I was set astride behind him and, with my father on foot, we all set off to the fields. My grandmother prayed aloud for God to keep us safe from harm and grant us success in our task.

5. Battling the Shifting Sands

My grandfather's fields and vineyards lay at the very edge of the Qo-Qo Steppe. This was east of Mahallayi Bolo and adjoined the fields of the village of Qarakhonī even farther to the east. The Qo-Qo Steppe lay south of the former course of the Shofirkom canal, and up to that time had been considered some of the best-watered arable land in the whole region. When we reached it, we saw nothing but a sand desert. To the northeast we could see enormous mounds of shifting sand, and to the southwest the sand gradually diminished until at the nearest extremity of the plain it lay no more than knee-high.

All over the plain people were working like ants: in the fields and vineyards to the northeast they were tying up broken branches, digging out newly-sprung vines that had been buried beneath the sand, and where the sand lay piled high on top of the vines or crops they were shoveling it into sacks and carrying it off to empty over less affected areas.

We reached my grandfather's orchard. He owned two orchards, one unwalled with an area of two *tanob*, and another of one *tanob* enclosed on three sides by a mud wall. The unwalled orchard was completely covered with sand, the vineyard section lying under a huge dune. The partially-walled orchard lay next to the river, which the shifting sand had first completely inundated; it had then risen to the height of the wall, flooded across this and spread over one third of the enclosure. Although the weather had cleared and the wind had dropped, there was still a danger that the sand would continue to creep south-westward and a tidal wave of sand, like water from a rain-swollen torrent, would surge in slow motion over the orchard wall and gradually advance until it had smothered all the newly-budding vine shoots in its soft embrace.

Grandfather spread out his *khurjin* and blanket and sat down under an elm that stood by the pond in the walled orchard, where he used to sit up until two days ago watching the orchard and the river. Only now there was neither pond nor river, just a pile of sand that reached almost as high as the branches of the tree. Father instructed my uncles to cut off the broken branches of the willows, poplars, mulberries and elms and to make two piles of them, one by the enclosure of the walled orchard and a second to the north and east of the unwalled orchard. The brothers started to take the broken branches up to the wall, while Father with his pruning knife trimmed the longest branches into poles and set them upright in a line outside the wall, between this and the sand, then interlaced the smaller branches and twigs between them to form a wicker wall. This done, he said to my uncles, "It will take you the whole day, but if you carry the sand from in here and dump it outside, this orchard will be saved."

Then he went up to the unwalled orchard and here, too, on its northern and eastern edges, he erected a number of poles and told my uncles to weave branches between them.

Until he had done all this, my father did not stop to eat or drink. My uncles of course followed his lead; and once the wicker wall was completed, they all huddled next to my grandfather and ate lunch. After the meal, Father told Grandfather, "I'm going now—the lads have learned pretty well how to weave a fence, they can finish it themselves. As for clearing out the sand and cleaning up the vines, that's a long and arduous job: you get it started, and your boys will finish it."

Grandfather, old and all but bedridden, bade Father farewell with profuse prayers and thanks, and once we got on the road my uncle Qurbon-Niyoz said, "Brother-in-law, I wish I had your energy and efficiency!"

"If you want to, you can be even more energetic and efficient than I—don't just talk about wishing, put your wishes into action! If the lazy and flabby only knew how work toughens the body and eases the mind, they would never again sleep in the shade of idleness."

*   *   *

We rejoined the highway. But instead of heading back toward the village, my father turned upstream, along the canal that was utterly choked with sand. When we arrived at the village of Boloyi Rūd we saw that from the fertile spot it had been up until yesterday it had turned into a frightful wasteland. All the houses were covered with sand; here and there, only the corner of a roof was visible. Women, girls and young boys stood huddled together in the open on top of the piles of sand, and in between these forlorn groups of homeless people could be seen blankets and rugs, quilts and cushions, pots and trays. "They look like refugees from another village," my father said to himself, but loud enough for me to hear.

We reached the house of Usto Barot the halva-maker. Of this, only the roof of the halva-factory—the tallest building not only of this residence but of any in the village—was still visible. Three sides of it were covered by the sand right up to the roof, and only the south wall was to some extent clear. The gate and gatehouse were blocked by sand, and from no side was there any access except over piles of sand. Father waded through the sand to the wall of the house and called, "Usto Barot! Where are you?"

"I'm in here, buried alive with my sons," came an answer from inside; then Usto Barot came out through the same door as Ergash and I had gone in to buy halva, and exchanged greetings and news with my father. In reply to Father's inquiries, he explained with tears in his eyes that when the sand had swept in and engulfed their living quarters he had moved his wife and small children with their things to the halva shop, while he and his sons had gone up to the roof and set about shoveling off the accumulated sand, just as they shoveled snow off the roof in winter. In this way they still had a roof—if not over their heads—at least under their feet.

"Thank your lucky stars," my father consoled him. "Others have been left without any shelter at all." And we continued on our way.

Next to Usto Barot's house there was no canal and no bridge across it, no mill stream and no mill that I could see. Nevertheless my father went straight to where the mill had been. The old building had collapsed into the millpond under the weight of the sand, together with all its machinery, and from outside only a heap of sand could be seen. We reached the miller's house. At the doorway we were met by my other grandfather (Father's father), Usto Amak. He had gone to the village of Tezguzar[8] a few days ago to do a building job and had returned only that day. He told my father that the farmlands of Boghi-Afzal, Tezguzar, and Qarayaghoch—together with the village of that name—plus the northern part of Dehnavi Abdullojon, Muhammad-Boqi, and a part of Kochi-khūron had been completely buried by the sand. There were reports that the sand had reached as far as the village of Sayid-Ato and Vardonzé Hill.[9]

"The canal doesn't exist any more—it's been utterly drowned in sand," my father said. "That means there is no hope of saving even those places that were not directly in the path of the sand. We can say right now that the province of Shofirkom has become a waterless, grassless desert." And we went home.

After she had been told all about my father's progress through the devastation, my mother said: "Today you went to help out my father instead of seeing to your own affairs; whereas you've always said that the wheel in hand has to be finished first." At these words, Father nodded and half-smiled. Then, his expression growing grimmer, he said, "This mill wheel was ordered by the

---

[8] *Tezguzar* means "passing quickly" or "begone!" This village and the (folk-etymological) origin of its name are mentioned in the second volume of Aini's reminiscences (in the chapter *Sayohati sahro*; see *Bukhara*, pp. 43-44).

[9] *Qūrghoni Vardonzé*: *qūrghon* (Russ. *kurgan*) means (1) burial mound, tumulus; (2) (ruined) fortress, and refers here to the ruins of the ancient town, still largely unexcavated. Vardonzé (also Vardona, Vardonzi), northwest of Bukhara city, was a pre-Islamic city-state perhaps even older than Bukhara. At this time (1880s) it was still a flourishing market town and handicraft center, noted for its pottery.

miller on the bank of the canal. He gave me twenty *tangas* deposit and asked me to finish it for him in one week. That's the day after tomorrow. Only now there's no need for the wheel, since the mill and its stream are no more. Now I have to find the money to give the miller his deposit back."

He asked my mother to fetch tea, and settled down to go over my brother's homework with him.

6. In Soktaré

Before I tell about life in Soktaré I should first describe the house we had in that village.

Our house in Soktaré was situated north of the village mosque, and was reached from the main street through a narrow lane running west of the mosque. On the east side of this lane was a school, the mosque and its garden, and on the west side was a large house that could be entered only from the main street. At the end of the land, on the west side of a more open area, were a few other houses, but only the gate of our house opened directly onto the lane. This house, however, did not belong to our family alone, for all our relatives lived there, and each of them owned a part of the large building and grounds. The whole property was about one hundred and fifty yards from east to west, by about two hundred yards long. This area was divided into four parts. The part that was directly in front of the entrance gate was ours. The other three parts, to the east of ours, belonged to my father's uncle and cousins.

The southern section of the house was separated from the mosque garden by a low mud-brick wall. The east and west sides were bordered by the neighbors' walls, and to the north lay the open fields, beyond a low mudbrick wall which had openings for each of the adjacent houses. At the time of my earliest recollection, we had in our inner yard an old wooden building as our living room and a mud-brick building to house the weaving loom.

Our immediate neighbor on the east side of the yard was my father's uncle, who at that time was said to be ninety years old. In his inner courtyard he had a dilapidated house which was home for his his son's wife and his niece, and in the outer yard there was a square-built *mehmonkhona* with slender, carved pillars, like a mosque, in which he himself lived.

This old man, who was called Abdullo Khoja, had been a carpenter and had owned a little piece of land. But his son was irresponsible and lazy, and had neither farmed the land nor learned carpentry. When Abdullo Khoja grew old and could work no longer, he and his son sold their land and spent all the money. This poor old man had absolutely no income and relatives provided him with food. He used to sit all day in the *mehmonkhona* without saying anything to anybody, and would only emerge to go to the lavatory or wash.

His son wandered from village to village. He was able to read and write and people said that he wrote healing-prayers, but he was evidently not much good even at an easy job like that. Every two or three weeks he would return home, with barely enough food for his wife and niece, and there was never anything left for his father. My father called him an incurable scoundrel.

The name of this son was Ibrohim Khoja. Once my father cursed him out for not taking care of his father, finally saying, "The prophet Ibrohim would have sacrificed his son to God, and you have sacrificed your father to your laziness.[10] Shame on you and the curses of the world upon you!"

Unaffected by this bitter denunciation, Ibrohim just mounted his donkey with a tight-lipped smile and rode off on his travels again.

To the east of my father's uncle lived an old woman whom everyone called Tūta-posho, "Princess Tuta." I did not know her real name, and anyone hearing this glorious epithet would have assumed that she was a very grand lady who wore regal clothes, sat on many layers of quilts, and had lots of servants.[11] Actually, she was nothing of the sort. She wore a single dress and pants that were worn and patched. The only furniture in her house was an old sheepskin that had lost much of its fleece, a torn felt carpet,

---

[10] I.e., the patriarch Abraham, who was prevented from obeying God's command to sacrifice his son Isaac by the last-minute substitution of a ram caught in a thicket (Genesis 22:1-19). Abraham is venerated by Muslims as a precursor of the Prophet Muhammad, and God's testing of him is commemorated in the annual Festival of Sacrifice (*idi qurbon*). The Koran's reference to this incident (37:100-111) does not name the son involved, and Muslim tradition ascribes the role to Isma'il, i.e., Ishmael.

[11] *Posh(sh)o* (cf. Turk. *pasha*), from literary persian *pâdshâh* "great king," in later times came to denote a less exalted local ruler, and is a favorite element in women's names in some parts of Afghanistan and Central Asia (cf. Sulton-posho, below).

and a few bedraggled bolsters. She was more than eighty years old
and so hunched that she had difficulty either walking or sitting;
when she sat, her knees came up to her chest. Because of this she
always slept on her back with pillows under her head and more
pillows under her legs, so that she maintained lying down the same
posture as when standing up.

Tūta-posho was the widow of my father's uncle Abdulquddus
Khoja, who had died long ago. She had a son called Sharof Khoja
who, like Ibrohim Khoja, was a ne'er-do-well. After his father's
death Sharof Khoja sold the piece of land he inherited and left for
Qarshi,[12] where we also had relatives. He came to see his mother
once a year, bringing barely enough food to last him the two or
three weeks he stayed; it was obvious that he did nothing but loaf
in Qarshi as well. After he left, Tūta-posho's neighbors and
relatives would provide for her.

In the farthest section of this yard lived my father's cousin,
then about fifty years old and an accomplished carpenter. It was
said that even in Bukhara it would be hard to find his equal in all
kinds of woodwork. His name was Hidoyat Khoja, but people
called him *Usto* Khoja because he was such a skilled craftsman.
He was literate, had a sense of humor, and got on well with people.
He had two sons by a previous wife: the older one, Sayid-Akbar
Khoja, was the same age as my older brother and took lessons
from the *khatib*, while the younger one, Ikrom Khoja, was barely
literate and helped his father with his work.

After the death of his first wife, Usto Khoja took a second wife
who bore him two daughters, both of them still children. His wife
was young, and very proud of being descended from a long line
of *khojas*,[13] so she never did any work except cooking. Apricots
fell onto her yard and lay there rotting, but she would not
condescend to gather them.

Despite Usto Khoja's great talent and his rarely lacking for
commissions, he was no better off than we were. Nevertheless, he
never begrudged Abdullo Khoja and Tūta-posho a helping hand.

---

[12] A city some 100 miles southeast of Bukhara. During this period, the
region was generally governed by the successor-designate to the Bukhara
emirate. It was a thriving market town for the nomads of the surrounding
steppe and a center of trade and communications with the eastern half of the
emirate.

[13] *Khatchagi*: a *khoja* (q.v.) with a documented pedigree, hence one of the
cream of the Bukhara aristocracy (*khat[t]* "writing, document").

*   *   *

Each year when the mulberries began to ripen, my father used to move us from Mahallayi Bolo to Soktaré. The year that the Shofirkom canal was choked with sand and Mahallayi Bolo was left without water, we moved to Soktaré early, even before the mulberries began to fruit.

In Soktaré my brother and Sayid-Akbar Khoja began to study with the village *khatib*, and I played in the many streams and canals with other boys my age. My father decided not to move back to Mahallayi Bolo that winter, since drinking water was scarce there and had to be drawn from a village well and carried to the house. Accordingly, he demolished our tumbledown living quarters and built a new house of mud brick, with a storeroom, a kitchen porch, a cattle stall and a barn for hay. Usto Khoja assisted him with the construction, and Ikrom Khoja and Muhyiddin helped as far as they could in mixing the mud; but despite his father's pestering, Sayid-Akbar refused to help, claiming that he wanted to be a calligrapher and if he soiled his hands with mud and bricks they would be spoiled for the pen.

That year I and my playmates Hamid Khoja, the nephew of Ibrohim Khoja, and the daughters of Usto Khoja, spent most of our spare time with Tūta-posho, who would tell us strange and wonderful tales. She knew by heart the stories of Rustam, Isfandi-yar, Siyavush, and Abu Muslim,[14] and would repeat them for us endlessly. We would each bring her bread, mulberry raisins, or some other delicacy to entice her to talk. She would lie back with pillows under her head and legs, and tell us stories. Once she told us the following tale of the clever orphan and the wicked landlord, which I have never forgotten.

---

[14] Rustam, Isfandiyar and Siyavush are mythical heroes of the Iranian national epic; Abu Muslim is a historical figure, who has become the hero of a folk epic (*dâstân*) still transmitted orally in Afghanistan and Central Asia (see separately in Glossary).

7. The Clever Orphan and the Wicked Landlord

Tūta-posho told us that once upon a time there was a deceitful rich landlord. He always managed to get hired hands to work for him for free. Should one of them demand his due, the rich man would accuse him of some misdeed and would force him to work in order to pay it off. Then, after the laborer had worked off his fictitious debt, the rich man would find another pretext to put him in his debt again. The workers found themselves stuck in this situation, from which the only release was death.

In time the landlord's tactics became so widely known that no one trusted him or would work for him. They called him a liar and a scoundrel and refused to be taken in by his offers. When all his old servants had died and he no longer had anyone to work for him, he called all the poor people of the village in front of the mosque and swore a solemn oath[15] before the imam, that whoever agreed to work for him would be paid fully and without question. Still the poor people would not believe him, for all his oaths.

The rich man thought long and hard until he hit upon a scheme. In the village was a young orphan,[16] whom he invited home. There he told him: "My boy, you don't have a father and I don't have a son. If you move in with me and help me I will adopt you as my son, and when my only child, my little daughter, comes of age, I will marry you both. That will make you my son-in-law, and all my wealth and property will be yours when I die."

With this, he brought out his five-year-old daughter and showed her to the orphan. "Here is my sweet, pretty daughter, wh will one day be your wife," he said.

The orphan boy accepted the rich man's offer and became his servant that very day.

Days, weeks, months, years passed. The orphan served the rich man like a son from the bottom of his heart; the rich man's profits and losses were his own. He kept telling himself, "Some day I will be his son-in-law and all this will be mine." The orphan

---

[15] Specifically, swore that he would divorce his wife if he broke his word—a common, and originally solemn, oath in Muslim countries. If a man divorced his wife by triple public declaration of the same, he could not remarry her until she had subsequently married and divorced another.

[16] *Yatim*, "orphan," is the same word used in Tajik to denote a seasonal or casual farm laborer.

made all sorts of toys for the landlord's little daughter; he told her wonderful stories, looked after her, and did all he could to make her happy. The little girl truly loved the kind, gentle, fun-loving boy, and would not be parted from him for an instant. When the girl came of age she remembered her father's promise to make the orphan his son-in-law, and when she thought of him as her future husband and life-long companion, her love for him grew even greater. She helped him out to lighten his work load and no longer called him "brother," but "sweetheart."

The orphan loved her more than ever, and there came a time when he found it very difficult to be apart from her. Whenever he left the house to go to work in the fields, he would keep turning round and looking back longingly, as though he had left something very dear and precious behind. From the very start he had worked especially hard in order to soften the rich man's heart and hasten the marriage. The rich man, too, treated him well. He never ordered him to "weed the field" or "reap the wheat," but rather he would say "weed *your* field," or "reap *your* wheat."

At last the girl grew impatient and asked the boy to send a go-between to her father with the request for her hand in marriage. The orphan refused, saying, "It would be better if he made the match without my asking for it."

When the girl turned seventeen, bride-scouts and matchmakers started coming from everywhere. From behind the door the girl could hear how her mother received them: she did not say "my daughter is already betrothed," but instead haggled about the cost of the wedding and the very high bride price that she had fixed. The mother would tell them that even if destiny decreed that they were the best in-laws that could be found, nevertheless her husband insisted: "I have traveled all over this province and have attended many weddings—and for my daughter's wedding day I require ten *man* of rice with all the fixings." She added that certainly the clothes and money for the wedding would have to be worthy of their daughter. If a suitor could provide all that, the rich man and his wife would gladly give him their daughter a hundred times over.

The girl understood from all this that her parents had no intention of marrying her to the orphan; they were looking for a rich son-in-law to sell her to for a good price. So, when she saw the orphan again, she told him about the matchmakers and what her mother had said to them. "You'd better hurry up and send a proposal to my father soon, because if you don't, and my father decides to give me to another, I'll kill myself," she told the boy.

"God forbid! If your father refuses me and gives you to someone else, I'll kill myself first," the orphan replied. He then went directly to the imam, informed him of his claim against the rich man's promise, and asked him to act as mediator. The imam consented and presented his case to the rich man. The rich man laughed, and replied, "Leave it to me. Just tell the boy to come and see me." The rich man went straight to the orphan and told him, smiling, "No need to be upset, my son, nor to involve other people in our affairs. I have everything in hand for your wedding, so you will both live happily ever after. Don't worry about the coming and going of these matchmakers. You're very lucky that your betrothed is so beautiful and in such great demand. We don't want to hurt anybody's feelings, so instead of refusing the matchmakers outright, we discourage them by setting such a high price for her that they think we really don't want to marry her off at all. This way we can get rid of all the matchmakers without offending them."

The orphan believed the rich man and convinced the girl that it was true. She was reassured, and the boy began to work even harder from that day forth.

One day a train of camels appeared at the rich man's gate. All of them bore fine new rugs as saddle cloths, and silver bells dangled around their necks, legs, and tails. Some camels carried sacks of rice, others sacks of flour, sugar, and sweets. There were also camels laden with silks and satins, velvets and brocades, cloth of silver and gold. The camels were couched in front of the rich man's house, and their cargo unloaded and brought inside. It was obvious that the landlord had betrothed his daughter to another rich man, and that these goods were the price and paraphernalia for an impending wedding.

When the orphan saw this, all grew dark before his eyes, and his whole body trembled; he felt as if the sky had fallen on him like a millstone, grinding him into flour. At first he determined to kill himself, but then he thought, "Suicide is a last resort; so long as I'm alive I have to try to save both of us. If I fail, then I shall kill myself."

With this in mind the orphan slipped into the inner yard, while everybody was busy admiring the newly-brought wedding gifts and clothes. Seeing the girl, he signed to her and drew her aside. When they were alone together, she burst into tears and pulled out a dagger from under her dress, saying, "As soon as I have a chance I shall stab myself to the heart and kill myself!"

"I was going to do the same," the orphan replied, "but then I came up with a plan that will save both of us."

When the girl heard this she threw her arms around the orphan's neck and kissed him for the first time, crying, "Oh, please tell me quickly, or I'll die of happiness!"

"Be patient now. Let everyone think that you agree to the wedding, but be ready to run away at a moment's notice. When the opportunity comes I will come to you in secret and we'll escape," the orphan said. "But I can't bear to stay for the betrothal feast, which will be our mourning day. I will hide somewhere and prepare for our escape. But after the betrothal, I'll ask your father to give me my due for twelve years of service. Since he took a solemn oath to divorce his wife if he broke his word, he has to honor it. In any case, after we run away we'll need some money until I find work."

From that time on the orphan was absent from the village. A week after the betrothal was celebrated, the orphan came to the village, where the rich man was sitting with the imam and the village elders in front of the mosque.

The orphan faced the rich man and said, "Uncle, I ate so much of your bread and salt, and worked so little for you, now it's time for you to settle with me. If you give me my due it will be the last favor I ask of you, and I will be very obliged."

"What due?" The rich man asked angrily.

"The wages for twelve years of service, the payment you promised under the oath you made before his Honor the Imam here."

The rich man's eyes popped open wide. "Since you ask for your wages, you shall have it," he said calmly. "This morning I brought half a sack of wheat out of the barn to take to the mill. It's standing by the barn door. You can have it."

"Is half a sack of wheat all I get for twelve years of labor? For this, you would divorce your lawful wife?"

Upon hearing the orphan say this, the rich man was afraid of disgracing himself by public perjury. Embarrassed, he looked to the imam for help, since he had been a witness to the oath. The imam quickly came to the rich man's rescue, asking the orphan, "How much did your master promise to pay you every year when he hired you as a hand?"

"He didn't promise me anything except that he would make me his son-in-law."

"That doesn't count. How much money or property in compensation did he promise you?"

"He never promised me anything."

"Very well," said the imam, "in that case whatever your employer considers fitting is what you'll get for your service. Since he offers you half a sack of wheat, you should accept it gratefully. Even if he gave you a single bowl of wheat you would have no right to ask for more, and this man's obligation would still be fulfilled. According to the *shariat*, so long as he has compensated you and not made you work without pay, his oath is good, and he need not divorce his wife."

At first when the orphan heard the imam's legal finagling he was very angry, but then this gave him a new idea. Controlling himself, he said to the rich man: "Very well, I accept whatever you consider fitting. But what should I do if your wife won't let me take the sack of wheat?"

"If she doesn't believe you, then tell her to come out to the gate where she can see me, and I'll tell her she can give it to you."

The orphan ran to the rich man's yard, saddled the horse, and told the rich man's wife, "My uncle told me, 'Take the wheat to the mill, and take your sister with you so that she can see the mill before her wedding.' Tell my sister to get ready and come out."

"You're lying," said the wife. "He would never send his newly betrothed teenage daughter out with you!"

"If you don't believe me, go out and ask him from the gateway," the orphan replied.

The wife put a *jomacha* over her head and went to the gate with the orphan, from where they could see the men sitting talking in front of the mosque. The orphan waved to them and shouted to the rich man, "You see, she doesn't believe me, she won't let me!"

The rich man raised his hand in acknowledgement and shouted to his wife, "It's all right, I told him he could."

The orphan reentered the yard and, after loading the sack on his horse, he helped the girl, who had been waiting in readiness for just such a chance, to mount the horse behind him. The orphan rode out of the gate, spurred his horse in the opposite direction to the mosque, and galloped away. By the time the rich man found out and set off after them, the orphan and the girl had disappeared from sight. They rode till they reached a faraway land, where they lived happily ever after.

*   *   *

Tūta-posho told this story charmingly, in clear, simple, colloquial language, and despite the youth of her audience we were all enthralled by the tale. Alas, I cannot remember the old woman's exact words, and now, over sixty years later, I am obliged to write it in my own words; but I have tried my best to keep the story simple. I always think fondly of that illiterate, eighty-year-old woman as my first composition teacher.

Tūta-posho was indeed a very skillful story-teller. One evening before dark my mother gave me a plate of *shir-birinj* to take to the old woman. I brought her the rice, and she told me, "Sit awhile, I'll eat the rice and give you the plate to take back to your mother and she can wash it with the other dishes."

I sat down. Soon Usto Khoja's son Ikrom Khoja came in and sat down beside me. He asked the old woman to tell a story, but she said, "I'm not in the mood to tell stories tonight. I feel weak because I was so hungry and I couldn't sleep. After I eat this rice I'm going to sleep."

Ikrom Khoja was a rather rude and impudent boy, and he especially liked to tease the old woman. "If you don't tell us a story," he threatened, "I won't let you eat the rice," and he snatched up the plate of rice pudding and ran some way off. The old woman was forced to promise us a story. She took the rice back from Ikrom Khoja, finished it, and began.

8. A Time and a Place for Everything

Once upon a time, said Tūta-posho, there was a poor mullah. He lived in a cell in a madrasa. He had a friend who always used to invite him to dinner. This poor mullah always wished he could get a chance to host his friend in return. One day a wild pigeon chanced to fly into his cell. The mullah quickly got up and closed the door, trapping the pigeon. He caught and killed it, plucked and cleaned it; then he went to his neighbor in the next cell, explained what what had happened, and asked him for a spoonful of oil so he could cook the bird and feed his friend.

His neighbor gave him the oil. The mullah cooked the pigeon, put the lid on the pot, and went to fetch his friend. When the mullah left the cell, his neighbor brought in a live pigeon, substituted this for the cooked one, and left the pot covered as before.

Soon the mullah returned with his guest, seated him in the place of honor, washed his hands, rolled up his sleeves, washed the plate, and put it on the tablecloth. He picked up the ladle in his right hand, and with his left hand lifted the lid—and the pigeon flew out of the pot, fluttered round the cell, and vanished through the open door. The mullah, seeing his hopes so suddenly dashed, nearly fainted. He dropped the spoon, raised his hands and eyes heavenward and cried, "O God, for you to bring the dead back to life is right and proper, but everything has its place, don't you think? By resurrecting this cooked pigeon of mine you have embarrassed me in front of my guest and deprived us of a delicious meal!"[17]

When she had finished her story, the old woman said to Ikrom Khoja, "My boy, just as the mullah said, story-telling also has its time and place, and you shouldn't badger me to tell stories when I'm sick."

I heard a lot of stories from Tūta-posho, and I may well introduce more of them in the course of my reminiscences—at the proper time and place! Here I must note that this eighty-year-old woman had a hard life, and the telling of one or two anecdotes or legends would tire her out. But the children always insisted that she tell more. Ikrom Khoja in particular pestered her constantly to tell stories, Sometimes he would take the pillows from under her head and legs and run off with them, leaving the old woman in considerable pain.

Whenever this happened, the old woman would begin to tell stories of demons and evil spirits, in order to be rid of her tormentors. When the boys heard this kind of tale they were so scared they would run away, and Tūta-posho, with a relieved glance heavenward, would double herself up and go to sleep with her head and legs propped up on the pillows.

The story of the seven-headed *dev* was particularly scary. Although in the end this fierce, wicked, child-stealing demon is killed by the legendary Rustam on Mount Qof, the beginning of

---

[17] This well-known *witz* occurs also in Jewish folklore. In Muslim versions, the protagonist is often Nasreddin, the most popular trickster figure of Persian and Turkish folk literature. The thrust of the protest to God may vary: thus in a Turkish version, the Hoca (Khoja) has been cooking quails, and when live birds fly out of the pot he protests that God is entitled to bring the quails to life, but what gives him the right to make off with the Hoca's salt, pepper, vegetables, etc.? (Tokmakçioglu, Tale No. 94).

the tale was terrifying. Of all the boys, I alone listened to the story of the seven-headed *dev* to the end.[18]

As for the adults, the wife of Ibrohim Khoja, who was called Sulton-posho, was always avid for more when stories of demons and fairies were being told. She and Tūta-posho were neighbors, and on summer nights the two of them would sleep out on their *sufas*, which were next to each other. Sulton-posho did not care for ordinary stories, but whenever she heard Tūta-posho begin a story about *devs* or jinn, she would get up and come and sit in front of the old woman and encourage her.

Sulton-posho would repeat these stories to the women and children, adding a few tidbits of her own along the way. She claimed to have seen every kind of demon and fairy, including the seven-headed *dev*. She used to say that behind the *mehmonkhona* of Abdullo Khoja, her ninety-year-old father-in-law (whom she called Amak Bobo) lurked the seven-headed *dev* himself: first he would appear in the form of a cat, then a dog, then a wolf, a donkey, and finally would change into a black, evil-looking man with seven heads on his shoulders, who would gradually grow taller and taller until his heads reached the sky. If at that time he happened to see anyone, particularly a little boy, he would grab him and, hoisting him up to the sky, tenderize him between his hands, fry him on the sun, then tear him into pieces and eat him.

I asked her, "You saw him, but he didn't see you? Is that why he didn't pick you up and eat you?"

She answered, "Your uncle the mullah" — meaning her husband, Ibrohim Khoja, the would-be prayer-healer — "taught me the Greatest Name of God.[19] Whenever I see the seven-headed *dev*

---

[18] This encounter with the seven-headed *dev* is not part of the literary canon of Rustam's adventures.

At this point in the text, Aini notes that during World War II he wrote an article in which he compares Hitler and the Nazis to this same seven-headed *dev*, who would be vanquished by the Rustam of our time, i.e., the Red Army. It was published in the Tajik newspaper *Tojikistoni surkh* of 24 August 1941, in the Russian-language *Kommunist Tadzhikistana*, and in the Uzbek paper *Lenin Yūli*; it is also reproduced in the Aini anthology *Aknun navbati qalamast*, Vol. I, pp. 351-5.

[19] *Ismi a'zam*: there are conventionally ninety-nine known names of God (strictly, epithets, such as *al-majid* "the Glorious"); the hundredth name is not generally known to mortals, and anyone to whom it is revealed can use it to work magic.

I recite this as a charm and he can't hurt me." Then she added, "Don't you go telling stories about demons and evil spirits anywhere, or something dreadful is sure to happen to you. Tūta-posho and I aren't afraid of them, because we know the Greatest Name and nothing can harm us."

From that time forth I became very timorous, and as darkness fell I would tremble at anything I heard or saw for fear of demons and *jinn*. And since Sulton-posho had warned me not to repeat these stories, I dared not tell my parents anything.[20]

9. Demons and Dragons

Soktaré, which was known as the village of exorcists (*devband*) and prayer-healers (*duo-khon*), abounded in tales of jinn and dragons. Some four hundred yards northwest of our house lay a ruined mausoleum, consisting of a mound of earth and rubble, the summit and sides of which were covered with graves. In the northwest corner of this mound was a cave. Lovers of tall tales used to say that in this cave lived a dragon, which would leave its lair at night while all were asleep and go down to the banks of the Zarafshon river. Here it would dip its lower lip into the water and open its mouth wide, damming the river so that all the water flowed into its maw. Having drunk its fill, it would return to its den. Anyone who chanced upon the dragon while it was abroad would be swallowed alive. The only thing this beast feared was the wind: whenever the wind blew, the dragon would howl.

I believed this tale, and whenever the wind rose I would listen at the edge of the cemetery. And indeed, during high winds, a howling would issue from the cave.

On the west side of the cemetery was a low hillock called Gharib-Mazor, the "strangers' cemetery." Here were buried the bodies of people from outside Soktaré. This ground was overgrown with tangled, impenetrable undergrowth. At night a noise of howling and wailing could be heard coming from there, too; the storytellers held it to be the voices of jinn. 1 was scared of that undergrowth, too.

*   *   *

---

[20] This situation is expanded as the background to Aini's battle against superstition in *Ahmadi devband* (Appendix I, Section vi).

Once my mother left Soktaré to visit her parents in Mahallai Bolo, accompanied by my elder brother. 1 was left alone with mv father in the house at Soktaré. Father had sown a crop of wheat in the kitchen garden beneath the saplings, and had begun to harvest it. In those days, farmers used to be careful to water their wheat or barley fields on a windy day, so that the chaff and rubbish would be blown to one side and the soil would thus be cleared. One evening when we were on our own, since the wind had risen at sundown, my father started to water his wheat field; but before he had finished, the wind dropped. He left me sitting alone on the *sufa* while he swished the chaff out from between the stalks of wheat with a leafy branch.

While my father was away it grew dark, and I recalled Sulton-posho's story of the seven-headed *dev*. At the end of the *sufa* there appeared a cat; then, in quick succession, various dogs and donkeys, and among them one or two cute little donkey foals such as I had been longing to have and ride for myself. As I gazed at these foals, all the animals suddenly bunched together and changed into a black, seven-headed man, who started to grow taller and taller. All at once I screamed: "Help! Murder!"

"What happened? What's wrong?" came my father's voice; and as soon as I heard it, the seven-headed giant disappeared. Father came running up to see what was the matter, and I told him how I had seen the very seven-headed demon · in Sulton-posho's story.

Father laughed, and said, "There was once a great man, a scholar, Shaykh Sa'di, who said: *devs* have no dealings with men, fear them not—Fear rather devilish men!" This means that demons cannot harm humans, and that man is stronger than any other creature. If ever anything like this appears to you, don't be afraid, and remember these words of Shaykh Sa'di, because he always told the truth."

I asked him, "But who are these 'devilish men' that I have to be afraid of?"

"There are 'devilish men' everywhere. But they're especially numerous in our village—those who have set themselves up as professional prayer-healers and fool people into thinking them to be 'exorcists,' these are 'devilish men.' First they frighten people into believing in demons, then they take money from them on the pretext of exorcizing the same demons." My father was silent for a while, lost in thought; then he went on, "That cousin of mine, Ibrohim Khoja, has turned into a 'devilish man.' Only he's a stupid one—whereas the others get rich practicing their prayer-healing and exorcism, he can't make enough to feed himself. Nevertheless, he persists in this trade. And as if he isn't enough, his wife has also become a 'devilish woman' to aid and abet her husband's business! Don't you go to Sulton-posho any more, and don't listen to her tales; if she talks about demons and fairies, don't believe her."

These words of my father's greatly encouraged me. But I was still uneasy about the dragon in the cave and the jinn of the Gharib-Mazor, since I had heard the howling from the cave and the wailing from the undergrowth with my own ears. So I asked my father about these phenomena. He told me: "The noise you hear from the undergrowth of the Gharib-Mazor is the howling of jackals. That place is their den; the jackal that stole two of our hens this year is one of that pack. As for the noise you heard coming from the cave, I'll show you what causes that tomorrow."

*   *   *

Next day, my father made ready to take me to see the "dragon's lair." Before we set off, he brought me an empty water-jug and said: "Put your mouth near the edge of the jug and blow steadily." I did so, and from inside the jug came a loud, muffled booming. "Now remember that noise," said Father. "It will come in useful when we get to the cave." And he took me to the cemetery, up to the mouth of the cave.

Until then, I had never gone near the cave out of fear of the dragon. On that day I saw a porch-like hollow dug into the northwest side of the mound, about fifteen feet above ground level, its ceiling shored up with a column of baked bricks; and in front of the entrance to this, a cave—or perhaps a man-made shaft—leading steeply down into the hillside. My father pointed this out to me and explained: "Whenever a high wind blows into this porch, it is deflected back into the mouth of the cave, and since its way is still blocked, it comes rushing out again. The howling that can be heard coming from here on a windy day is just the wind rushing in and out of this cave." He reminded me of when I blew across the lip of the jug, and went on, "You heard what a noise the jug made when you blew into it—well, the wind is thousands of times stronger than your lungs, and the cave is much wider and deeper than that jug of ours. So when the wind blows, there's a fearful howling from the cave. That's all—no dragon's voice, and no dragon."

My father did in fact believe in the existence of demons and jinn, but differed from other people in his conviction that these creatures could not harm mankind, in confirmation of which he would quote those lines by Sa'di of Shiraz.

Thus it was that my father succeeded in dispelling my fear of supernatural beings, which was a considerable boon to me. From that time forth I was not afraid of being alone, or of the dark. Once when I was older, I made a bet with the boys who feared the "haunted" undergrowth of Gharib-Mazor that I would go there at night, and did, leaving my knife behind to prove I had been there. (This and other adventures on the same theme are recounted in my story *Ahmadi devband*.)[21]

10. Khaibar

That autumn, my father and Usto Khoja took counsel together and decided to send their eldest sons to school in Bukhara. My father undertook to accompany the boys there and see that lodgings were found for them. Early in September, before the start of the academic year at the Bukhara madrasas, he took Usto Khoja's eldest boy, Sayid-Akbar Khoja, and my elder brother Muhyiddin, to Bukhara, and left them in the charge of my uncle Mullo Dehqon, who in furtherance of my father's promise had undertaken to see them settled in.

After this, I was the only boy in the family and the sole help. I did have a younger brother, Sirojiddin, but he was still small and my father considered him as yet no more than an infant. So I always strove to assist my parents to the utmost of my ability, so that they would not miss my elder brother.

With the fall, the jackals of Gharib-Mazor intensified their raids on the villagers' poultry. Their first victims belonged to us and to our immediate neighbors, since our houses lay on the northern edge of the village, adjoining the open fields and the jackals' territory. And so that year my father bought a purebred shepherd dog from a shepherd uncle of mine in the village of Mahallai Bolo. His name was Khaibar.

Khaibar was a highly intelligent dog. In a very short time he understood everything we said to him and thoroughly knew his

---

[21] See Appendix I: the episode of the seven-headed *dev* is told in Section vi, that of the visit to the Gharib-Mazor in Section v.

duties. He realized that this family's chief concern was that the jackals should not make off with the chickens; accordingly he always mounted guard under the trees where the birds habitually roosted, and would now and then patrol the area in front of the gate to forestall any approaching jackals.

One day in spring, when the apricots were coming into flower and Khaibar was nearly one year old, my father went off to the mosque an hour after first light for morning prayers. I was already awake. Suddenly I heard the cackle of a chicken, followed by the sound of something heavy falling from the roof onto the ground. I got up at once, dressed, and called Khaibar. He didn't answer, and was not to be seen. I went over to the trees and checked the chickens; one was missing. Evidently it had been stolen by a jackal. I went out through the yard gate into the field. By now it was broad daylight and I could see far into the distance. About two hundred yards away I saw Khaibar facing toward the house; when he saw me he gave a peculiar bark, as if to call me over. In answer I called him to me. He picked up something in his mouth and started to trot toward me. About halfway he stopped, put down his burden, turned round and stared back the way he had come. Then he dashed pell-mell up to me, grabbed my shirttail in his teeth and pulled, whining strangely, then let go and raced back to stand over the object he had put down.

I realized that the dog had rescued the missing chicken from the jackal's clutches but, judging it too risky for the chicken to bring it back in his teeth, was urging me to go and pick it up myself. I walked over to where the dog stood, and indeed there was the chicken, alive, lying on the ground. I picked it up, and there on its body were the faint marks of a jackal's teeth and claws. I carried the chicken back to the house, with Khaibar romping around me happily all the way. When we came in to my mother, Khaybar rolled over on the floor, as if both to apologize for his remissness in letting the jackal get away with the bird and to express his joy at having been able to recover the captive.

Khaibar used to stay awake all night until my father left the house at daybreak to perform his ablutions before prayer. Only then would Khaibar contentedly climb onto the roof of my father's mill-wheel shop, which was strewn with straw, and settle down to sleep. The jackal, which had never been able to approach close enough to catch a chicken for fear of Khaibar, had apparently cottoned on to this habit of the dog's and, even though it was broad daylight, had been bold enough to creep up once the dog was asleep and snatch a bird. Now that Khaibar had learned how a jackal was capable of mounting a sneak attack like this, he would no longer go to sleep at daybreak, but maintained his watch until the whole household was up and about and the hens had come down from their roost.

Khaibar was a dog of considerable dignity and self-respect. One day he came into the kitchen and sniffed at a tray that was there. Mother saw this and gave him a whack with a stick of firewood. After that, he would not eat; all day he slept on his straw, and at night came down to guard the chickens. My mother told my father that Khaibar must be ill, as he had been off his food for two days. This news greatly upset me, since I had played a large part in his training and had grown fond of him, especially after the incident of the chicken and the jackal. So I took a piece of bread and went to see how he was. He was up on the roof, and came down when I called him. I tossed him the bread, and he ate it. I told my parents. Father told my mother to take him some bread, which she did; but the dog didn't even look at it. But when I gave him some, he ate it again.

Seeing this, my father said to my mother, "You seem to have offended Khaibar; I wonder how?" Mother told him about the incident when she had hit him. "In that case," replied Father, "The dog has a right to be offended. He's a shepherd dog; shepherds never prevent their dogs from approaching the cooking pot, so he wasn't shy about coming up to your kitchen tray for a sniff. You should have showed him gently, by words and gestures, that what he was doing was wrong. Since he didn't realize he was doing anything wrong, naturally he was offended that you hit him."

Khaibar was indeed deeply offended, and for several days more he refused to eat anything my mother offered him.

*　　*　　*

When we moved to Soktaré, my father had my mother set aside a bowl of whatever she cooked for his uncle Abdullo Khoja, and detailed me to take it to him and at the same time see to it that his water jug was kept full. Accordingly I would go to see "Amak Bobo," as we called him, several times a day. He was tall and thin, with a ruddy complexion, a fair-sized beard (which was not very gray, despite his ninety years) and long, bushy eyebrows. His eyebrows were so long that they covered his eyes; if he wanted to look at anything or anyone, he had to lift his eyebrows out of the way with the back of his hand. Not that he did look at anyone or talk to anyone; he always sat silently in the outer room. He was robust for his age. Once or twice a day he would come out into the yard, wash his hands and face, take a stroll, and return to his quiet corner. He was said never to have had a day's illness in his life. And even at his death he did not fall ill. One evening I brought him a bowl of stew, and the next morning went again with some bread and milk. He was lying at full length, with the stew bowl empty in front of him. I didn't put the bread and milk down in front of him in case the cat got it, but took it back and told my father that Amak Bobo was sleeping.

"He never used to sleep at this time," said Father; "He would always get up two hours before sunrise. I'd better go and see if anything's wrong." He got up and I went with him to Amak Bobo's room.

Before hie went inside, my father looked at the water jug that stood by the door. "The jug's empty," he observed. "That means he did get up this morning." He went in and sit down by Amak Bobo's side, and checked first his pulse and then his heart. "He's dead," he announced. "Recently—his body is still warm."

Father told me to go and call Usto Amak. I fetched him, and the two of them got the dead man onto a shutter, then wrapped him in a shroud. His son was away, no-one knew where, so he could not be told. The villagers were informed, and on the same day, after the afternoon prayer, they carried the corpse to the courtyard of the mosque and held the funeral service. Then they all grabbed hold of the cloth that covered his coffin and began tearing it into pieces, which they took away with them. I asked my father why they were doing this, and he replied: "The fools think that his coffin-cover will bring them good luck. It doesn't matter that none of them ever once asked after him while he was alive—now that he's dead, the cloth that covered his coffin (which I brought from my house!) is suddenly a talisman for them."

11. Usto Amak

In winter, when house-building came to a standstill, Usto Amak (Usto Khoja, to give him his proper name) would be out in the porch of his courtyard, making doors. The doors he fashioned were of elm; he would polish the planks until the reflection was dazzling, then on their iron-hard surfaces he would carve designs with a variety of steel chisels. So delicate and beautiful were the figures he carved that you would swear they were the work of a master miniaturist working with a pencil brush on paper.

Usto Amak was broad-browed, courteous, articulate, and a first-rate jokester. There wasn't an ounce of deceit or arrogance in him; he addressed young and old, great and small, with the same unassuming good humor, and treated all as his equals. He would regard me, a small child, with a serious eye when I asked him about his work, and answer every question in detail, taking pains to explain the intricacies of his craft. His work, which appeared very boring to me, bored him not at all; from first light to evening dusk he never stirred from his carving.

"Uncle," I asked him one day, "Who taught you to carve so beautifully? Who were you apprenticed to?"

He replied: "My relatives are all woodworkers. You see, your father's a master carpenter, so is your uncle, so was your great-uncle—well, our grandfathers and great-grandfathers were all master craftsmen too; but not one of them was ever apprenticed to anyone—they learned from watching one another. Then each according to his own talent and industry became more or less specialized. I learned to cut timber from my father and grandfather; later I expanded my skills on my own. I got my first patterns for woodworking from the stones of our mosque, then I invented more fitting and beautiful designs out of my own head." Usto Amak showed me a design he had drawn on a piece of paper, and explained: "This pattern is called *duvozdah-gireh*, 'twelve knots.' This one," he went on, showing me another, "is the same 'twelve knots' with the difference that in among the twelvefold knot designs there are stars and almond shapes. You see how much prettier and more striking this *duvozdah-gireh* is than the old one? Well, I invented these extra curlicues and cmbined them with the traditional twelve knots.'"

Usto Amak put away the papers with his designs on them in his leather wallet, and went on: "If a pupil were content to learn only from his master, no craft on earth would make any progress. Successful craftsmen are those who invent things out of their own heads and integrate these with the techniques they learned from their masters. Wait here, I'll show you something interesting." So saying, he stood up and went inside, to return with a length of cane some eighteen inches long with a bore of about a quarter inch.

Usto Amak took his cylindrical file and reamed the bore. Then at one end of the cane he cut a rectangular opening about half the size of a man's fingernail. Next he shaved a piece of sheepskin very thin, cut from it a bit large enough to cover this opening, and sewed a length of thread to one end of it. With an awl, he pierced a hole near the upper end of the opening; he inserted the thread attached to the piece of leather inside the cane until it was level with this hole, then pulled it through from outside with a small wire hook. He pulled firmly on the thread until the leather flap lodged against the inside of the cane, hanging so that it completely blocked the rectangular opening from within. Next he cut a piece of wood as a stopper, and plugged the end of the cane nearest the opening. Then he fetched a dry mulberry twig; at one end he fashioned a double crosspiece at right angles to the stem, then pared down the stem from the neck of this to the end. He cut out another flap from the sheepskin, of a size to cover the bore of the cane, pierced the center, pushed the twig through it and fixed the flap to the crosspiece. At the other end of the cane, near the mouth, he bored a hole and stuck a weaver's reed into it. He next poured some water into a bucket, inserted the twig (which he called the "handle") crosspiece-first into the cane, and placed the end of the reed in the water, holding the other end upright. When he moved the plunger up and down, water entered the cane, rose, and started to pour out of the weaver's reed at the top.

I was amazed, and asked Usto Amak how the water got into the cane and came up to the top. He explained: "When we pull the plunger up, the leather flap fitted to the crosspiece at the end pushes up the air inside the cane. Once the bottom of the cane is emptied of air, the water forces its way through the opening, water pressure pushes the leather valve away from the opening, and water replaces the air inside the tube of the cane. When we push the plunger down, the water pressing back against the valve closes it tight against the opening, which won't let the water flow back into the bucket. As the plunger is pushed down, the water pressure forces the leather flap away from the crosspiece, so that water gets past and into the top part of the tube. So with two or three up-and-down actions of the plunger the cane fills with water and it starts to pour out of the reed."

At the close of his explanation Usto Amak gave the apparatus to me, saying, "This will be a good plaything for you. We can call it 'Water Pump, Mark I.'" I was all agog at his cleverness, and asked him, "Did you think up this toy out of your own head?"

"No," he replied, "The original of this water pump was made by my father, Sayid-Ahmad Khoja, your grandfather—that is, your father's father. What he did was to saw a long, thick Samarkand poplar log lengthwise in two—the kind of poplar that in

Samarkand is called *shamshod*—then hollow out each half like a trough and glue them together to form a tube. He also fitted a couple of iron hoops so that it would hold under pressure of the water. When he'd completed this, your grandfather took it down to our mosque on Friday, when everyone from the district was gathered there for public prayers, and used it to pump water from the pool of the mosque up to the roof. Everyone was astounded. But my father's pump was so powerful that the plunger couldn't be operated by one man. They fitted a pole across the top, which was pushed and pulled by two hefty young men, one at each end; then the water came splashing out as if from the spout of a jug."

Usto Amak sat down by his handiwork and, sharpening his chisels with his whetstone, went on: "That year the water level of the Zarafshon river was low to start with, and in summer it dried up all together. The fields by the riverside that are usually not watered and get by on river seepage alone looked like drying up, too. At that point the villagers brought this same pump of your grandfather's down to the bank of the Zarafshon and used it to water their fields from the puddles in the riverbed."

Usto Amak recommenced his carving and said, "It was none other than your grandfather who invented that machine; I was only seven years old at the time. But I remembered how it was made. You seem like a handy lad, so I've made this toy for you, modeled on the same pump. Off you go and play!"

Ten years after this, I saw a professional-looking metal version of this apparatus, which had been brought from Russia; it was used for pumping kerosene out of barrels, and was known by its Russian name of *nasós*.[22]

* * *

Usto Amak wished to make his younger son, Ikrom Khoja, into a skilled craftsman. But the latter paid no heed to his father's instruction and deliberately spoiled any of his father's wood-carving commissions that he had a hand in. One day Usto Amak

---

[22] The usual Russian term for a (suction) pump, from the root *sos-* "suck," and now in general use in Tajik. Usto Amak's own term was *ob-kashak* "water-drawer." The suction or piston pump described here was used in mines in medieval Europe, and was first described in Agricola's *De Re Metallica* of 1556. Aini made a similar one from memory during his student days (*Yoddoshtho* Part 4, sixth chapter).

was complaining to my father about his sons. "Sayid-Akbar, true to his name, has grown too big for his boots.[23] He doesn't care to learn the craft, and considers this work to be beneath him. Very well, I said to myself, since he doesn't want to be an artist and a man, to hell with him, he can go and be a mullah or the like, and sent him to learn to read. But then this younger brother of his is even worse: I struggled to teach him myself for two years, and he stayed in the *maktab* for another three, but apart from basic reading, he didn't learn a thing. As for handicraft, he won't have anything to do with it. At this rate he'll make neither a man nor a mullah; by and by he'll end up an ass."

"Better an ass than a mullah," my father answered.

Ikrom Khoja was indeed very stubborn. One day his father traced an interlaced chain design (*islimi*) on a board for him to practice carving. But he chipped out the places he should have left, and left untouched the places he should have cut out. Every time I reminded him of his father's instructions he refused to listen, telling me I didn't know how to do it. When he showed his handiwork to his father, the latter saw red and, brandishing an ax handle on which he had been working, yelled at his son, "Get out of my sight before I thrash you!" Ikrom Khoja stepped back a couple of paces. Usto Amak, still bent on mayhem, stood up and repeated, "Get out, or. . !"

Ikrom Khoja fled toward the inner yard, pursued by Usto Amak. I was scared that if the carpenter hit his son with that stick he would cripple him, and I ran after them, crying, "Uncle, don't hit him!" Ikrom Khoja ran out of the inner courtyard and stopped at the outside gate. Usto Amak reached the middle of the yard and sat down a moment to catch his breath, then got up again and shouted, "If I catch you. . !" Ikrom Khoja took off through the gate, Usto Amak hot on his heels, while I yelled "Don't hit him!" In this way father and son completed two laps round the adjacent fields. Finally, Usto Amak shouted to his son, "Come on, I won't hit you now—I've calmed down. But from now on, do a proper job."

He turned back toward the house and I followed him. On the way he said to me, "You were afraid I was going to beat your poor cousin Ikrom, but I wasn't. An ass doesn't beat its foal, an ox doesn't beat its calf, so why should a man beat his child? I just wanted to scare him into learning to carve properly. Don't tell your father about this, or he'll have a good laugh."

---

[23] *Akbar* in Arabic means "bigger, greater" -- A.

Figure 4. Wood carving: portrait of
Sadriddin Aini (B. Nuriddinov, 1958)

Apart from their being brothers, Usto Amak and my father were very close friends. They thought alike and shared the same attitude toward others. The only difference was that Usto Amak was soft-spoken, courteous, and appeared not to take things too seriously; he would counter others' harsh deeds with good-humored words. For instance, we had a neighbor called Aziz Khoja. Once he tied his son, E'lom Khoja, to a tree and started thrashing him. Usto Amak heard the boy's cries and went over to their house. Seizing Aziz Khoja's arm, he said, "That's enough, Uncle, the lad is sorry, he won't disobey you in future."

"He's a madman, he doesn't know the meaning of 'sorry,' what he needs is a beating to bring him to his senses!" raved Aziz Khoja, breaking free of Usto Amak's grip and laying into his son again. Usto Amak countered: "Uncle, you're a strange man; it's no great matter to have two madmen in the house—why, I know ten houses in our own village with two or three madmen in each of them!"

With these words, Usto Amak had called Aziz Khoja himself a madman, and by the same token had taken a sideswipe at the self-styled exorcists of the village. But all this was said with such good humor that the listener, though he knew full well who was meant, was at a loss for a suitable retort.

My father, on the other hand, was rather more direct and sharp-tongued; he made it abruptly clear when he did not find someone's conduct to his liking, and had no compunction about offending the other party.

12. Lutfillo Gūppon

Another person in Soktaré who attracted my attention, despite my youth, was Lutfillo Gūppon.[24] He was the stepson of our immediate neighbor, Avez Khoja. Avez Khoja was a landless peasant: he worked as a day laborer (*koranda*, or "sower"), or as a share cropper (*choryak-kor*) for one quarter of the harvest, in the fields of landowners who did not or could not work their own

---

[24] *Gūppon* means "big, tough; champion." Aini notes later in the chapter that Lutfillo (more formally, Lutfullo) Gūppon is also portrayed in *Ahmadi devband*; actually he appears there under the name of Niyoz-Gūppon, and in quite different episodes (see Appendix I, Sections iv-v).

land. He had two young sons of his own: the elder, Nizom Khoja, he had sent to school, and the younger, who was my age, was still too young to work. Avez Khoja himself was a man who talked much and worked little, and the twenty *tanob* he had contracted for was worked single-handed by Lutfillo Gūppon.

The farmers of Soktaré generally used a type of mattock made by Usto Dūstboi of Ghijduvon, which weighed nearly nine pounds. There were said to be ten men who had ordered an eleven-pound mattock from Usto Dūstboi the mattock-caster; one of them was Lutfillo Gūppon. The locals, however, distinguished between Lutfillo and the nine other wielders of the "great mattock": Lutfillo, they said, was "possessed." They told how he would hack away steadily without a break from early morning until lunch, and from lunch until sundown, and that for lunch he ate four times as much as the other laborers.

One day I was playing with my toy pump on the bank of the Mazrangon stream, which flows through the village. A certain Abdushukur Khoja, of the Sayid-Atoyi Khojas, with a couple of other youths, came along with the intention of damming the stream and diverting the water to his orchard. But his men were unable to manage it; every time they shoveled mud and earth into the stream, the current washed it away. At this juncture Lutfillo Gūppon appeared, and after watching their attempts at damming the stream for a while, he said to Abdushukur Khoja, "Uncle, what will you give me if I dam this stream for you on my own?"

"A loaf of bread and a *qabza* of halva," replied Abdushukur Khoja.

Lutfillo accepted, stripped down to his loincloth, and set to work. First he piled up earth on both sides of the stream. The problem was that there was no turf or firm clay available; the bed of the stream was composed of sand, and the banks of loose sandy earth. Nevertheless, Lutfillo Gūppon waded confidently into the stream and raked down the earth he had piled up on one side, blocking one third of the waterway. Then he waded over to the other bank and in the same way blocked off another third. Now came the hard part: squeezed through the central third of the passageway, the stream redoubled its force and began to wash away the loose, newly deposited earth.

But Lutfillo was not about to let it: he lay down at full length across the gap, holding in place the earthen bank on one side with his head and neck, and on the other with his legs and feet. His body formed as it were a central weir, over which the water rushed foaming. In this position, Lutfillo plied his great mattock in the streambed on the upstream side, shoveling up earth and plastering it over his own body. His arms moved so fast, I had never seen anything like it. Much later, when the railroad ran across the Bukhara steppe and I saw the locomotive's pistons flashing back and forth, I was reminded of the speed with which Lutfillo Gūppon's arms moved, and at that moment saw a perfect parallel between the two.[25]

Once the central dam had risen higher than his own body, Lutfillo got up and knelt behind it and, holding the dam in place with his belly, with the same speed and agility as before, raked more mud onto the dam from upstream so as to raise and reinforce it. Then he climbed out of the water and shoveled dry earth onto the top; there was now no risk of its being washed away.

Usto Amak, who had also witnessed this spectacle, turned to Lutfillo and cried, "Well done, lad! God grant you live a thousand years! May you live for ever!"

Abdushukur Khoja burst out laughing and said to Usto Amak, "Usto Khoja, you have wished something for Lutfillo that he cannot possibly accept and which is no earthly use to him—who on earth could live a thousand years? Who is there that is not mortal? You would have done better to wish him wealth and a full stomach."

Usto Amak answered Abdushukur with his habitual good humor. "Permit me, dear *eshon*, to explain the meaning of my prayer."

"Please do," said Abdushukur Khoja.

"By wishing someone a thousand years of life, I mean not that he should spend a thousand years of his actual existence, but that in his day-to-day life he should do such deeds as another might do in a thousand years, were he to live so long; and similarly, by wishing that he might never die, I do not mean that, like the legendary drinker of the Water of Life, he should live out a life worse than death until doomsday, but that he should do such deeds as will make his name live on in the world."

---

[25] The Transcaspian Railroad, extended from Krasnovodsk on the eastern shore of Caspian Sea, reached Ashkhabad in 1885. The emir of Bukhara was obliged to permit the Russians to build it across his territory; the line reached Samarkand, via Bukhara, in 1888, when Aini was ten years old, though he would not have seen it until his adult years.

Abdushukur asked, mockingly, "Fine—and what deeds could Lutfillo perform that another might do only in a thousand years, and which would make his name immortal?"

Usto Amak replied, "Lutfillo has lived thirty years, and during that time, ever since he took up his mattock, he has kept a whole family fed by his labors. Whereas you in your sixty years of life have not filled your own belly by your labors, let alone a family."

"Oh yes?" Abdushukur retorted sarcastically. "I spend my time chasing up students, and earn between a hundred and two hundred *tangas* a month teaching them. From this work, I and my family live like kings. What more should I do?"

"Bravo," laughed Usto Amak. "You've admitted it yourself. 'Chasing up students' is hardly a job of work. Certainly, hunting game or trapping birds is a trade, but 'chasing up students'—hunting humans—what do you mean by that?"

"Catching gulls," said a voice from the back. "Tricking people into his snare." Everybody laughed; Abdushukur turned bright red with embarrassment, and joined in the laughter. "Come on, enough of this talk—now we'll watch Lutfillo eating the halva he got from his labors." And so saying, he ordered one of his men to bring a loaf of bread from his house and a *qabza* of halva from the Urgenchis' store.

* * *

Gūppon divided the flat loaf into four, then likewise the halva, wrapped the one in the other, swallowed all four mouthfuls, cupped his hands and drank from the stream, then recited: "Lip says 'Here it is,' Mouth says 'In it comes,' Belly says 'What gives? Where's it gone?'" Everyone laughed, and one young man asked him: "Hey, Lutfillo, how many more handfuls of halva could you eat right now?"

"Right now, three more; later, four more."

"Nonsense," sneered another. "You couldn't eat even one more."

"Bring on the halva and you'll see how much I can eat," Gūppon retorted.

"I'll bet on it," shouted another youth. "Where's the extra halva?"

"Whatever you're betting, I'll take you on," said Lutfillo. "Get the halva."

"Three *qabza* of halva cost three *tangas*," said the youth who had proposed a wager. "If you can eat them, *bon appétit*, you'll get three *tangas* into the bargain. If you can't, you give us the three *tangas* for the halva and three *tangas* forfeit. What do you say?"

"I've already said it: bring me some halva in addition to what I've already polished off, so's I can eat my fill, that's what I say!"

They brought the halva. Lutfillo set to; after each mouthful of halva he took a gulp of water, and when he had eaten it he took three *tangas* from his challengers. "You've really won six—no, seven *tangas*," said the man who had brought the halva, and explained: "Three *qabza* of halva weighs just three *nimcha* (two-and-a-half pounds). I actually bought four *nimcha* (five pounds) and cut it into three 'handfuls' to fool you—cost me four *tangas*!"

You did me a favor," said Lutfillo, and added pointedly to Abdushukur Khoja, "My friend the *eshon* fools people and takes their money, you fool me and give me money. Much obliged to you!" All laughed, got up and went their separate ways.

*   *   *

In Soktaré, whenever my father had finished his field chores, he would get on with some weaving. Mostly he wove cotton canvas. He would give a length of this to the fuller to be bleached and softened, and from this he would have a suit of tunic and trousers made for himself. The rest he had made up into quilt and cushion covers, tablecloths, and other household articles, then sent to the dyer to be block-printed (dyers usually chose a color and design appropriate to each article, so the cloth had first to be sewn and then printed). When he wove *qalami*—in which the warp threads were already dyed—he would have tunics and trousers made for us boys, and shirt-jackets for both himself and us. If he had woven *alocha*—a red, white, and green striped material—he would provide us all with tunics and trousers, including himself. For my elder brother, who would be going to Bukhara, he bought machine-woven material and had a woollen tunic-and-trouser suit made and a chintz shirt-jacket. The rest of us wore homespun, hand-woven clothing. My father also dyed most of the stuff he wove in home-made dyes: from dyer's weed he produced beige, from pomegranate rind, black; by mixing dyer's weed with something black he produced pistachio red; from madder he produced bright red—and so on. The only colors he needed to order from the dyer were olive green and blue, which were made from indigo.

My mother helped greatly with all these tasks. Apart from picking fruit, she spent most of her time spinning yarn and thread and winding skeins and spools, and also dyed the yarns under my father's supervision.

As winter drew to a close, my father made ready to go to Mahallayi Bolo in order to fashion mill wheels from lumber he had stored there, and to sell the wheels he had made and take orders for new ones from the mills of the district. My mother was fearful of staying by herself with two young children in a dilapidated house, but my father paid no heed to her remonstrations. "The wolves won't eat you," he said, "and even if they do come close, there's Khaibar." And off he went.

13. A New Channel for the Shofirkom

Spring was here. Apricot saplings burst into flower, Balkh mulberry bushes put out green berries on their twigs, and the large mulberry trees had their leafy branches chopped off to feed the silkworms. The Mazrangon stream, swollen by the spring meltwater, was a roaring, muddy torrent. The villagers yoked up their teams, ploughed, harrowed and sowed. The swallows fashioned wet clay into something like huge cotton bolls and with wonderful dexterity constructed their keel-shaped homes under the eaves of the houses. The storks built their nest atop the mausoleum gateway, and brought home their dinner of water snakes they had caught among the reeds on the riverbank. Peacock-hued pheasants, their irridescent wing feathers wonderful to behold, flushed out by the storks, scampered from thicket to thicket, their raucous cries warning their fellows of danger. In short, everything—people, birds, plants—was astir.

On one such day, when a spring cloud was momentarily shielding the toilers in the fields from the sun's blazing rays, my father returned from the village of Mahallayi Bolo. I was in the back alley by the mosque, playing "horsey" astride Khaibar, who welcomed him with wagging tail and joyful barks. He tethered the donkey under a mulberry tree, took off the *khurjin*, and went into the house. Khaibar and I had preceded him and told Mother of his arrival; she rushed out, took the saddlebag from him, and asked how things had gone. He came in with no more than a perfunctory response to her welcome, and passed on greetings from her parents. Mother put the *khurjin* in an alcove of the kitchen, took my father's coat and satchel and hung them on a nail in the wall, spread a quilt over his usual sitting place and arranged bolsters on either side. In the same subdued tones, he told my mother to heat up the samovar for tea and to take the meat out of his satchel and put it away so the cat would not get it; then he rearranged both bolsters at one end of the quilt and lay down. 1 sat down silently where I could see his gloomy face.

When she had brewed the tea, my mother spread a tablecloth in front of him and served bread and dried apricot jelly. My father roused himself and squatted to eat, but even then his expression remained troubled. Trying to elicit the cause of his depression, my mother asked, "Didn't you manage to sell the wheels?"

"Yes, I did," he replied. "I also bought two elms and had them cut to size, so I can go and make wheels out of them in summer." And he relapsed into silence. "Then I hope you haven't fallen sick, that you're looking so pale and unhappy?" my mother went on.

"I'm sick all right, but not from any illness—sick at heart for the people of Shofirkom," he replied, and fell silent again.

My mother had found the end of the thread in the tangled skein of my father's preoccupation. She now needed to unravel it, so she went on probing: "There's been talk of their digging a new canal in Shofirkom. Is it true?"

"It's true," said Father; "and I wish they hadn't. Excavating that new watercourse has only caused new problems for the people there, on top of the woes they suffered from the sandstorm—'sentenced to death, plus one hundred lashes,' as the saying goes." Father had relaxed a little, and began to explain. It seems that last autumn the people of the Shofirkom region had attempted on their own initiative to dig out the old channel and start it flowing again, but without success. They had shoveled out the sand several times and had gotten a trickle of water flowing as far as the Qo-qo steppe, but barely two days later the banks had collapsed again and buried it. Thereupon the elders and landlords and *amins* of the *tuman* had petitioned the emir to provide them with a new watercourse, for which they would furnish the labor and expenses. The emir sent instructions to the four administrative heads of the *tuman*—the *qozi*, the *ra'is*, the *amlokdor*, and the *mirshab*—to carry out the project forthwith. They determined the site to be excavated, called on all able-bodied persons to join in the labor, and set to work.

Figure 5. Collective farm workers with mattocks, 1930

From the beginning of winter up to the present time—four months—they had scarcely excavated half a *sang* (two miles) of the proposed channel, but already everything the people of Shofirkom still owned after the ravages of the sandstorm had gone to defray the four officials' expenses. The irrigation scheme, in my father's words, progressed as follows.

"One day I went to the work site, to see how the unpaid labor was going. The four officials and their entourages, plus the *arbobs* and *amins* of the *tuman*—about two hundred people in all—were encamped over a wide area of the steppe. Hundreds of laborers were sleeping all over the place. Butchers were slaughtering sheep, cooks were preparing rice and mutton stew, bakers were turning out thick loaves of flat bread. The horses of the two hundred-odd supervisors were tethered by their masters' tents, munching fresh clover-hay, with bags full of barley for their evening meal standing by. Village headmen were bringing in donkey-loads of rice, barley, and flour. All over the campsite, huge samovars were boiling. The two hundred bosses were enjoying their rice and kabob and tea. The day was well advanced: about two hours remained to sunset. At this point the *amins* emerged from their tents and called to their respective foremen to round up their men and get them to work. This took nearly another hour. Once the work started, each gang had dug one or two feet more in its sector when dusk began to fall, and the foremen relayed the *amins'* instructions to stop work for the day, warning them to start earlier the next day or else they'd have to pay a fine! And that's how the work is going," Father concluded.

"But what good is it to the four officials to have the work drag on like this?" my mother asked.

"If the job gets finished, where will those two hundred bosses get their daily bread, pilaf and kabob, and what will their horses do for clover and barley?" my father answered. "And it isn't just a free lunch they get out of it—of ten thousand *tangas* per day they collect for the laborers' expenses, they steal the half of it in cash before they cook and eat the other half."

My father drank a cup of tea and was silent for a while, but his eye held a gleam of defiance. He looked at my mother and said, "I *have* done something—I don't know whether it will work or not. But I think it might." However, he did not tell us what it was, and fell silent again. My mother waited a little; then, seeing that he was not about to volunteer anything further, asked, "Well, what *did* you do?"

"This isn't the time to tell anyone anything about what I've done; don't you tell anyone, either," he said, and started to explain. "I saw that the residents of the *tuman* would be pauperized and that the new watercourse would never be dug anyway. So I wrote a petition to the emir, a whole sheet of the largest size paper. In it I described the way the work was proceeding, as I told you just now. And I requested that he appoint an honest man to see that the work is finished sooner. I pointed out that the delay harms both the people and the government; for if the channel is not dug, and the water does not flow, the fields must remain unsown, and then where will His Highness get his taxes and revenue?"

"In whose name did you write the petition?" asked Mother.

"In my own behalf," Father replied, "but anonymously. I wrote: 'The petitioner owns no land in this *tuman* and has no need of water. The situation has been brought to Your Highness' notice purely in hopes of benefiting both people and state.'"

"Have you sent the petition to the emir?" asked my mother, in relieved tones.

"It will definitely reach him," said Father. "After I had written it, I gave it to your brother Qurbon-Niyoz. He's a bold and intelligent fellow. When he goes to Bukhara, he'll stand in the crowd outside the palace on Friday when the emir rides out to go the the mosque, and will hold up the petition as the emir passes; an outrider will take it and hand it to the emir. When he reads it, the emir will have to do something about it, since it's in his own interest."

Once my father had described what he had done, his petition seemed to have a practical effect on him. His spirits rose, his brow cleared, and not a trace remained in his demeanor of the gloom that had marked his arrival, as he busied himself with his day-to-day tasks as usual.

* * *

Two weeks after my father's return from Mahallayi Bolo, my elder brother Muhyiddin and Sayid-Akbar Khoja, having finished their schooling in Bukhara, came home from the city. After a couple of weeks' relaxation, they both recommenced their studies with the village *khatib*. A month after that, my uncle Mullo Dehqon came to visit his sister, my mother. He told us that in Bukhara he was the classmate of the son of the kadi of Ghijduvon, Qozi Abdul-Vohid, and that after graduating they had both gone to Ghijduvon in order to continue their studies under the kadi.

However, the kadi had received a "Hallowed Rescript," that is, a commission from the emir, to go to Shofirkom and supervise the excavation and irrigation of the new watercourse, ensuring that the water would be flowing by the end of the summer and the farmers should be able to use it for their autumn sowing.

On hearing this news from my uncle, Father seemed to shoot up from where he sat until he was ten feet tall, his head held sky-high and his chest thrown forward, as if the joy that this news obviously produced could not be contained within his heart, and his chest was seeking to expand in order to accommodate it. Nevertheless, except for a satisfied smile and a meaningful look directed at my mother, he said not a word about his petition. He merely asked my uncle, "Well, now that they've appointed a new director, how is the excavation coming along?"

"While I was in Ghijduvon," my uncle replied, "these orders arrived for my master the kadi, and he immediately laid aside his teaching and went to the site. I stayed on a few more days with my classmate, the kadi's son, then came straight here to see my sister; from here, I'll be going to visit my parents—so I've no idea how the work is going. I have heard this much—that the emir has dismissed the four officials who were in charge of the project up to now, and confiscated all their wealth and property!"

*   *   *

Ten days later, my uncle made ready to leave in order to go and see his parents, and my father decided to go along with him and see how the excavation of the canal was progressing under the supervision of the kadi of Ghij duvon. I asked him if I could go too. Father consented, and the three of us journeyed to Mahallayi Bolo and stayed at my grandfather's house. The village elders came to see my father and uncle, and all to a man spoke highly of the new head of operations at the canal site. They reported that the kadi of Ghijduvon had ordered the workers all to be ready at daybreak, and to work through the day until dusk, with a one-hour break for lunch. Each worker was to bring his own food from home, and the *arbobs* and *amins* were likewise to bring their own food and not to extort expenses from the peasantry. Even the kadi came to work with only two men, a courier to convey his written and oral instructions around the site, and a personal servant, and also brought his own food. In the space of the ten days since Qozi Abdulvohid had taken over direction of the excavation, it had progressed as much again as it had during the previous six months.

On hearing this, my father was happier than ever, and suggested to my uncle, "Let's go and see the excavation too, and encourage the workers!" My uncle agreed, and my father took me along.

The channel had been dug as far as the village of Rūbaho, less than a mile to the south of Mahallayi Bolo. When we arrived, the kadi was standing on the bank of the channel, his robe hitched up about his waist, a long willow staff in his hand. He was a slim man, of medium height, with a medium-length white beard, and eyebrows long and bushy like those of my late great-uncle Abdullo Khoja. My uncle bowed deferentially to his teacher, exchanged greetings, then introduced my father as "my brother-in-law, who has come to pay his respects."

The kadi shook hands with my father, then asked my uncle, "Isn't this the person who taught you to read and write and sent you to the madrasa ?"

"The same," replied my uncle.

The kadi looked at my father and said, "I have heard from my son, who is your brother-in-law's classmate, that we have you to thank for educating this young man," and he clasped my father's hands again. Then the kadi's eye fell on me, and he asked my father, "Whose son is this?"

"He's my boy," answered Father.

The kadi lifted me up to his eye level, then put me down and said, "God grant that you grow tall, and become a learned man!" He took out from his purse a piece of locally-made candy wrapped in red paper and gave it to me, asking my father, "Does the lad read?"

"We're sending him to school this autumn," my father replied.

My other uncles—Qurbon-Niyoz, Ravshan-Niyoz, and Niyoz Khon—were among the workers in the trench, and came up to greet my father and uncle. "Who are these men?" asked the kadi.

"My brothers-in-law," answered Mullo Dehqon.

"Fine, they're good workers," said the kadi; and, turning to my uncles: "All right, go back to work now—you can talk to our friends here this evening." He asked Qurbon-Niyoz, however, to stay behind a minute, and after my two other uncles had returned to work he said to Mullo Dehqon, "This brother-in-law of yours"—switching from the formal to the familiar pronoun—"is a phenomenal worker! There are only ten others like him out of all the rest of the volunteers, but he exceeds them in intelligence and self-confidence."

Standing and talking must have tired the old kadi for, leaning on his stick, he sat down and signed to his companions to sit too. He continued: "On my first day in charge of the project, I ordered the *amins* to find ten master carpenters so that we could be building bridges, weirs, and catchment basins as the excavation progressed. One of the *amins* told me, 'Each carpenter will cost five *tangas* per day; ten will cost you fifty *tangas*. Since you've stopped us collecting expenses, where will you find the carpenters' wages?' At that, this young man"—the kadi indicated Qurbon-Niyoz—"spoke up: 'Begging your pardon, sir,' he said—'Go on,' I told him—'Well,' he said, 'there are fifty carpenters and joiners digging in the trench with the rest of the volunteers; if they were let off excavating and put to wood-working, they'd gladly do it for free.' So I at once gathered the carpenters together, selected the ten most skilled, and set them to making bridges, weirs, and basins to keep pace with the excavation of the watercourse. This young man's intelligence and forthrightness impressed me; if he had been too shy to speak up, his intelligence would have availed him nothing, and he wouldn't have been able to advise me in front of those smug *amins*. So you see, one needs self-confidence as well as intelligence! And conversely, ignorant self-confidence is just as useless."

The kadi turned now to my uncle, Mullo Dehqon. "If you'll appoint this brother-in-law of yours as my assistant, I shall be grateful," he said; then, as an afterthought, "Can he read and write?"

"No," admitted Mullo Dehqon.

"Never mind. Smart and forthright as he is, he'll do well enough, and he'll learn a lot for himself."

The kadi let Qurbon-Niyoz return to work, and had his servant bring tea. The servant unhooked a leather bag from the branch of a tree and took out of it a china cup and a brass teapot, poured out a cupful and handed it to the kadi. The latter drank it in a couple of gulps and told the servant to give his companions a drink. To my father he explained, "We brewed this tea in Ghijduvon before we came here, so it has gone cold. But not to worry, it's better than having only cold water to drink." When my father and uncle had each drunk a cup of the cold tea, the kadi stood up, and the others followed suit. "Come," he said, "let's wish the workers godspeed."

The kadi set off, my father and uncle on either side and a little to the rear, while I tagged along behind them. The kadi stopped for a moment by each laboring gang of volunteers to call out a word of encouragement, and directed a special "bravo!" or "well done, keep it up!" to the more industrious ones before moving on. The *arbobs* and amins who were sitting in the shade would see the kadi approaching in the distance and get up, hurry to the edge of the trench and yell instructions. At one point a very fat *amin* heaved himself to the edge of the trench and started telling the workers how to dig in a voice loud enough for the kadi to hear. When the kadi reached him he greeted him and bowed humbly. The kadi told him: "Foreman, you have grown far too fat. Your obesity is a burden to you and makes you uncomfortable. And the sort of work you are doing for me, like the other *arbobs* and *amins*, will not lighten your burden. You ought to pick up a mattock sometimes from one of the laborers and do some digging, to lighten both your own load and that of the laborer."

The *amin* said "Yessir," hurried to the trench, took a mattock from one of the laborers and started to hack at the earth. After a dozen or so lunges, however, he was so drowned in sweat that he looked as if a bucketful of water were cascading over his head, and he slumped to the ground exhausted, while the laborers guffawed. The kadi told him, "You see how much more difficult it is to work than to give orders. And you people can't even perform the easy task of giving orders—you lie in the shade scratching your bellies!"

We moved on. After walking for some distance, the kadi looked back. All the *arbobs* and *amins* were bustling about at the edge of the trench.

Leaving the village of Rūbaho, we reached a spot at which the Mahallayi Bolo channel debouched from the northern bank of the watercourse and the Istamzé channel from the southern bank. In front of these outlets the carpenters had already constructed sluice gates, and were now planing the sides of the planks to make them sit flush. For about fifty yards below the sluice the watercourse was already excavated, and further downstream work was continuing. The kadi ordered the laborers to raise a high earthen dam at the end of the trench, and told the *mirob* to go and open the Qo-qo dam and let the water flow. "Yes sir," said the *mirob*, unhitched his horse from a tree, mounted up and galloped in the direction of the Qo-qo Steppe. The kadi said to my father, " I have arranged things like this—that the trench should fill up with water right after the laborers have dug it—for a purpose. A worker who can see the fruit of his labors before him in the midst of his hard toil will work with a double will. Every stretch excavated will be filled with water the next day. Tomorrow we will lead the water as far as Rūbaho, and the day after up to Dehnav."

The kadi squatted against a tree, and his companions hunkered down in front of him. Sometimes the kadi said things I did not understand at all, then explained them in Tajik, but I did not understand the explanation either. My father listened to him respectfully, like a schoolboy, at times so excited by what he heard that his whole body would rock to and fro. Meanwhile the *mirob* came back with the news that the water was on its way. The kadi and his companions stood up and went over to the sluice.

The water, driving its dirty yellowish foam in front, raced up to the sluice planks where, balked in its course, it began to surge up to the top; even though it flooded between the planks at the bottom, this did not prevent it from spilling over the top as well. As soon as it reached the top of the sluice, it flowed into both the Istamze and the Mahallayi Bolo feeder channels, then roared over the wooden weir and was brought up short by the earthen dam.

My father and uncle took their leave of the kadi to return home. We walked slowly along the edge of the channel, keeping pace with the water's flow. My father said to my uncle, "Besides being the most learned, intelligent, wise and just scholar of our time, that man also has a body of iron. At his age he doesn't tire of squatting, standing, or walking—and he must be over seventy."

"According to his son, he turns seventy-six this year," said Mullo Dehqon.

We entered the village along with the water. The children in the streets were clapping their hands and running up and down the banks of the channel, shouting "Here comes the water—just like it oughter!" We went in to see my grandfather. There, the chief topic of conversation was the expertise and achievements of the new boss of the canal project. The talk came round to his appointment of my uncle Qurbon-Niyoz as his assistant. My father was of the opinion that this was a wise move, and although he disapproved of officials and courtiers—especially kadis --having personal servants, he acknowledged that in this case it would be an education for Qurbon-Niyoz.[26]

---

[26] This Qozi Abdul-Vohid is the same who wrote poetry under the pen-name Sadri Sarir, and whom I have memorialized in my *Representative Sample of Tajik Poetry*, pp. 385-391. -- A.

14. The Greening of Shofirkom

That same autumn, once the new canal was in use, the farmers of
Shofirkom *tuman* set to work with fresh heart born of this realization of their dream. They sowed winter wheat, cleaned out the
irrigation ditches and dug new ones in preparation for the spring
sowing. Even though the head of the new Shofirkom watercourse
was supposed to draw more water from the Zarafshon river than its
predecessor, the farmers by their own efforts and without any
guidance from the emir's government cleared the bed of the old
Shofirkom of sand,too, and diverted water into it from the new
channel; they cleared most of the sand-covered fields and
irrigated them, thus adding them again to the total of arable land.
By this means, even those peasants who had left after the sand
deluge and migrated south were enabled to return to their original
lands and work them again. Moreover, the landless peasants on
their own initiative excavated the Jilvon river, on the fringe of the
desert, which for years had been a dry riverbed, then directed the
abundant water of the new Shofirkom canal into this too, irrigated
the lands along its banks that had deteriorated into scrub pasture
and turned them into arable fields.

In this way, during the second year of operation of the new
watercourse, Shofirkom *tuman* was blooming like a garden. This
garden, however, became the focus of the owl-like gaze of the
Emir Muzaffar.[27] He appointed as tax collector of the *tuman* a
certain Murodbek, who had made a name as a tyrant, and as kadi a
mullah named Safi who had impressed the emir with his erudition.
These two plunderers with their locust-swarm retinue and diligent
apprentices reduced that freshly-flowering garden to a wasteland.
On the pretext that the residents of Shofirkom *tuman* had not paid
their land tax for the past several years (the years of the sand
inundation and consequent drought), they not only took the
whole of that year's crop as back taxes, but then forced the peasants to take out a "government loan" which they would have to
repay in future years as a bigger proportion of their crop.

---

[27] In Iranian folklore the owl is a bird of ill omen, presaging the destruction
of cities and the devastation of the sown. (For the Emir Muzaffar, see
Glossary.)

Qozi Safi, whose primary duty was that of administering justice, plundered the people in the name of upholding the religious
law in order to return to his patron in even greater favor. Be also
took the field as assistant to the *amlokdor*, as follows. The system
of tax collection under the emir was for the *amlokdor* to go out to
the fields when the crops were ripe and record the amount of tax
in kind due from each farmer. At the end of autumn, when the
harvest was in, the kadi would submit the market rate for each
crop to the emir, whereupon the emir would instruct the *amlokdor*
how much tax to take in cash from each grower on the basis of the
rate reported by the kadi. In this case Qozi Safi lent his aid to the
amlokdor, and hence to the emir's treasury, by artificially
inflating the market price in his submission of the rates: for
instance, if the going rate for one *man* of wheat was twenty *tangas*,
he increased it to twenty-five before submitting it to the
emir—who sent out decrees for the collection of taxes on that
basis.

This precedent of Qozi Safi's then became the general practice
for all the kadis of Bukhara's dependencies. Oddly enough, the
emir was fully aware that the rates he was given had been falsified:
he would brazenly justify his continued use of them, in private, by
claiming that he held himself personally innocent of this ma-
nipulation before God, and that on Judgment Day it would be the
kadis who would have to answer for it.

As a result of this method of taxation, farmers who had been
royally plundered once already—at the time of the assessment—found themselves totally destitute when the time came to
pay. Some were forced to sell their lands cheaply to rich landowners, and others had to sell their draft animals and household
effects in order to pay off the tax. Some were even forced to sell
off their sons and daughters to the rich landowners in order to pay
off the "government loan," or to give their children directly to
the government itself, in lieu of taxes, to serve as maids (*dukhtar-
khona*) and pages (*ghulom-bacha*) of the emir's court. (The emir
Muzaffar toward the end of his life had collected so many of these
slave boys that he formed them into a corps of private guards.)
Those who had access to none of these recourses and could not
meet the government's demands were sent to prison, or went
underground and were forced into thieving, or fled to Russian
Turkestan[28] and become vagrants.

---

[28] Southernmost of the three administrative areas (*guberniia*) set up by
Russia in 1867 in the occupied Kazakh region immediately to the north of

Nor did Murodbek and Qozi Safi spare the newly-cultivated bank of the Jilvon. The farmers there had no work animals and had to reclaim their dead lands solely by dint of mattock and spade. The *amlokdor* assessed their dues at the same rate as for land long cultivated. Unable to pay, they were obliged to contract a "government loan," which they had to pay off by collecting and selling firewood --their original occupation (a situation I depicted in the second part of my novel *Ghulomon*). The kadis, in accordance with an unwritten law of the Bukhara emirate, confiscated abandoned property as *luqata* "escheat," and declared it the property of the ruler. Qozi Safi took full advantage of this "law," leading his pack of retainers down to the bank of the Jilvon to pick up *luqata* where it lay. The peasants' goats and sheep, left to graze on the fringe of the steppe while their owners went off to gather firewood, were seized as abandoned property and driven off to the kadi's court to be legally escheated. Even if the owner of the flock arrived on the scene as his animals were being driven away, he could do nothing to recover them: the kadi's attendant would wave him off, telling him, "I'm taking these in to the kadi's court—if you want them back, bring a trustworthy witness and file a claim!"

Naturally the owner of the livestock could not bring a witness, sue the attendant, and recover his property, since the judge of Islam would reject his witness either as legally incompetent (if he failed an examination in the prescriptions for religious observances, such as prayer and fasting), or on suspicion of being an accomplice of the plaintiff (if he came from the same village) or of being a hired perjuror (if he came from a distant village). And once the animals had been committed to the kadi's custody, the claimant no longer had any right to protest; this would mean bringing suit against the kadi, which was categorically forbidden.

As a result of all this, the old Shofirkom canal and the Jilvon soon became the dry gullies they had been before. Even those fields watered by the new canal that belonged to small or medium farmers either went untilled and reverted to scrubland, or passed into the hands of rich farmers with large holdings, where the surplus water from the Shofirkom canal flooded hollows and collected into stagnant malarial swamps. (The old Shofirkom watercourse and the Jilvon remained disused until recent times. After the Great October Socialist Revolution, however, in the

---

Bukhara. By this period (1880s) it included all of the left bank of the Syr Darya, Khiva and Ferghana.

period of land reform, both these waterways were re-excavated and the lands on their banks irrigated.)

*   *   *

Qozi Abdul-Vohid Sadri Sarir, who considered himself the architect of the Shofirkom *tuman*'s recovery, and cherished its fertility as a monument of his old age, could not endure this situation. He was like a gardener whose green saplings are being chopped down and carted off, his roses trampled and strewn abroad, and his flowerbeds turned into pasture before his eyes. In consequence he became embittered not only against Qozi Safi and Murodbek, but against the emir and the office he held from him: without submitting a letter of resignation, he publicly renounced the kadi-ship of Ghijduvon and returned home to Bukhara, where a few days later he sickened and died. (Qozi Abdul-Vohid Sadri Sarir was a kindred spirit with Ahmad Makhdum Donish. However, he was no activist; he could not express his social indignation openly, but smoldered inwardly until it burned him to death.)

15.   Schooldays

I have published a detailed description of my adventures at the village school in a work titled *Maktabi kūhna*.[29] Here I shall recall only those episodes that were omitted from the earlier work or mentioned only briefly. As I wrote in *Maktabi kūhna*, when I was six years old my father put me in the village school which was attached to the mosque. Since I made no progress there, he transferred me to the girls' school. This was located in the home of the village *khatib*, and run by his wife, whom we called Bibi Khalifa. The only other boy there was Abdullo, who came from Ghijduvon. Since Abdullo was older than I, and also somewhat more uncouth, the girls did not like him and avoided him. But they were very sweet to me and treated me like a little brother.

During my second year there, a girl called Habiba, from a village named Raboti Qazoq, joined the class. Raboti Qazoq lay

---

[29] Written some fifteen years earlier, and translated here as Appendix II, "The Village School."

almost a mile southwest of our village, so Habiba did not go home after school, but stayed at the *khatib*'s house, in the same room as the khatib's daughter. Habiba and the khatib's daughter, Qutbiya, were the same age, and were the oldest girls at the school. But Habiba was smarter, more talkative, and better at her lessons than Qutbiya. My father told me that Habiba's father was the imam of his village, one of the most literate imams in the region, and had himself taught his daughter to read and write. In fact my father was surprised that she had been sent to school here, with the wife of the *khatib*; what more could she teach the girl? He likewise voiced his surprise that, though the girl was now twenty, her father had not yet married her off. Habiba was even nicer to me than the other girls. She taught me her lessons and made pretty dolls for me. Although I was unable at that age to appreciate the erotic content of lyric verse, whenever she read me the *ghazals* of Hafiz she would explain the love imagery. For the terms *yor* "(inseparable) companion," *dildor* "captivator," *ma'shuqa*, beloved" or *shohid* "beauty," she would point to the khatib's daughter as an example; and when a word such as *oshiq* "lover," *oshufta* "distracted," *dildoda* "devoted," or *dilshuda* "enamored," came up, she would claim herself as an example. The khatib's daughter was visibly embarrassed by Habiba's behavior. She would scowl and look daggers at her, yet at the same time smother a smile and say, "Stop it now, or I'll tell my mother, and she'll beat you harder than your father has ever beaten you—and I wouldn't be surprised if they threw you out of school when they know what you get up to!" Habiba would answer, with a sigh, "Oh, if only they would!" in such a way as to leave no doubt that she was serious.

The other girls would discuss among themselves the relative beauty of Habiba and Qutbiya, some maintaining that Habiba was prettier and others voting for Qutbiya. Nevertheless, none of them liked either of the two girls. They would find fault with both behind their backs, decrying Qutbiya for being spiteful, gossipy, haughty, and thinking herself better than her parents, and Habiba for being flighty and overly talkative, singing love songs like a professional crooner, and being wrapped up in her own beauty. None of these criticisms, however, made any sense to me, since I had never been ill-treated by either girl, and had never witnessed Qutbiya being spiteful, nor sensed any haughtiness in her. The fact that Habiba sang love songs like a professional, which the other girls particularly held against her, was something I especially liked.

One day we were reading the ghazal of Hafiz that begins:

> I'll not give up my suit until my heart's desire is won;
> Either I win my one true love, or else my life is done.[30]

The teacher delegated Habiba to go over the *ghazal* with me while she went home to do her housework. Habiba had me repeat it several times, then she picked up the book and recited the *ghazal* so sadly and hauntingly that her own eyes brimmed with tears and my spine began to tingle—especially when she reached the verse:

> Not for me another lover at a moment's whim;
> At my darling's door I'll lie till death, constant to him.

She looked so distressed that I thought she would fall into a faint on the spot. She closed her eyes and was silent for a while. The tears I had seen in her eyes while she was reciting trickled down her cheeks. Then she opened her eyes and gave me an embarrassed smile. Even though I was then completely ignorant of love and romance, I was touched; I sensed that she was suffering some inner pain, and wished I could do something to end or at least ease it. Of course, I could do nothing, and did not even know the nature of her suffering.

I don't remember whether it was that same day, or the next, that Habiba asked me after school had finished, "Do you have roses at home?"

"Yes," I answered.

"Tomorrow morning, bring me a fragrant, freshly-blooming rose."

I promised I would, and went home. I felt a thrill of pleasure at being entrusted with this errand, and thought to myself that by bringing her the rose I would perhaps be easing her pain and fulfilling the wish I had conceived when she was reciting the love-poem.

There were two rosebushes by our front door, one bearing white roses and the other pink ones. Next morning, before sunrise, I crept out to pluck a rose for Habiba from one of them. Both bushes were full of freshly blooming roses, and each was equally

---

[30] Persian *dast az talab nadâram tâ kâm-e man bar âyad*. The text and a translation by Gertrude Bell are given in Arberry's *Fifty Poems of Hafiz* (No. 24).

fragrant. I couldn't make up my mind which sort to take; which would she like better? I examined both kinds of roses closely. The pink roses closely resembled Habiba's complexion and, especially with the drops of dew still clinging to their leaves, looked very enticing; they seemed as beautiful as Habiba's tear-stained face when she was singing. I decided on the pink roses, and picked three. Then it struck me that she might prefer the white ones, and I picked three of these too, then ran off to school. When I reached the gate of the *khatib*'s house, I hid the roses under my arm in case the other girls should grab them. As I went in, Qutbiya met me in the corridor. "What's that under your arm?" she asked.

"A book," I answered, in an effort to keep the flowers a secret. But I myself was nervous of such an obvious lie, since my book was in my hand. If she realized I was lying, she only had to pry my arm away from my side to reveal the roses. Wondering whether she believed me or not, I looked closely at her face for the first time. It was entirely different from Habiba's face: if Habiba's complexion resembled a pink rose, that of Qutbiya was like a white one. I did not care for white roses as much as pink ones; my father had strictly forbidden me to pick the pink ones, since he would take them to the perfumier in exchange for rose-water—but whenever I could get away with it, I always did.

At any rate, Qutbiya appeared not to suspect anything, and without looking under my arm she went off into the nearby cow-shed. I went on into the classroom. None of the children had arrived yet, and Habiba was sweeping the floor. I held out both sorts of roses in both hands. "Bravo!" she cried, and snatched the pink ones from me. First she sniffed them, then stuck two of them under her- headsquare, one above each ear, looked in the mirror, then pinned the third at her breast. Next she took the white roses and sniffed them. Looking rather annoyed, she thrust them back at me and asked petulantly, "Why did you bring these?"

"I thought you might like them too," I answered.

"Which do *you* like best?" she pursued.

"The pink ones!"

"Why?"

"I don't know, I just like them."

Habiba held a white rose against her cheek and asked, "Which ones suit me best—the pink or the white?"

"The pink ones," I replied.

"Why?"

"Because the pink ones are the same color as your face."

On hearing this she laughed out loud, "Oh, you imp!" And she hugged me tight and kissed me on the cheeks. Indicating the white roses, she asked, "Whose face is the same color as *these*?"

"Auntie Qutbiya's!" I replied. This seemed to delight her even more than my first answer, for she laughed loud and long, hugged me again, and smothered my face with wet kisses. Then she let me go, saying: "Look at me. Don't tell *anyone* what you just told me, that pink roses match my face and white roses match Qutbiya's, do you hear? If you do, I shall be very cross with you. Now go and sit in your place and get on with your lesson."[31]

*   *   *

In spring, when the mulberries were ripening, my brother Muhyiddin and Sayid-Akbar Khoja returned from Bukhara. After a few days' rest, they started their lessons with the *khatib* as they did every year. Sayid-Akbar Khoja was too proud to speak to most adults, but he became my "playmate." He used to sit in the porch of his father's house, which opened onto the forecourt of the mosque, and whenever I came out of the girls' school he would call me over, give me toys he had made, and ask me how school was going and how some of the neighbor girls were doing in their lessons. Incidentally, he would also ask after Habiba. I, in my childlike innocence, would answer all his questions as best I could.

One morning, as I was passing Usto Amak's house on my way to school, Sayid-Akbar called out to me. This was contrary to his usual practice of calling me over on my way home. I told him I would be late for school, and continued on my way. "You won't be late," he called. "I just want a quick word with you." So I was obliged to go back and see what he wanted. He handed me a sealed letter, saying, "Give this to Habiba and bring me her reply. Take care not to let anyone see you giving it to her."

I took the letter from him; naturally I had no idea then what it all meant. During the course of the day I found an opportunity to hand it to Habiba. She took it to one side and after a little while came back to me, her eyes flashing angrily, her lips trembling as if with fever, and the muscles of her cheeks and around her eyes twitching. She stared at me. I still had no idea what was going on and, assuming that she was upset about something else, asked her

---

[31] A character-sketch of Qutbiya appears near the end of the novel *Ghulom-on* — A.

when she would give me an answer to the letter. Her eyes flashing more angrily than ever, she glared at me and stood up. "Come here!" she snapped, and stormed out into the corridor and along to the cowshed, dragging me after her. In the cowshed she took off her shoe, rubbed it in the cowdung, and handed it to me, saying, "Take this shoe and slap the writer of your letter in the face with it, and tell him this is my answer!"

Of course I didn't actually take the shoe and carry out her instructions; but when Sayid-Akbar called me over on my way home and asked me if I had delivered his letter and brought an answer, I told him about the shoe. Sayid-Akbar was furious, and when he opened his mouth to speak, a foam of spittle preceded his words. "That Habiba is a stupid, flighty baggage," he said in a strangled voice, "and you—you shovel up the shit she hands out, bring it all wide-eyed innocence, and fling it in my face!" And he slapped me hard across the face.

I was first of all surprised, then angry, and finally I burst out laughing—surprised, because I never expected this kind of reward for my errand; angry, because it was utterly undeserved; and amused, because with his own words he had made himself ridiculous. Naturally I conceived a deep grudge against him. But I could do nothing about it there and then, a young boy against an older and stronger youth. I was forced to await an opportunity for revenge. As it happened, this opportunity soon came my way.

*   *   *

Ibrohim Khoja, my father's uncle's son, after his father died, took to practicing prayer healing and exorcism in the porch of his house, where his father had used to sit. One day they brought a lunatic from the village to see him—a tall, robust, full-bearded man of between thirty and forty. Ibrohim Khoja locked a horse-hobble around the lunatic's ankles, passed the end of the chain around the bottommost beam of the wall, and tied it to a pillar that stood in the middle of the room. The patient could thus sit on the *sufa* of the porch, or stand upright, but could not move from the spot.

Ibrohim Khoja's procedure for curing lunatics, like that of all the other healers, was quite simple. He gave the patient nothing to eat other than a piece of dry bread once every twenty- four hours, and twice a day, morning and night, bared the patient's back and flogged him with a horsewhip. The flogging would invariably continue, not up to a specified number of blows, but until the exorcist's arm was tired. This procedure Ibrohim Khoja began to apply. The lunatic, in tears, would plead with anyone, far and near, who came within his range of vision: "Please, for the love of God, give me a bite of bread, I'm a man like you, a creature of God, it isn't right to starve me to death, have pity on me. . ."

I felt very sorry for him, and each mealtime I slipped him a piece of bread and saved him a handful of dried apricots or mulberries. Little by little the lunatic grew to trust me, and I used to sit in front of him without any fear. He would say some odd things, but they seemed more the words of a wag than of a lunatic.

For instance, he often stood upright and addressed the sun, imploring it tearfully to set him free and to take him up to live with it, so that he too might float freely about the sky and look down and see everything on earth.

One day the lunatic asked me, "Please, tell your uncle the *eshon* it wouldn't do any harm to let me loose for a bit once a day; I could take a walk in the forecourt of the mosque. I promise I won't run away, and I'll come back and put the hobble on my leg myself and lie down here again. If you do this favor for me, I'll catch the sun and give him to you, so you can ride him everywhere and see everything."

At this very moment I noticed Sayid-Akbar Khoja approaching, on his way home from the mosque school. This, I thought, is my chance to get even! I pointed him out to the lunatic and said, "The *eshon* was going to set you free, but that man wouldn't let him; if I let you loose, you can go and hit that man, and that'll teach him to make the *eshon* keep you locked up!"

"Let me loose," growled the lunatic, his eyes blazing like those of a wolf that has caught sight of a sheep. I went into the porch and untied the chain from the column; the lunatic pulled the end through from behind the wall beam, coiled it up in his hands, and stood up. He turned and started to walk toward the forecourt of the mosque. But walking with the shackles on was not easy: his legs were so closely hobbled that he could not put one foot more than a handsbreadth in front of the other. At this rate, there was a fair chance his enemy would be out of sight before he could reach him. With this in mind the lunatic, instead of walking, put both feet together and hopped forward, each hop taking him the equivalent of two or three normal steps. Sayid-Akbar Khoja had not yet reached home when the lunatic was upon him: picking him up in both arms he flung him to the ground and squatted on his chest, pummeling him with his knees. At the instant he was lifted, Sayid-Akbar let out a piercing shriek: "The lunatic's got me, help, murder!"—then either he lost consciousness or his breath failed him, for he uttered not another word. At the first cry, however, his father came running out from the house and other men from the mosque; they rescued him from the clutches of the lunatic and took the latter back to the *eshon*'s porch and shackled him again.

By then I had realized my mistake, for if the rescuers had arrived a moment later, Sayid-Akbar would certainly have been killed. I had wanted to exact the just revenge of one wronged, but my vengeance had gotten out of hand. I had not told anyone about Sayid-Akbar's hitting me, out of fear of my father, for if he knew I had been slapped as a consequence of acting as a go-between, he would first have punished me for taking a billet-doux from a young man to a girl. Similarly, out of fear both of my father and of Sayid-Akbar, I told no one of how I avenged the slap.

*　　*　　*

In addition to his own woodcarving, Usto Amak also created suitable designs for other craftsmen. Potters, cotton dyers and plasterers would order templates from him for their work. For the potters and dyers he would draw the designs on paper then prick the outline of each flower or other motif with a pin; his customers would then place the paper over their artifacts, dust over it with coal dust, take away the paper, and there would be an outline of the original design for them to color as they chose.

One of the potters in the village of Qazoqrabot[32] produced excellent decorated bowls and plates. He would order fresh designs from Usto Amak for every batch. This potter had a son twenty-four or twenty- five years old, who as a child had fallen out of a tree and broken his leg, and as a result of faulty bone-setting his left leg was two inches shorter than his right. He walked only with great difficulty, and consequently rode everywhere on horse- or donkey-back. Once a week he would come to Usto Amak to order new designs, and the next day would return to pick up the finished templates. Recently, however, the frequency of his orders had greatly increased: he would arrive every day to order new templates and would sometimes stay overnight to take them back the

---

[32] The same as Raboti Qazoq, mentioned above; Aini has (perhaps unconsciously) slipped from the Tajik to the Uzbek syntax of this compound name ("Kazakh Inn").

next morning— then come straight back to order more. Everyone was amazed at this profligacy. Usto Amak observed that ordinary potters generally bought a total of two templates per year, one for bowls and one for plates; famous craftsmen would use one design per batch of bowls or plates. But the Qazoqrabot potter was using so many templates that just about every bowl and plate must have a separate pattern— which would boost the cost of his clay pots to ten times that of fine china. Why on earth was he doing this?

Then something happened that clarified for me, before anyone else, the reason why the Qazoqrabot potter's son was ordering so many templates. It came about as follows.

After the excavation of the new Shofirkom canal, my uncle Qurbon-Niyoz entered the service of Qozi Abdul-Vohid, the kadi of Ghijduvon. Meantime another uncle of mine, the much-traveled Ali-Khon, had become engaged to a potter's daughter in Ghijduvon. My grandmother, since her son was in the kadi's service, got him to invite his family to the wedding. Since I had been favorably received by the kadi, I asked if I could go along with my grandmother as well, and my father agreed. We went to Ghijduvon and stayed overnight at the potter's house. In the middle of the night there was a disturbance and cries of alarm, as if thieves had been discovered, which however soon subsided. But everyone was awakened— the men, who were sleeping in the courtyard, and the women, inside the house, who started whispering together anxiously. The potter's son came and reassured the women with the news that it was not burglars but guests who had arrived.

Early next morning my grandmother rolled up her belongings in her tablecloth and went to the kadi's residence-cum-courthouse and I, in hopes of seeing again that kindly, white-bearded old man, tagged along behind. When we went in, the kadi's women servants took my grandmother's bundle and led her into the women's quarters. But since I was a boy, albeit a young one, they would not let me in with her. I remained in the courtyard, squatting with my back against the door of the stablehands' quarters. From where I sitting I could see the kadi, who looked old. He was sitting in front of the porch— his courthouse— trying a case. He didn't see me or, if he saw me, didn't recognize me or, if he recognized me, didn't think it necessary to acknowledge me. Whatever the case, he did not show me the kindness I had expected.

At this juncture the potter's son from Qazoqrabot came limping in. At his side was a girl wearing a *jomacha* over her head and holding tightly onto the skirt of his overcoat. The kadi's house-hold staff and onlookers from the street crowded into the courtyard, talking excitedly to one another; I heard the words "eloped" and "runaway wedding." I got up from where I was squatting and joined the back of the crowd gathering in front of the *sufa* outside the courthouse, but it was no use—I couldn't see a thing. Suddenly I heard the kadi's voice: "Who has led you astray, my daughter?"

"No-one has led me astray. 1 want to marry this man of my own free will." It was the girl's voice, excited and close to tears. Came the kadi's second question: "If your parents hear of this, what will they say? Will they consent to this action of yours?"

"This man is now both father and mother to me. I don't care whether my parents consent or not." The girl's voice was now more self-assured.

The kadi began to recite the marriage invocation. After he had finished the Arabic lines and their Tajik version, he asked the potter's son in Tajik: "Do you, being adult and of sound mind, before these here assembled, take this girl in lawful Muslim mar-riage to be your wife?"

"I do," came the voice of the Qazoqrabot potter's son. The kadi then addressed the girl: "Do you, being adult and of sound mind, before these here assembled, give yourself to this youth in lawful Muslim marriage?"

"I do, gladly," came the girl's voice—now calmer, and sud-denly familiar to me, though I still couldn't place it.

The crowd started fighting over the bowl of water that is tra-ditionally part of the wedding ceremony.[33] The potter's son and the girl rose from the kadi's *sufa* and headed toward the gate, the girl still holding on to the youth's coat at his side. In two bounds 1 had beaten them out of the gate and onto the street, in order to see who that familiar voice belonged to. I turned to face the kadi's house, and could not believe my eyes: the girl coming out of the gate side by side with the potter's son was Habiba. I was so dumb-founded that I stood stock still, blocking Habiba's way as she reached me. She saw me too, but unlike me, maintained her com-posure. "Well, you imp," she said, "what are you doing here? You're the first to find out—give them all my regards!" And

---

[33] A bowl of drinking water was placed before the newly-weds, who each drank some at the end of the ceremony. The guests would each try to drink a drop from the same bowl, to bring good luck -- especially unwed youths and girls, who hoped thereby to hasten their own wedding day.

bride and groom swept gaily on by me, mounted a horse that
stood tethered in the street in front of the courthouse, and rode
away.

Now at last I understood why Habiba had always wept when
she recited that *ghazal* of Hafiz beginning:

> I'll not give up my suit until my heart's desire is won;
> Either I win my one true love, or else my life is done.

That courageous girl, trapped in the conventions of a medieval,
feudal tyranny, had by sheer strength of will overcome all obstacles and won her true love. Though, truth to tell, her true love was
not at all my type—as well as being lame, he was ugly; but then,
the groom's being less than ideal only emphasized the bride's
love, zeal, constancy, and strength of will.

Now it was clear to me why the potter's son had been placing
so many orders for Amak Usto's templates during the past week.
It was, of course, so that he could arrange a secret tryst with his
beloved and go there more often under the pretext of ordering
templates. Now, too, it was clear to me that the mysterious
"guests" who had arrived at my uncle's house like thieves in the
night were none other than the runaways, fleeing from Soktaré,
who had sought a night's shelter from the groom's fellow artisan,
and when day broke had left for the courthouse. Finally, it was
also clear to me why Habiba's father had sent her to Bibi
Khalifa's school even though she could read and write perfectly
well. It was, of course, to stop Habiba and the potter's son seeing
each other.

*   *   *

When I grew up, I saw quite a few runaway weddings in the kadi's
courts of Vobkand, Zandané, Jondor and Qarokūl.[34] I have included Habiba in these memoirs both as a real person known to
me, and at the same time as being typical of those young women
who courageously rebelled against the tyranny and oppression of
the days of the Bukhara Emirate, eloped with the man they loved
to the kadi's court and demanded out loud their right to be married.

---

[34] Towns near Bukhara city. Vobkand and Qarokūl. are generally spelled in
the Russian fashion as Vabkent and Karakul'.

16. Secondary Schooling

I completed school; but I was still illiterate. I could read things I had read in school, and from the same book I had used at school, but I couldn't read things I hadn't read before, or even things I *had* read before but in a different book. Nevertheless, my father sent me to the village imam to start my education in earnest. I began under the village *khatib* with a booklet in Tajik called "Principles of Knowledge" (*Avvali ilm*), in which religious matters were expounded catechism-style, and after working through this (which took roughly one month) I started on a book with the title "Know" (*Bidon*). "Know" was a Tajik exposition of the rules of Arabic grammar.[35] I got nothing out of either of these books; I just repeated parrot-fashion after my teacher and learned them by rote. The prerequisite for progressing from one lesson to the next was that I should be able to recite the previous lesson word perfect, without any faltering or hesitation, before *domullo*, as we called the teacher. But I was never asked whether I understood those Tajik terms and idioms intermingled with Arabic proverbs, nor did I myself think it necessary to understand them, even though the book called *Know* began with the injunction "Know . . !" On the day we started reading it, the teacher made us commit to memory some questions and answers germane to the new lesson. The first question was "Why did the author write 'Know,' and not 'Read'?" The answer: "Because it is not necessary to know in order to read, but it is necessary to read in order to know. Therefore the author wrote 'Know,' not 'Read'."

Naturally at that time I did not follow this reasoning, but the wonder is that my late respected teacher did not understand its practical import or, if he did, never asked whether this "knowing" applied to my lessons. Even more remarkable is that my father, for all the pains he took with my schooling, never asked whether I understood my lessons. He simply emphasized each night that I should memorize my lesson perfectly, so as not to be shamed before the teacher on the next day. Sometimes my father even heard me recite my lesson; if I recited fluently and without error

---

[35] An anonymous Arabic primer in Tajik, widely used in Central Asian *maktab*s during the nineteenth century. For *Avvali ilm*, see Glossary.

he would say, "Well done! That's the way you should always learn your lessons."

In all this elementary and secondary schooling, only two things made a proper impression on me. One was the numerical system called *abjad* which, as I described in detail in *Maktabi kūhna*,[36] my father taught me when it came up at school. Applying the rules of *abjad*, I used to enjoy working out the values assigned to the twenty-eight letters of the Arabic alphabet over and over again, and adding them up by using the nine figures and zero of the so-called Arabic (originally Indian) numerals.

The other thing I enjoyed was reading Tajik poetry. Even though at that time I did not fully understand the meaning of the poems, their music enchanted me; I used to repeat to myself in private the verses I had learned by heart, and my pleasure in them grew. I was especially affected by the poems whose romantic content Habiba had interpreted to me, notably the ghazals she had recited at the girls' school in melancholy tones "like a professional singer." When I read those ghazals over again, the vision of Habiba singing sadly would appear before my eyes and plunge me into a sweet melancholy. Then I would recall the episode of Habiba "winning her true love," and that slender, fragile beauty would be transformed in my fancy into a fairytale heroine, a champion whose example fired me to emulate her and "not give up my quest."

I wanted to understand fully all the verses I had memorized or heard. My one help in this was my father, who answered all my questions fully and intelligibly. But when the question concerned erotic imagery, his brow would furrow and he would say with a frown, "The time is not yet ripe for you to understand such things; as you grow older, you'll come to understand."

At that time I did not know that there were poets in our own time and our own country. I imagined that to be a poet one must be a *vali*, or saint, and that in our time, which is the "latter days," it was not possible to be a saint, and therefore not possible to be a poet. This belief had been inculcated in me by Bibi Khalifa. But then something happened that completely discredited this dogma and brought me to a realization that poetry could indeed be produced in our own days. It came about as follows.

One day my father had gone to the mosque for the noon prayer, but suddenly came back and called to me from the corridor to come quickly; then he hurried out again, with me running

---

[36] See Appendix II, Section v, and Glossary.

after him. In the courtyard he lifted me up and stood me on top of the low earthen wall that separated our house from the forecourt of the mosque. He himself stood behind the wall and said, "Your big brother's *domullo* is about to come out from the madrasa. Keep watching and I'll point him out to you." Before long two people came out: one was the village *khatib* I took lessons from, and at his side was a man of medium height and slender build, with a sallow complexion and a grey beard, wearing a small white turban and a white shirt coat. This was the man Father pointed out to me as my brother's teacher, adding that he was a very great man, an eminent scholar both of religious and secular sciences, and a skilled poet.

Puzzled by my father's description of him, I asked, "How can you say he's a great man and an eminent scholar, when he isn't all that tall and his turban is smaller than our imam's?"

"A man's greatness is not measured by his physical stature, nor his learning by the size of his turban," was my father's reply. "Most mullahs of little learning wind their turbans large, so that the common people will be fooled into thinking them great scholars. But a learned man and true *mullo* ties his turban small, and his greatness is shown by his scholarship."

Though I knew the word *she'r* (poetry) and what it meant, this was the first time I had heard the word *sho'ir* (poet). "You called him a 'poet'," I asked Father; "What does that mean?"

"A poet," explained my father, "Is someone who composes—that is, makes up and recites—poetry." I was about to ask what sort of poetry he composed, but missed my chance; it must have been time for prayers to start, for my father lifted me down from the wall and—perhaps guessing the question I had in mind—said, "Go back home now. When I get back from prayers, I'll read you some of his poetry." And he ran toward the mosque.

When he returned, he took me indoors and from an alcove took down a book in which he had written various things in his own hand. In the back of the book, written slantwise across both sides of a few sheets of paper, were a couple of *ghazals*. He showed them to me, saying, "These are the work of your brother's teacher," and began to read. He read the *ghazals* through one after the other, pausing to explain occasional verses where he judged it might be helpful—or at least harmless—for me. At the end of each ghazal there occurred the word *iso*. Father pointed it out to me, explaining, "Iso is the poet's name, the one he has chosen as his *takhallus* or pen-name."[37] The refrain (*radif*) of one of the ghazals comprised the word *qashshoqi* (poverty, indigence) and my father repeated the following verse from it:

> I'm thirty now, and still constrained to be almighty thrifty;
> Perhaps I'll slip the hooks of hock by forty, or by fifty![38]

"Iso composed this poem at the age of thirty, and in it he expresses the hope that by the age of forty or fifty he will have escaped the trammels of poverty. But alas, forty and fifty are behind him, and now that he is over sixty he still hasn't escaped 'the hooks of hock,' and spends his life tutoring and copying manuscripts for people." My father went on to generalize: " A learned man can in fact escape from penury, but pity those born to poverty who have no opportunity to learn to read! the sons of the rich—especially the *makhdumon*, the sons of the important mullahs—are mostly fools or good-for-nothings; even though they can read. most of them never amount to much, or if they do they turn out bad. Not without reason has it been written that knowledge in the hands of an evil man is a sharp sword in the hands of a drunkard."

My father fell silent, sunk in thought. Sadness clouded his face, and he sighed: "If I had completed the madrasa, I might well have amounted to something. But alas, this same accursed poverty never gave me the chance. Study, son, whatever hardships it entails, study! I never made it—maybe you will."

Father quoted a couplet from another ghazal of Iso:

> Why waste away and die of idleness, when the prescription
> Is in your hand?—Fill it, and cure yourself!

He explained it to me, adding, "You see how wise this man is—he equates idleness with death, and urges you to work at *something*,

[37] This was Iso-Makhdum "Iso" (1827-88), a Bukharan poet of the second rank, who wrote conventional mystical-lyrical verse; as Ayni notes later, a brief biography of Iso with examples of his verse may be found in *Namunai adabiyoti tojik*, pp. 418-28.

[38] The Persian couplet contains a play on the homonyms *shast* "hook" and, by implication, *shast* "sixty," which cannot be directly reproduced in English. Significantly, Aini used *qashshoqi* as a pseudonym in some of his early poetry.

whatever it is." Next my father picked up two or three scattered sheets of paper from the alcove shelf, turned them this way and that, and located the following verse, which he read out to me:

> Don't load your burden upon Providence —
> Know as your benefactor your own diligence!

After explaining it, he went on: "You see how great men think alike. Bobo Soib, who died two hundred and fifty years ago, and Iso, who is our contemporary, express the same view, urging men to forsake fatalism and indolence and get down to work." (My father was very fond of Soibi Isfahoni; he read his verses with a sensuous pleasure, as children lick the candy called *nabot*, and referred to him by the respectful epithet *bobo*.)[39]

This observation was to have a strong influence on my subsequent life and thought. I came to despise the big turbans of the would-be scholars, and likewise acquired a horror of idleness. A more immediate result of the episode was my realization that it was possible to be a poet in our day and age. I still had one problem: was it after all not necessary to be a saint and miracle-worker to be a poet, or was Iso a saint? To settle this, I asked my father, "Don't you have to be a saint to be a poet?"

"Of course not!" he replied. "Why, I myself wrote a verse chronogram (*ta'rikh*) on the date of construction of the portico of our mosque, which your uncle Hidoyat Khoja built this year." And he recited:

> That peerless engineer, Hidoyat Khon,
> In the Year of the Fowl built this *aivon*;
> Should you desire the exact date to read,
> Give water to the fowl, and chickenfeed.

He explained it thus. The word *murgh*, meaning "fowl," gives a total of 1240 in the *abjad* notation, and if you add to it the values of the letters in the words *ob u dona*, "water and seed," a total of 63, you get 1303, which was the correct year in the Muslim

---

[39] Mirzâ Mohammad 'Ali Sâ'eb-e Esfahâni, also called Tabrizi (ca. 1601-76); generally regarded as the ablest of the post-classical Persian poets, an exponent of the baroque "Indian Style." He spent some time as court poet to the Mughal emperor Shâhjahân, and returned to Isfahan in the reign of Shah 'Abbâs II, who made him his poet laureate (see Rypka, Chapter X).

calendar. Since I knew the *abjad* system I was able to check the arithmetic for myself; and sure enough, it came out to 1303.[40]

Thanks to this conversation I was delighted to learn not only that my father was able to compose verse, but also that it was possible to be a poet without being a saint. Of this there was no doubt, since I knew that my father was not a saint. I wanted to hear more of my father's poems, and begged him to recite some. He replied, "I'm not a poet. A person doesn't become a poet by reciting one or two verses: anyone with a bit of sensitivity can do that The word *she'r* (poetry) and the word *shuur* (sensitivity, consciousness) certainly come from the same root; but to be a poet, a verse or two verses won't do. One must be able—like Iso, like Bobo Soib, like Bedil, like Hafiz—to compose good poems on every topic."

Since my father did not name any others of the poets of our time, I imagined that Iso was the only one. To verify this, I asked, "Are there any other poets nowadays besides Iso?"

"Of course there are," said my father. "Many. One of the good poets of our day and age is Abdul-Vohid, the kadi of Ghijduvon." On hearing this I was sorry that when I had met the kadi a few years ago, and he had been so kind to me, I had not been aware that he was a poet. Then I suddenly wondered whether I could be a poet or not. Of course I could find no answer in myself, so again I asked Father. He told me: "Yes, you could be a poet. But in that case you must read a lot of the poems of great poets, learn them by heart and write them down, and also talk with and learn from great poets. Now, while you are young, your duty is to do your lessons, read poetry, learn poems by heart and copy them down. Don't be distracted by planning to compose poetry."

Father's admonition aside, I really enjoyed reading poetry, only I could not read it properly from books. And as for writing, it was completely beyond me, since apart from the Arabic numerals I had learned from my father when he was teaching me *abjad* counting, I could not form a single letter. So I had to ask my father how I could learn to write. He undertook to teach me,

---

[40] 1303 *hijri* (i.e., according to the lunar calendar dated from the Prophet Muhammad's emigration from Mecca to Medina in 622 C.E.) is equivalent to the year October 1885–September 1886 in the Gregorian calendar. The poetical conceit, not explained by Aini, lies in the reference to yet another calendrical system, that of the Turkish twelve-year animal cycle (cf. Chinese usage). In this, 1303/1885-6 is the Year of the Fowl (Uzbek *tovuq*, Tajik *murgh*). See also under *abjad* in the Glossary.

adding that once I had learned to write, my reading skill too would improve and I would be able to read anything. During that same session, I did memorize a few verses of Iso's that I liked. Here are a couple of verses taken from them:

> The heart's glad for one debt repaid,
> And patient of long cruelty;
> Disdainful pride, unbend, I beg,
> And show some common courtesy!
> Flirtatious Spring winks openly—
> Open your eyes to dalliance!
> The garden's leaves are music sheets—
> Spring to your feet, and join the dance!

17. Learning to Write

When I begged my father to teach me how to write, he told me, "My own handwriting is not good—if you copy me, you'll develop a poor hand. Wait until Sayid-Akbar returns from the city,"—he was then studying in Bukhara with my elder brother—"He has a good hand, and you can practice under him."

Now, although the marks of Sayid-Akbar's slap had long vanished from my face, its inner effects were still with me. Learning to write at the hands as such as he was the last thing on my mind. However, I reasoned that, in the first place, it was necessary to undergo a few hardships in order to acquire a skill; and, in the second, I had already taken more than my revenge—albeit indirectly, by means of the lunatic—so why should I still bear him any grudge? With these thoughts I gladly accepted my father's suggestion.

Father accordingly admonished me first to prepare the tools and materials of penmanship, quoting in this connection the verse mnemonic:

> If pens were sticks and ink were water,
> Paper were earth, with straws for rules—
> Who could write a lovely hand
> With such a silly set of tools?!

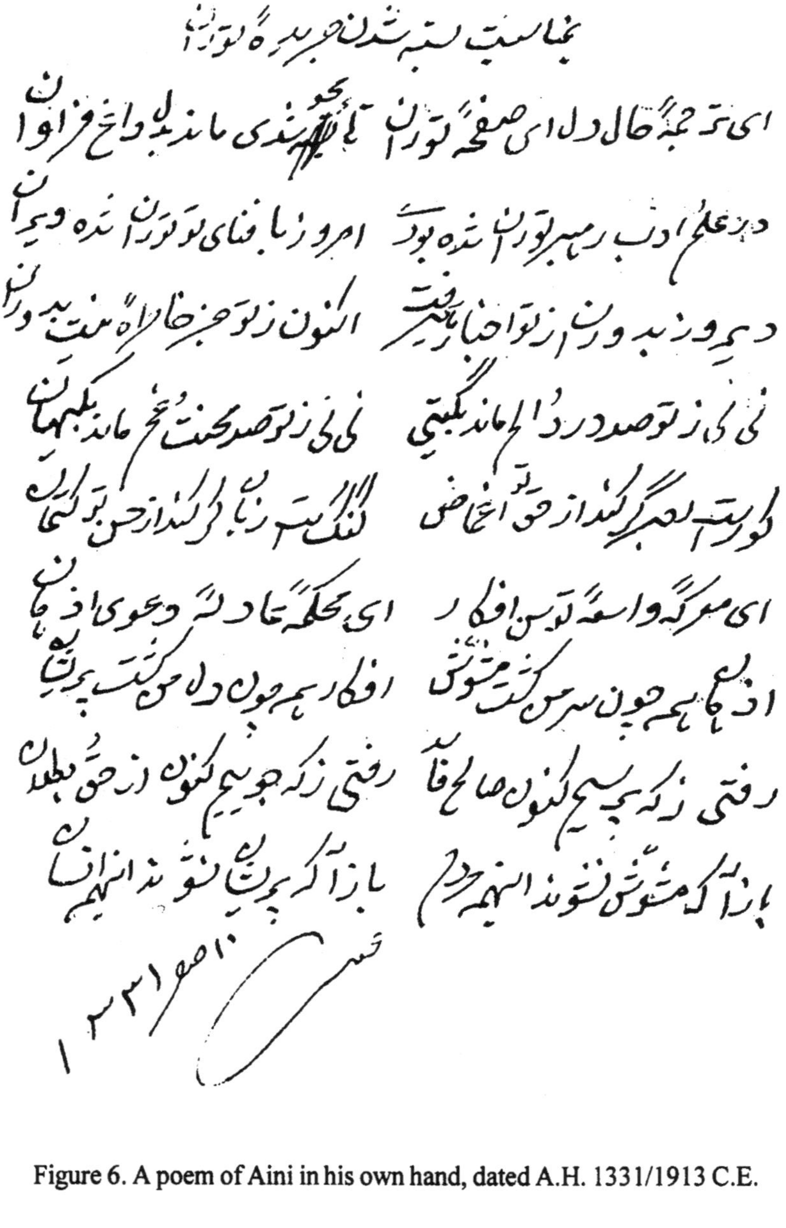

مناسبت بسته‌شدن جریده تورک‌اوا

ای تو جمله حال دل‌های صفحه تورک تا کندی ماندی واخ فراوان

در علم ادب رهبر تورک شده بود امروز با فنای تورک شده ویران

دی موز به ورن زتوآحبان رفت اکنون زتوحزه جان‌اله منت برورن

نی که ز تو صد درد الم ماندگی بتی نی نی ز تو صد محنت نخ ماند بهان

لورثه بعمر گذر کنداز حق اخلاص لئک به رنا از کندازحن برکنه

ای مرگ واسعه تویی افلا ر ای حکله تا دلر دعوی‌ای ذی جان

اذ جاییم چون سرس کرد متوین افکار سم چون دلای کتب یقشا

رفتی زکه پیچ کنون هلا حقا رفتی زکه جوییم کنون ازحق بطلان

بازا که مشوش نشوند انهم دلم بازا که برش نشو بدانهم انف

۱۲۲۱ صه ۱۰

۱

Figure 6. A poem of Aini in his own hand, dated A.H. 1331/1913 C.E.

With this in view, Father took me along with him one Ghijduvon market day when he had to go to Mahallayi Bolo. At the bazaar he bought me a pencase, two pen-reeds, a penknife, a bone nib-trimming board, a leather document-wallet, a bunch of silk threads (to put in the inkwell, so as to keep the pen from drawing too much ink), and four sheets of Kokand exercise paper. Then he sent me off to Soktaré and himself continued on to Mahallayi Bolo. I got onto the donkey—which did not have saddlebags—and, holding in front of me the wallet and writing paper rolled up around the pencase containing all the writing implements, I left the bazaar and set out along the road in high spirits. But my happiness was not to last.

As I turned out of the alleyway of the Ghijduvon bazaar, the saddle cloth slipped forward; I would have to dismount in order to tighten the girth. There was a low wall to my left, so when I got down I put my bundle of writing materials on top of this. I was just reaching out to tighten the girth when the pen case slid out from inside the bundle and tumbled into the ditch on the far side of the wall. I had inadvertently placed the bundle on a slope, and the light pen case had slithered through the smooth tube of rolled-up paper and over the wall.

I left the donkey's girth and looked over the wall. There was no water in the ditch, and no pen case either. In the middle of the ditch, however, a deep oblong pit had been dug, and there was my pen case—my precious pen case!—down at the bottom of that pit. There was no way I could get into the pit to retrieve it. All I could do was to sit by the edge like a bereaved mother mourning over the grave of her lost child, and burst out sobbing. A passer-by stopped and asked me why I was crying.

Through my sobs I told him about the pen case. "Don't cry," he said, starting to take off his coat; "Crying won't get your pen case out of the pit—I'll get it for you." I calmed down somewhat. The man stripped off his coat, turban, and shoes, and placed them on top of the wall. Dressed only in his shirt he made his way to the edge of the pit, climbed down the steps that had been cut into its sides, and within a minute came back up carrying the pen case tied to his waistband.

Now my joy knew no bounds. Twice in one day—rather, in one hour—a simple pen case had made me enormously happy. Happy and grateful as I was when my father bought me the pen case for one *tanga*, I was now infinitely happier and more grateful to this stranger. After all, the one who had bought me the pen case was my father—I had a right to ask him for anything, including a pen case; but this man I had no claim on whatsoever—he was not even a neighborhood acquaintance—yet he had done this good deed for me. Young as I was, I realized this, and a great feeling of gratitude welled up within me. But I was too young to know how to express this properly; I could only wipe my tearful eyes on my sleeve and smile at the stranger, but I felt that my eyes as well as my smile were sufficiently expressive of my heartfelt gratitude.

The pen case had not suffered serious damage from the water: the side was slightly scuffed at one point, but the water had not penetrated inside. When I told my father of the incident and expressed surprise that the pen case had come out unscathed, he told me that the case was the work of Mir Odil, a master book-binder and stationer (*sahhof*). (He was the father of Qorî Ibod, who worked in the Department of Oriental Manuscripts at the Uzbekistan State Library in Tashkent, until his death in 1944). Though Mir Odil's pen cases were made merely of papier-mâché, he invested such skill in their construction that they were as strong as wood and quite waterproof. The outer layer was of Samarkand oilpaper, which repels moisture. The scuff mark, said my father, was obviously not water damage, but the result of the pen case's having hit a sharp piece of wood or stone when it fell into the pit.

*   *   *

Sayid-Akbar came back from Bukhara, and I started to learn to write under his tuition. As was usual with calligraphy teachers, he would write out on a sheet of paper a few words of Arabic in large letters with a broad-nibbed pen. Even as he was writing, it became clear that, though he might write legibly enough in a smaller hand, his broad nib calligraphy was poor. Now, for the beginner, copying a large hand is obligatory, and the teacher must be able to demonstrate to the student how to form these letters in practice. My teacher wrote the large letters with a crooked sweep and angular curlicues, then with the tip of his penknife he scraped a layer of plaque from his teeth and applied it to the offending parts of the letters, scraped off plaque and dried ink together, then inked in the corrections with the tip of his pen; so that there emerged a line of script which the casual observer could not fault. This calligraphy Sayid-Akbar handed to me, with the instructions: "Take this home and practice until you can copy my script exactly. Then write out a fair copy and bring it to show me tomorrow. If you've written it correctly, I'll give you a new piece to practice. If you haven't, you'll have to copy the same one again."

I took the exemplar home. Without any prior practice, I picked up a pen and with a quavering hand wrote the letters straight onto the fair-copy paper. The letters, however, were so crooked and ugly that they looked more like the result of an ink spill than conscious writing. But I wasn't in the least worried by this—like my teacher, I scraped plaque off my teeth with the tip of my penknife, applied it to the crooked parts of the letters, scraped them clean and—like my teacher—inked them in again. As a result, recognizable letters emerged.

When I showed this first copy of mine to my father he praised it, since he was unaware of my subterfuge. Amazingly enough, when I showed it to my teacher the next day, *he* praised it too, never suspecting that I had learned from him how to fake writing before learning to write. So on the second day he set me to copying the second exemplar. In this way I progressed in a short time from forming single letters to writing cursive groups. When I embarked on this stage, the teacher wrote out the following verse as an exercise:

> Once you've learned the lines and loops,
> Time for ligatures and groups!

Now that he was writing with a small pen, Teacher Sayid-Akbar had no need to pick his teeth. But I, who had never practiced at all, had to resort to the same stratagem for cursive groups.

When I finished my writing lessons, I had attained my primary purpose in learning this skill, which was to be able to write down a few poems. But my writing was so bad that no-one was able to read it but me—and after a few days, some of the words I had written were illegible even to me!

Although in course of time, by dint of much writing, my hand did improve somewhat, I am still an extremely poor penman. This is the result of my teacher's setting me the bad example of his own short cut.

18.   Fasting and Breakfasting

The month of Ramadan fell in the season of ripe apricots, corresponding to June. The days were at their longest. And in those
long, hot days, my mother encouraged me to observe the fast. I
complied, but by ten o'clock on the first morning I was overcome
by hunger and thirst. I asked Mother to let me drink some water
and eat a little bread, but she refused: "Anyone who breaks his
fast commits a sin, and will burn in Hell," she told me. I pointed
out that seven days of Ramadan had already passed, during which
I hadn't fasted; so long as it was assured that I would burn in Hell
fire, I didn't see how one day more or less could save me from the
inferno, and again begged Mother to let me break my fast. She
explained: "So long as you haven't *vowed* to fast at the
beginning of the day, then, since you're only a child, no harm will
come to you if you break the fast. But since you solemnly
undertook this morning to fast all day, once you break your fast
you have broken your word—your *niyat*—and you become a
sinner."

I held out for another hour, but could not go on. My mouth
was parched from throat to lips, and in my belly was a gnawing
pain as if a fiery, famished worm were demanding food and drink
and, if I failed to satisfy its demands, would burn and consume me
utterly. At this stage of my distress, my father emerged from his
weaving shop, to get a spool of thread from my mother; he saw
how pale and ill I looked and asked me what was wrong with me. I
told him about my fasting and repeated what my mother had said.
Laughing, he said to my mother, "The boy has not yet reached
years of discretion, he isn't permitted to undertake any religious
obligations. You don't know the *shariat* yourself, so why punish
the child in the name of the *shariat*? Be quick and give him
something to eat!"

That day I ate more than usual, since my eyes were as hungry
as my belly. Inevitably, as a result of eating too much too
quickly—and especially, too many apricots—that night I was sick.
Naturally my mother saw this as a punishment for my breaking
the fast, but kept this opinion to herself for fear of what my father
might say.

Nevertheless my mother persisted, and tried to persuade me to
fast at least three days in the month so that I would get used to it

and fast fully when I grew up. But I took no further notice of her urging. Finally she devised a ruse to make me submit to fasting; to whit, the fair at Darveshobod.

In those times, every year during the month of Mizon (from 23 September to 23 October) an all-night fair was held once a week at Darveshobod, one of the quarters of Ghijduvon.[46] To anyone who had not seen it, a description of this fair would seem as strange and wonderful as the tales of the Thousand and One Nights. The accounts of the fireworks displays and rockets, donkey races and ram fights that went on there were as incredible and exciting as any fairytale. Rare indeed was the resident of Ghijduvon district who had not been at least once a year to the Darveshobod fair. Even poor peasant boys whose fathers could not afford to take them used to try to earn a few *tangas* by doing odd jobs so that they could go and see the fair. As the time of the fair drew near, they would pick cotton for neighbors or tote melons for rich farmers for a daily wage, and if they could not find paid work they would steal stuff from the fields to sell.

I, too, had longed to go to this fair, and every year I asked my father to take me. Initially he would tell me the fair was a bad place, though he knew I didn't believe him. Later he used my youth as an excuse, telling me that I couldn't go on my own, that he didn't intend to go and it would cost him too much to send someone with me: "Wait till you're older, then you can go—if you still want to."

My mother decided to make use of this inordinate desire of mine in order to get me to fast. "If you fast three days," she told me, "I'll give you one *tanga* for each day; that will make three *tangas*, which you can use to go and see the Darveshobod fair." I accepted this challenge, and resolved to fast. That same day my mother made me sleep during the day so that I could stay awake at night, eat a hearty breakfast before daybreak, and sleep through the next day unaware of its passage. Since I agreed, my father did not object. "If you can do it, go ahead and fast," he said. "It's no business of mine."

I stayed up all night and ate a good breakfast with my parents. In the forenoon too I stayed awake, playing with the

---

[46] *Mizon* (Ar. "scales, balance," i.e., the zodiacal sign Libra) is the seventh month of the Iranian solar calendar as used in Afghanistan and Central Asia. This fair evidently had its origins in the old Iranian festival of Mihrgân, celebrated at the autumnal equinox (ca. 21st September).

neighborhood boys, until it began to grow hot. Feeling sleepy, I came home to lie down. Mother had made up a bed for herself and for me outside, on the ground under the apricot trees; but I preferred the empty house, and took my bedding inside. My father used to take his Ramadan siesta in his workshop.

I closed the doors, lay down, and soon fell asleep. All of a sudden I woke up, feeling hungry. I closed my eyes again and tried to go to sleep, so I would not notice the day go by. But my poor empty stomach would not let me. I called to mind the food we were to eat to break our fast that evening: the warm unleavened bread fried in butter that my mother had promised to make, and the mulberry syrup that she always made when the mulberries ripened and put aside especially for Ramadan, seemed particularly appetizing. I mentally reviewed these delicious dishes in hopes of appeasing my growling stomach. But it had the opposite effect, and I craved a bite there and then. I could not help but open my eyes and look toward the outside wall to see if the jar of syrup was still where my mother had put it. It was. At the sight of it my craving increased. Mother usually kept the Ramadan syrup hanging from a nail near the top of the garden wall, out of reach of the ants, and every night she would pour out as much as she needed and hang it up again.

I rose and approached the jar, but 1 was not tall enough to reach it. I brought my bedding over, piled quilts and cushions one on top of the other, and climbed up them; now I could reach the jar. Next I opened the bread bin and, breaking it off bit by bit, took out a loaf of bread. Hitching up the hem of my tunic, I tucked the bread underneath my arm, clambered atop the piled-up bedding, tool off the lid of the jar. and held onto the nail with one hand while with the other I took bits of bread from underneath my arm, dipped them into the syrup, and ate them. As the load under my arm grew lighter, my stomach grew fuller. I replaced the lid on the jar, went to the doorway and washed my hands and mouth from the water jug—drinking as much as I needed at the same time—remade my bed inside the room and went to sleep. When my mother woke me up it was almost sundown, and she was setting out the warm bread and syrup for "breakfast."

In this way I "fasted" for three days and earned three *tangas*, which were to pay for my forthcoming trip to the Darveshobod fair.

19. The Darveshobod Fair

Came the fall, and time for the fair at Darveshobod. My father refused to let me go during the first week it was on, claiming that the first week nothing worth seeing ever happened, and promising to send me during the second week. The second week, Father's cousin Ibrohim Khoja was due to go to Darveshobod. Father gave him my three *tangas* and asked him to take me along, and his young nephew Homid Khoja as well, so we could share the fun of the fair with each other. He also instructed Ibrohim Khoja that in Ghijduvon we should stay at the house of my uncle's father-in-law, the potter.

The fair generally started early on Tuesday morning and went on until mid-morning on Wednesday. We set off early on Tuesday and reached the potter's house where we were to stay the night. It was full of people—not overnight guests, but fellow potters and kiln-workers, all excitedly and noisily making fireworks. Some were cutting lumps of dried clay to size, others were mixing gunpowder, some were sifting iron filings into the powder, and others again were assembling the finished products.

The fireworks comprised a cast iron container something like a water jug without a handle or spout and with a hole in the base. The hole was plugged from inside with a bung of dried clay, and a combustible powder was poured in at the top and tamped down with a sort of wooden pestle. The powder consisted of gunpowder mixed with all kinds of metal filings, including iron, to provide the colored sparks. Our guide Ibrohim Khoja stood watching the gunpowder-mixing and firework-packing for a while, then asked them, "How much money do you spend on this?"

"Ten *tangas* for each firework," came the answer.

"Who pays?" Ibrohim Khoja pursued.

"We, the pottery-workers, and the iron-foundry workers, and others like us."

"What do you get out of it?"

"If we beat our rivals, the Vobkand men, at the fireworks display, it'll be a tremendous coup. What more could we wish for?"

On a quilt atop the *sufa* squatted our host, the master potter of Ghijduvon. He winked at Ibrohim Khoja, and joined in the conversation with a mocking grin. "These people, and the young factory workers too, are called the 'mad lads.' They don't have to care for wives and children, or worry about food and clothing. Their one delight is to let off fireworks twice a year, once at the Darveshobod fair and once on the eve of Ramadan. They are the luckiest kids under the sun—I wish I could spend my life enjoying myself like that! A pity that worldly concerns, a wife and children to look after, and other personal worries, deprive me of this carefree existence!"

Ibrohim Khoja was evidently about to dispute this view but the potter anticipated him and, with a meaning wink, went on: "But though I'm denied the pleasure of this sport myself, I compensate by helping these lads."

"What?" exclaimed Ibrohim Khoja, "you mean you even pay for this out of your own pocket?"

With another wink, the potter replied, "Well, what I do amounts to the same thing. A year's wages, for most of these lads, won't stretch to a twice-yearly fireworks spree. So when any of them need fireworks-money, I give them an advance against their future work. And for someone who's short of cash, that's a great help."

For a while the potter silently surveyed the activities of his workers, then went on: "Don't imagine that the only benefit of the advance is to enable them to play with their fireworks. Oh, no. That's just one of the happy results. The basic benefit is that it ties the workers to the one pottery—'the tree flourishes in one spot,' as the poets say—and they gain daily in experience and skill. If God favors them, they too will have the chance to become master potters with their own workers. Just as I went through my youth as an apprentice and journeyman. If it wasn't for this advance, these self-styled 'mad lads' would be traipsing every day from one pottery to another in search of an illusory extra *tanga*. This nomadic existence would hinder them from improving their skills, and in consequence employers would be reluctant to hire them. They'd end up as vagrants, gamblers, even thieves."

I was depressed by our voluble host's lecture, and begged Ibrohim Khoja to hurry up and take us to the fair.

*   *   *

We went to the fair. The fairground was situated on the western side of the main road that ran from the Ghijduvon cattle market toward Bukhara. From the market gate to the Chubin Madrasa[47] of Ghijduvon, this road stretched straight and broad as a ceremonial avenue, but devoid of trees on either side. On the western side was a twenty-five acre rectangle of land on which the fair had been set up. This land consisted of individually-owned vegetable patches each no larger than a half to one-and-a-half acres, but at the beginning of September the farmers would harvest their crop and clear the ground for the fair. The rent they collected from the fairground stallholders repaid them twice over for any loss incurred from an early harvest.

This stretch was crossed from north to south by alleyways, lined on either side with tent-like booths constructed of laths and rush matting; some were teahouses, some sold meat dishes, others fish, and so on. We strolled the length of these alleys, watching what was going on. It seemed to me, however, that this was nothing more than an ordinary village bazaar, and I wondered what on earth people found to see here. If it was the teahouses and food stalls, then there were better and more attractive ones in the back streets of Ghijduvon itself, and they were open every day. Even the teahouses in the little bazaar of Sari Puli Eshon near our home were better, prettier, and—thanks to the proximity of a pool and a grove of trees—pleasanter to sit at. Feeling bored, I asked Ibrohim Khoja, "Aw, come on, take us to see something exciting!"

"Very well," he replied, and led us to the end of the alleyway, away from the rush matting stalls, up to a wall that separated the fairground from the highway that led from the Chubin Madrasa to the high bridge over the Khoja Khomon creek. The space before the wall was packed with people standing around in circles. Our guide took us to each of these circles in turn and showed us what was going on. In some they were spinning tops, in others rolling up and unwinding straps,[48] in others they were playing cards or the like—all were forms of gambling, in which half-stupefied men crowded around the participants wagering away the pittances they must have saved with enormous difficulty in order to spend at the

---

[47] Named for one Khoja Muhammad Safi Chubin, a fifteenth-century Bukharan mystic.

[48] *Tasma-bozi*, "the strap game": a leather strap is folded lengthwise and rolled up tight, then a nail or other small metal object is inserted into the roll at an arbitrary point. One player then unrolls the strap with a snap of the wrist; if the nail turns up outside the fold, he wins, and if it appears inside the fold, the challenger wins.

fair. "This is nothing worth watching," I complained to my guide in somewhat disappointed and petulant tones.

"You're just like your father, moody and hard to please," Ibrohim Khoja grumbled irritably. A moment later he regained some of his composure, and announced: "All, right, I'll take you to the best sport of the fair."

He led us back through the alleyways between the stalls, to the northwest corner of the fairground. Here there was a pond, on the northern side of which were stalls selling bread, sweets, and fruit. The bakers had fixed large wooden ladders against the trees by the pond, and on the rungs had set out rows of large flat cookies made of extra-fine flour and eggs, a Ghijduvon delicacy. The sweet-merchants, too, had laid out boxes of their wares in every direction and from top to bottom of the rungs, and had wrapped the top layers of candies in colored tinfoil, all of which made for a most appetizing display. To the north of the path skirting the pond lay a low hill, on top of which was the mausoleum of Khoja Darvesh, in whose honor this annual fair was held; and to the east of the pond stood a *sufa*, adjoining which an open-air teahouse had been set up.

I could not see anything exciting to watch here, either. True, the flat cookies and foil-wrapped sweets looked very attractive; but, provided one had money enough, he might buy as much as he needed and take it home to eat—it was certainly not necessary to go to a fair, or to have a fair at all, just for this. However, I refrained from voicing this objection to my guide, who had so recently chided me as "moody and hard to please." Nevertheless, he seemed to have guessed my thoughts from my expression, for he explained: "The fair really gets under way at night—at the moment, people are just strolling about, snacking and drinking tea. We'll get something to eat, too, then go home and come back tonight."

Our guide bought two flat cookies for eight *pul* and half a *tanga*'s worth of soft halva wrapped in gold foil, and took us over to the teahouse by the pond. We ordered tea and started to eat. At the far end of the *sufa*, a *maddoh* had set up his pitch in a small open space and was regaling his audience with the exploits of Khoja Darvesh. According to the tale, Khoja Darvesh was a poor man, but even if he had to go hungry himself he would give everything he acquired as alms to *maddohs* and beggars. One snowy winter's day, he went out into the street dressed in little more than an overcoat. Here he came upon a *maddoh* plying his trade, who asked him for his coat. Khoja Darvesh gave it to the man, and went on through the severe cold to his anchorite's cell dressed only in his tunic.

On concluding his tale, the storyteller made the rounds of his audience, asking them first to spare him clothing, then silver coins, and finally copper coins. Everyone gave him something. Ibrohim Khoja, too, joined the throng and gave him a *tanga*. This surprised me, since my father always said that Ibrohim Khoja lived off the charity of others. So I asked him why he had given money to the *maddoh*. He looked at me quizzically, and said: "Did it cross your mind, perhaps, that the *tanga* I gave the storyteller was one of the three that your father gave me to spend on you at the fair? Well, it wasn't. That money came from my own pocket."

This explanation did not entirely allay my doubts about Ibrohim Khoja's uncharacteristic generosity, and I still stood looking at him with open surprise and puzzlement. Seeing this, he expanded his explanation. "People need to be reminded to be charitable to others. The fact that I—who wear a white turban—gave money to the storyteller serves as an example to the others. They think to themselves, 'if it wasn't right and proper to give alms to the *maddoh*, then this person—a mullah, an *eshon*, who lives on charity himself!—wouldn't have given him any,' and so they join in this good deed as far as they can."

Close by the town of Ghijduvon, to the south, lay a village called Pa'mūza (for Pahn-mūza, "broad-boot"). Most of the adults there were *maddohon* like this one, and most of the boys were in training for the same profession. As can be seen in the example just given, these *maddohon* frequented bazaars and fairs, where they would recite a legend based on religious superstition and beg for alms; their young apprentices would make the rounds of teahouses singing for money.

After the *maddoh* had finished, two of these apprentices, together with a barker to promote them, appeared in the teahouse. The singers looked about sixteen or seventeen years old, the barker twenty-five or twenty-six. They would approach each party of customers, whereupon the singers would squat down and their barker, standing, would start off a song and the boys would join in. But neither the barker nor the other two ever sang a song through to the end; as soon as the boys had taken up the retrain from him, the barker would break off and start begging for alms. His manner of asking was quite impudent, somewhat as follows: "Come on, turn out your purses, cough up! Your tip should be as big as your moustache. Hey, you with the walrus whiskers—why don't you set an example?"

When the customers had been shamed or bullied into giving something, either by the persistent barker or by each other, the barker launched into a different spiel: "O ye who are nourished and protected by the Lord of the World, Khoja Abdulkholiq of Ghijduvon! I have come from Bukhara to entreat your hospitality, having taken a sacred vow. This year I wish to make the pilgrimage to Mecca. My name is Jūrachulak, and I live in the Street of the *Maddohon* in Bukhara. Whatever you have given so far was in appreciation of these two fine young singers, and is their property. Now I ask you in God's name for something for myself, for the journey to Mecca the Blessed! After the season of the Pilgrimage, if any one of you happens to go to Bukhara, let him pay a visit to the Street of the Maddohon and ask whether Jūrachulak went on the Pilgrimage or not; and if they say I didn't, then anyone who gave me one *tanga* here will get ten *tangas* back from me!"

And of course they gave the barker another contribution.

I really enjoyed the singing of the two apprentice storytellers; they had excellent voices and a masterly delivery too. It was a pity that the arrogant barker gave them no chance to sing properly, and had ruined all the listeners' enjoyment with his constant pestering and collecting.

*   *   *

We came late to our lodging, to find completed fireworks stacked up one atop the other like waterjugs at a potter's store. After a couple of hours' nap, off we went back to the fair. Large candles were burning in the teahouses and stalls, and in the open squares they had set out mortars full of oil with blazing rags in them, which lit up the surroundings like torches. We worked our way round the fair adMir-ing these lamps. Ibrohim Khoja bought us a string of paper firecrackers. All at once an excited hubbub arose among the fairground crowd: "The fireworks are starting!" Ibrohim Khoja took us to the top of the little hill. Apart from the mausoleum of Khoja Darvesh, there was another small building up there, built as an annex to the shrine. Between this and the mausoleum was a mulberry tree. A faint glimmer of light, as from a dimly burning lamp, came through a crack in the door of the smaller building. Ibrohim Khoja seated us in front of this building, at a spot from where we could see the pool and the stalls of the bakers, confectioners, and fruit sellers. "The fireworks display takes place right around this pool," he told us. "But it would be dangerous for you to stay down there—you might be frightened when the fireworks go off, or get trampled underfoot in the crowd. Up here you have a good view and can watch the fireworks safely." He took a box of matches out of his purse and gave it to his nephew Homid Khoja, with the words "If you get bored before the fireworks start, you can amuse yourselves by letting off one of your firecrackers now and then."

Ibrohim Khoja went away. Homid Khoja struck a match and lit one of the firecrackers. It went off with a bang, and at once a piercing shriek of "Help! Murder!" came from inside the small building. A confusion of voices followed, the door burst open and several people emerged. We took to our heels in fright. I went and hid inside the mausoleum; Homid Khoja, who had run in the opposite direction, was caught. The men from inside the building boxed his ears and cuffed him a few times, but when he apologized for setting off the firework they let him go, went back inside and closed the door.

I sidled out from the shrine and rejoined Homid Khoja. He was still crying but, presumably ashamed, stopped when he saw me, and suggested, "Let's see who's inside and what they're up to!"

We went up to the door and peered through the crack. Three or four pale-faced men were sitting with grubby kerchiefs spread out in front of them. On these lay something that looked like crumbled halva and raisins. At the side, one of them was crushing something in a small bowl. All of them had their heads bowed and their eyes closed, including the one with the bowl. One of them, without raising his head or opening his eyes, began to murmur in a soft drone, like the buzzing of a fly. Another, likewise without stirring, answered him in the same drone. Evidently they were conversing quietly, but the actual words could not be distinguished.

Without making a sound, Homid Khoja gripped my hand and signed for us to withdraw. Once we were back at our original spot, he said, "These men are opium-eaters. The things they're grinding up in the bowl are poppy seed pods; they drink the sap, and get high."

"How do you know all this?" I asked him.

"I know. I saw an opium den when I was in Rishti with my uncle. He'd gone there to recite prayers over one of them who'd gotten ill. They're scared of loud noises. Just you watch how I get my own back on them."

Homid Khoja put the string of firecrackers under his arm, climbed up the mulberry tree and slung the firecrackers over a twig at the end of a high branch. Next he took the box of matches from his purse and lit the fuse, scrambled down hastily, and motioned me to join him as he retired to a safe distance from the opium den and hid.

A moment later the fuse burned down to its end and the fire-cracker went off with a bang. As before, the opium-eaters rushed out yelling; but though they looked high and low they could find no trace of the culprit and, cursing, went back inside and closed the door. Once the coast was clear, Homid Khoja squealed with delight, "I really put the wind up those fellows!"

The firecrackers were strung together in such a way as to leave about an inch of fuse between each one. After one cracker had exploded, the fuse slowly burned on until it reached the next. The bang was repeated, as were the cries and alarums and excursions of the opium-eaters, and Homid Khoja's squeals of joy. When the third firecracker went off, the same scene unrolled again. I said to Homid Khoja: "But for this, I'd have left the Darveshobod fair without seeing anything worthwhile. Now I can say I really saw a sight at the fair!"

At that moment the fourth firecracker went off, and we were busy watching the opium-eaters rushing around yelling, when from behind us arose another hair-raising sound—a hissing, which went on and on—and all around us was bathed in light. We looked round toward the pool. The fireworks display had begun! On the narrow poolside path was such a dense crowd of people that, as they said in those days, "if you tossed a needle into the air, it wouldn't reach the ground." Inside the stalls, up in the trees on the western side of the pool, everywhere was full of people. At either end of the throng of spectators stood two tall young men, their sleeves rolled up to the elbows, each holding a firework in his right hand. The fireworks, like the dragons they used to tell about in fairytales, made a dreadful continuous hissing noise, and belched fire from their mouths. The fiery tongue of the firework shot straight up into the air like a fountain of water, blossomed open at its summit like an umbrella, and scattered sparks all around.

As these two youths advanced toward each other, their fire-works gradually died out; then from each of the directions they had come from, two more youths emerged—four in all—and each ignited a firework, which they bore toward each other. One of them was very young, and swayed forward like a dancer, whirling round and round with the firework in his hand like a spinning spool. On every side rose shouts of applause: "Bravo, Abdullo! Well done! You're the champion!"

In the glare of the firework I saw the young man's face, and could not believe my eyes. This Abdullo was the same boy who used to be my classmate at the girls' school and whose father, Botur-boi the dyer, had brought him from Ghijduvon to Soktaré in order to keep him out of mischief. After his arrival, however, he had fallen in with a bunch of the local "tough guys" and, young as he was, had earned quite a reputation through his prowess in combat with other toughs.

When these youths' fireworks had fizzled out, three more came on from each side carrying six lighted fireworks in all, as the crowd roared its appreciation. These fireworks flared up in different colors—red, yellow, purple, green, and blue—and blossomed out like a huge bouquet of multicolored flowers.

All at once, fire spurted out from the bottom of one of the fireworks, and both firework and bearer tumbled to the ground. Cries went up from the crowd: "It's backfired, one of the Ghijduvon fireworks has backfired!... The Vobkand team has won!... Throw them in the pond!... Hey, come on, Ironcasters, the Ghijduvon men are being routed!"

At the spot where the firework had backfired, several people whose clothes were smoldering were picked up bodily and tossed into the pond. "Ironcasters! Ironcasters!" rose a triumphant chant from one section of the crowd. From the opposite side came an answering shout: "The Vobkand ironcasters are ready to face off against the Ghijduvon ironcasters; this final heat will show which *tuman* is the best—don't crow too soon!"

From each side emerged eight bearers, and sixteen fireworks blazed up. But barely a moment passed before one of the Vobkand fireworks backfired, and simultaneously another one blew up with a deafening boom; and at that same moment, the bakers' ladder on which the huge flatcakes were displayed keeled over and fell into the pool.

Seeing and hearing this, Homid Khoja and I fell face-forward on the ground. The screaming and weeping and cries for help, combined with the hissing and crackling of the fourteen fireworks still going off, produced a terrifying spectacle. We had still not dared to raise our heads from the ground when the noise of the fireworks suddenly subsided and a few voices could be heard shouting, "Enough for now! The Vobkand team has lost! Next week we'll teach the Ghijduvon team a lesson, so don't crow too soon!"

After the voices had ceased altogether and an unhappy quiet came over the poolside, we raised our heads and Homid Khoja said, "I wonder what's happened to the opium-eaters?" He ran up to the building, and I followed on his heels. The door was ajar, the lamp was burning dimly, the bowl of opium lay overturned on the floor; the opium-eaters' kerchiefs and cushions were still in their places—but of the opium-eaters themselves there was no sign. Evidently they had retired somewhere apart at the first noise of the fireworks display.

A while later Ibrohim Khoja returned, turbanless and with his top clothes held dripping wet in his arms. We asked him what had happened, and were told: "When the Ghijduvon and Vobkand teams sent out four fireworks into the field, I went up close to the two Ghijduvon men and prayed that God would keep them safe from harm and bring them victorious from the contest. One of them promised me that if they won he wouldn't forget that it was thanks to my prayers, and so I said another prayer for him. But right after that his firework backfired, he was injured in both legs and collapsed, and his clothes caught fire too. Some of the onlookers picked him up, along with some of the spectators whose clothes had caught fire in the same mishap, and threw them into the pool. Suddenly I noticed that my clothing was burning as well; I took my coat off quick and threw it into the pool . . ."

"What happened to your turban?" Homid Khoja asked his uncle.

"I was just coming to that. After I'd extinguished the flames on my coat, I picked a spot in the stall of Fayzi-boi, the son of Nazrullo-boi the confectioner, so as to be able to watch the fireworks show more comfortably. And in fact it was a good deal better and safer, being out of the crowd and away from exploding fireworks. But when that unlucky Vobkand firework exploded, this spot was right in the line of fire. The baker's stall went tumbling into the pool together with the ladders leaning against it, and several people who were standing inside it were injured; the confectioner's stall caught fire, and some people in there were injured too; and since I'd already   suffered when the Ghijduvon firework backfired, I got out of the way when the Vobkand firework exploded. But after the explosion, someone said to me, "Hey, Mullo, your turban's on fire!" I took it off right away in order to throw it into the water, but I couldn't manage to—the fine gauze turban was well ablaze, and when I grabbed it off my head I burned my hands—so I threw it down at my feet, and it burned to ashes in front of my eyes."

According to what Ibrohim Khoja told us, the young man of Vobkand who was holding the firework that exploded had both his hands blown off at the wrists, and the rest of his forearms burned up the the elbows. He had passed out and been carried away; so far there was no news as to whether he was alive or dead.[49]

* * *

We went home and slept, and returned next day to the fair. At the poolside there was no longer any trace of the stallholders' displays of the day before, but at least the marks of the fire had been erased and the place to some extent cleaned up. We sat at the poolside teahouse drinking tea; the felt mats and kilims had faded patches on them in the shapes of the shade from the elm tree. We had not yet finished our tea when the *maddoh* of yesterday appeared, greeted Ibrohim Khoja obsequiously, sat down before us and addressed our guide as follows: "I heard that in last night's disaster your clothing was burned; so I have taken the liberty of bringing you one of the best robes that I acquired last night, thanks to the blessing of your encouragement, and I beg you to accept it as a gift." And he placed a bundle he had brought before Ibrohim Khoja.

"A good deed is not necessarily a good omen," the latter protested, nevertheless picking up the bundle. The *maddoh* took his leave, and once he was out of earshot Ibrohim Khoja said to me, "You see the result of my giving a *tanga* to the *maddoh* yesterday? My money, like that of a moneylender, has returned to me with interest."

After finishing our tea, we went to watch the donkey-racing.

* * *

---

[49] A similar fireworks contest that took place at Ghijduvon during the Ramadan night fair, when I was an adult, and resulted in many deaths, is described in *Ahmadi devband* -- A.

On the eastern side of the fairground, along the highway that ran broad and straight from the gate of the cattle market to the Chubin Madrasa, the donkey racecourse had been set up. Some fifty donkeys were entered for the race—all of them big, white, brush-tailed, sabre-maned, and prick-eared. Two or more donkeys were raced at a time, and a horse was run with them. The horse was ridden by an experienced youth, and the donkeys by boys of twelve to fourteen years. The starting line was the cattle-market gate, at the far end of the horse market, and the finishing post was in front of the Chubin Madrasa, where the judges also stood.

First came the amateur heats, with a few boys riding foals and ordinary working donkeys. Then came the turn of the professional donkey-dealers and celebrated amateur riders. When two of these men placed bets of ten or twenty *tangas* on their respective animals to win, the betting was declared open, and spectators would wager twenty, fifty, even a hundred *tangas* with each other on the outcome of the race. In this way, complete strangers would win from or lose to each other hundreds of *tangas* on the result of a race between somebody else's asses.

At last a boastful rider named Istam the Ass-killer swaggered onto the track. The ass he led was large and sleek and, moreover, in rut, so that it missed no opportunity to fight with its peers. Despite all Istam's efforts to hold the halter hard down with both hands, it would constantly rear and attempt to attack the other donkeys. After much lauding of his mount's prowess, Istam challenged anyone to ride against him for a stake of two hundred *tangas*. Nobody accepted, since all feared their own mounts were no match. Finally a stripling by the name of "Bucktooth" Rustam took up Istam's challenge. He was about sixteen or seventeen, with three of his front teeth jutting out over his lower lip. His donkey, compared with that of Istam the Ass-killer, was small, thin, and lopeared. Everyone laughed at the youth's temerity and told him he was throwing away two hundred *tangas*. The "Ass-killer," for his part, declared that it was an insult to expect him to ride against this bucktoothed kid and match his own sleek roan against that sack of dogmeat. Spectators told him that if he refused to race they would consider his ass beaten; to which Istam replied angrily, "All right, let him show me the money first, then I'll take the bet—how do I know I'll get the money out of this orphan when I've won?"

The boy had only one hundred *tangas*. He was obliged to try to stake his own donkey to cover the balance: if he won, he would give his backer one hundred five *tangas* in return for the hundred loaned and keep his donkey, but if he lost he would forfeit the donkey to his backer. Finally someone was found who would lend Rustam a hundred tangas against his donkey—a gray-haired former donkey-racer who had retired from the sport on account of his age. "Never fear, son," he encouraged Rustam,"your ass will beat Istam's; I'll get five *tangas* extra on my loan, and your ass will be yours." He counted out a hundred *tangas* from his satchel and gave them to Rustam.

Istam the Ass-killer, hearing this prediction, flared up like dry brushwood androunded angrily on the old man. "I bought this ass last year for two hundred *tangas*, and I've been training him up for this day all year! If my ass is passed by this carrion, I'll change my name from "Ass-killer" and I'll slaughter my ass with this very knife!" and he pointed to the hunting knife at his belt. The old man smiled and replied, "Don't lose your temper, little brother! 'A man's mettle is proved in the field, an ass's on the course,' as they say. Don't boast before you've started racing—once your donkey wins, you can boast as much as you like."

The race began. Istam's ass bounded ahead with abandon; Rustam, who had elected to ride himself rather than employ an unknown jockey, held the reins in and stayed behind his competitor. Istam threw his turban to the winds, whooping joyfully. When they had covered half the course, Rustam gave his mount its head, urging it, "Come on, beast, catch him up!" Rustam's ass swiftly made up the distance, and both animals disappeared from the spectators' view. A short while later the judges appeared, to announce Rustam's ass the winner. Rustam too walked back leading his ass, but with no flush of victory on his face. As for Istam, he could not bear the shame of this defeat; drawing his knife from its sheath, he plunged it up to the hilt in his ass's belly. As the beast collapsed, the old man told Istam, "There was nothing wrong with your ass—it was your fault, for over-fattening the beast. You should have slit your own belly!"

The spectators, horrified at this gruesome scene, dispersed and went their separate ways.

*   *   *

From the horse market we went to the open space by the sheep market, where the ram-fighting was to take place. Here, just as in the donkey-racing, the competitors bet against each other's animals and the spectators bet against each other on the outcome; as a result, a great deal of money changed hands. Finally a fat-tailed ram, with a tail that by the spectators' estimate must have weighed over fifty pounds, was brought out to fight. In the clashes with its massive opponent, the animal's tail was so badly shaken that it broke apart, and its owner was forced to slaughter it and sell its flesh and fat at the regular market rate.

With this, our stay at Darveshobod, which had lasted a day and a night, was over. I promised myself I would never again visit the Darveshobod fair, since it offered not a single enjoyable spectacle.

20. "Lord Provider"

One of the Mirakoni Khojas of Soktaré was a certain Qori Mahmud, a man of ready wit and a born prankster. When he was a boy his father had sent him to a school for Koran-readers to learn the scripture by heart, and from this had come his sobriquet of *qori*. When he grew up he served his apprenticeship as an attendant at the courts of the emir's provincial governors for a few years, then returned to the village and took up a practice as an *eshon* and prayer-healer.

One day I asked him, "Why was it that you gave up being a courtier and took to the life of an *eshon*? Even as a page, life at court carries a certain authority, whereas being an *eshon* and healer, even an eminent one, is still really a form of begging."

"As the saying goes," he replied, "'One eats meat dumplings for the meat.' Whether one is an outrider for the emir's officers, or a prayer-healing sheikh, the purpose is to get a regular ration of bread for one's belly. True, officers and courtiers command respect and force people to do what they want, yet the people know them all for the tyrants they are and hate the sight of them—especially their attendants, who are the immediate instruments of oppression in the hands of emir, minister, and governor. Though the people obey the orders of government hirelings out of fear, if ever they get the chance they won't leave one of them alive. I've had ten years of service at court to learn that. Now, being a sheikh and curing people by reciting prayers, that's a nice easy profession: it isn't all that different from fleecing them as a courtier, except that the sheikh handles a man's life with cotton wadding, and those who've been caught never even realize it. On top of that, not only do they not hate him, they revere him as their savior and always treat him with respect and affection. That's why I changed back from my former job to this one."

In our village there was another Mirakoni called Ubayd Khoja. He was a poor and unsuccessful individual, without a single desire or ambition in life. His worldly estate consisted of three acres of land and an apricot orchard. He was neither a courtier nor a prayer-healer himself, but he held both professions in great esteem, and would invent and elaborate stories to illustrate the "justice" of the most oppressive governors and the "miracles" of the most illiterate and fraudulent *eshons*.

Provided he found a willing ear, he could talk on and on in this vein the whole day long.

Qori Mahmud would listen to Ubayd Khoja's tales, ridicule him, and publicly refute his fabrications with facts that were common knowledge. Finally he told him: "Brother, you're a frustrated evildoer. If you were a government lackey or a practicing prayer-healer, I wouldn't blame you for spreading these tall tales; for—apart from me—'no Arab will admit that his own whey is sour,' as the saying goes. But you are an unpaid and thankless encomiast for both courtiers and *eshons*, and a procurer for their misdeeds, which is sheer stupidity."

One day I was sitting on the bank of the Mazrangon stream, which runs through our village. Qori Mahmud rode up to the other bank, dismounted and shooed his horse homeward, then squatted down at the water's edge opposite me and began washing his hands. I asked him where he had come from.

"From the village of Obkena, from a funeral," he answered.

"You must have gone to recite prayers over the dying man?" I surmised.

"Of course. I went, I prayed, I took my fee,[50] I buried him today and came back."

---

[50] Fee: *nazr*, actually a gift of alms made to a sacred institution or personage in return for intercession for divine favor or in fulfilment of a vow. Here, ironically, the *eshon* evidently expects such a gift even if the patient does not recover (Obkena is also mentioned as the site of the death of

"Well, when they saw that your prayers had no effect on his illness, did they tell you at the funeral that they still had faith in you?"

"The common people have an odd characteristic," he mused. "The washer of their dead, who is harmless, they consider a person of ill omen and bar from the funeral. But they put such trust in *eshons* and prayer-healers that they summon one in hopes of curing their sick, and ply him with votive offerings. If the patient recovers, they attribute it to the good fortune brought by the *eshon* and the efficacy of his prayers, and they give him repeated assurances of their devotion and present after present. But if the patient dies, they attribute it to God's will, and shrug it off as the man's fate. In that case, not only do they not lose faith in the *eshon*, they hold him in greater respect than other imams and mullahs, and if they give *them* one yard of wool or cotton print as a *yirtish*, they give *him* a whole bolt of gauze! At any rate," Qori Mahmud concluded, "*eshons* and prayer-healers are better off and more highly regarded than washers of the dead."[51]

* * *

The older youths in the village used to throw regular evening parties at one another's houses.[52] To one of these they invited Qori Mahmud, for his skill as a wit and raconteur, and Sayid-Akbar, because he was a student at a Bukhara madrasa, even though neither of them was a member of the "club." All of the regular members and the guests arrived early in the evening at the appointed place, except for Sayid-Akbar, who—perhaps to demonstrate his seniority, since older participants in a soirée of any sort generally arrive late—had still not showed up two hours later. Some of the guests, who were all on friendly and informal

---

a woman in labor, who failed to respond to the village schoolteacher's written prayers: see Appendix II, Section iv).

[51] This speech of Qori Mahmud is included in the novel *Dokhunda*, in the chapter *Janoza* ("Funeral"), as part of conversation between Hoji Ya'qub-boi and the *eshon* Sulton-khon -- A.

[52] This kind of soirée, where each regular participant plays host in turn, was called a *gashtak*. For the conventions governing similar communal entertainments (the *dangona* and *harifona*), and a description of a *dangona*, see Appendix I, iii-iv.

terms, grumbled to the host of the evening: "Come on, if you've prepared any food, dish it up, we're famished—and if you haven't, tell us straight out, so we can go home and get something to eat!"

The host answered that everything was ready, but he was waiting for Sayid-Akbar, who after all was a guest—they would have to wait a little while longer.

After a long wait, however, Sayid-Akbar still had not arrived, and the party went on without him.

The next evening, Sayid-Akbar was sitting together with a group of friends in the street when Qori Mahmud joined them and asked him why he had not come to the party last night. " A houseful of guests were waiting anxiously for you for two whole hours, and you never showed up. That's not right."

"I did go there," replied Sayid-Akbar. "But I came away without entering."

"Why?" asked Qori Mahmud in surprise.

"Because the ignorant host abused me behind my back. With my own ears I heard him say 'Sayid-Akbar isn't here yet.' For an illiterate person to take me to task by name me,—a theology student at a Bukhara madrasa!—isn't that impertinent? So I thought to myself, 'let him eat his dinner himself,' and turned back at the door."

Qori Mahmud laughed heartily, and replied: "Everybody and everything needs a name, which must needs be used even in the absence of said body or thing in order to talk about them. Since you are evidently ashamed of the name your father gave you, we'll give you a very grand name, one you needn't be ashamed of and one we'll know right away refers to *you* when we hear it used. I think this name should be 'Lord Provider,' which is one of the names of God and than which there is no grander name on earth. And since in your case the extra sobriquet 'Lord' (*khuĵja*) is tacked on to 'Provider,' that makes it even grander than God's name, as well befits you."[53] Everyone burst out laughing. Sayid-Akbar was incensed, but dared not say anything in front of them all. He could do nothing but stand up, fuming, and storm off

---

[53] Tajik *parvardigor-khūja: parvardegâr* "nourisher, provider, fosterer" is the Persian equivalent of Arabic *al-razzâq*, one of the epithets of God. *Khūja* is a colloquial (hence, mocking) variant of Sayid-Akbar's aristocratic title *khoja* (see Glossary).

home. He was not seen in public for several days after; but the nickname 'Lord Provider' stuck to him from then on.

21. My Father

I should like to devote a few pages to the life and character of my father, who, despite my being separated from him at an early age, exercised a profound influence on my life.

My father had a very poor opinion of the official clergy—imam, kadi, *rais*, and so on—and always dismissed them as being ignorant and unjust. The only kadi he liked was Abdul-Vohid Sadri Sarir, and the only imams he liked were a few whom I never saw. In the villages, quarrels were constantly erupting between my father and the imams, but my father would always emerge victorious. This was because he knew the so-called "head-scratchers"—the kinds of puzzle some people memorize in order to win battles of wits, such as rhyming riddles, enigmas, *abjad* puzzles and the like, or poems whose interpretation depended on a cryptic topical allusion.[54] The official village mullahs did not know this sort of thing; in fact some of them could not even read or write. So he would use this kind of question to discomfit them and mock them publicly for their ignorance.

The villagers, especially the women, took a very dim view of kadis. There was one kadi from our village, whom I never saw, though I did see his sons, whom people called the Qozibachas. This kadi was particularly disliked in our village. Most of the best land around Soktaré and Sayidkent was in the hands of his offspring. At the northern edge of Soktaré was a stretch of apricot orchard known as the "kadi's garden." At the time I remember,

---

[54] The genres mentioned are as follows. The *chiston* (lit. "what-is-it") is a traditional riddle, often posed in the form of a metaphor in rhymed couplets, e.g., *az du dara sel omad—panj javon pesh omad* "Torrents rush down double bed—Five young stalwarts stop them dead." Answer: wiping one's nose. The *muammo* ("enigma") is a literary riddle in verse, alluding to the target word by cryptic reference to the component letters; analogies in English are riddles of the type "What is the longest word in the English language?—'Smile', because there is a 'mile' between the first and the last letters." For *abjad*, see the Glossary.

the apricot trees had grown old and barren, and the kadi's sons had sold them to charcoal-burners, who set up several ovens in the orchard, felled the trees, and were burning them for charcoal.

During this same time Usto Amak's wife invited the women of the village to a celebration at her house. Since I was only a child, I was permitted to accompany my mother; and because I was known to be talkative and inquisitive, I was not left to play outside on the *sufa* with the other children, but was allowed to sit indoors with my mother and the other women.

The talk turned to kadis. One of the women characterized this class as "logs for hellfire" and claimed that kadis burn so well that they make Hell hotter than ever. Another declared that if God reserved a place in Hell the size of a single mattress for each sinner, then each kadi would have a complete house built for him, with the wall and door and living-room and all the furniture made of fire. Another woman agreed, adding, "But that would be for ordinary kadis. For our own kadi here, God has obviously decided to make a fiery orchard too, as well as a fiery house, seeing that He got the Qozi's sons to sell his trees to the charcoal-burners. The same fires that were kindled in their ovens are being used in the next world to feed the fiery orchard."

My mother, who through listening to my father had come to like Qozi Abdul-Vohid, joined in the conversation. "I think Qozi Abdul-Vohid will go to Heaven, because he's said to be just. Especially since he oversaw the digging of the new Shofirkom canal, which was a boon to the farmers of a whole *tuman*—that should guarantee him God's forgiveness."

The other women did not share my mother's view. The woman who had wished a fiery orchard in Hell on our local kadi said, "Once you become a kadi, you can't be just any more. If Qozi Abdul-Vohid has done a great many good deeds while he was a kadi, then he'll surely be spared the fiery house and garden in Hell. But at the very least he'll get a mattress-sized space in Hell along with the other sinners." Another of the women counted as one of Qozi Abdul-Vohid's misdeeds his marrying of Habiba without her father's consent.

The verdict thus voiced on Qozi Abdul-Vohid did not seem fair to me either, since I had liked him on first meeting him, and even more after he united Habiba with her true love; and when I learned that he was a poet, my admiration for him knew no bounds. I didn't like the idea of his burning in hellfire. So I asked my father about it.

Though he did not go as far as the women in allocating an infernal house and garden for kadis, he affirmed that they were "corrupt and unjust, the middlemen in the emir's sinful exploitation of the people, and therefore in accordance with the words of God and the Prophet they must go to Hell." My father was a religious man, in the sense that he believed in God and the Prophet, the Last Judgment, and Heaven and Hell

When I asked what he thought about Qozi Abdul-Vohid, he replied: "God have mercy on him, he was a good man." — the Qozi had died recently — "He will surely go to Heaven. At the close of every *namoz* I say a prayer for him." And he enumerated one by one the kadi's virtues and good deeds. He did not, however, include the fact of his being a poet.

"One of his virtues must have been that he was a poet," I reminded my father. He laughed at this, then resumed his serious air and said, "Being a poet is not always necessarily a virtue. Poetry, like education, is a sword: if you kill a bad man, an enemy, with the sword, that's good, but if an ordinary person is killed with that sword, then that's an injustice, and the killer should be executed. Likewise if poetry is used for good ends it is good, but if it is used for evil ends there is nothing worse."

"Did he do good deeds, or bad deeds?" I wanted to know.

"To marry a young man and woman at their request is in accordance with the *shariat*. Any kadi could do the same. The difference is that any other kadi, after marrying a runaway couple, would have agreed to hear the lawsuits that would inevitably have arisen as a result, which would have ruined the newly-established family. Because a lot of the kadi's income derives from litigation. Qozi Abdul-Vohid's good deed in this case was that after he had married Habiba he refused to hear the complaints prepared by her family and sent the plaintiffs packing. That was definitely a good deed!"

*   *   *

In those days it was the custom in Bukhara province for some of the poorer mullahs' sons to present themselves during the month of Ramadan before a noted kadi, who would send out these "students" of his to a village where there was no imam or regular schoolteacher (*maktabdor*), in order to act as a temporary teacher (*muallim*). At the end of the month the villagers would collect a sum of money to give to the student.

One Ramadan my elder brother, who was the classmate of a kadi's son, accompanied the latter to see his father the kadi, and was duly sent out to a village to teach. My father got to hear of this somehow or other and was enraged; he came home with his whole body trembling, as often happened when he was very angry, and told my uncle Qurbon-Niyoz (who was at that time staying with us): "Go to the city and bring Muhyiddin home. I'd go myself, but I'm afraid I might hit him in front of the mullahs and shame both of us."

Three days later my uncle brought Muhyiddin home. As soon as he came in and greeted us, Father picked up from the felt mat a stick that he had earlier cut and prepared, and rushed at him. But my uncle and mother shielded him, and insisted that this time Father should just give him a talking-to. My father was thus obliged to resolve the matter by admonition; but his admonition was more severe than a beating would have been.

"Kadis are swine," he growled. "They dig up carrion from anywhere, eat it, and feed it to others; any student who frequents the house of one of them is a swine in the making. If you want to be a man, then make do with any morsel of dry bread and any cup of water I can afford to provide you with; if you want to be a swine, then consider all parental bonds between you and me as severed."

My brother promised never again to go for work to a kadi.

*   *   *

The imam of our village was a sanctimonious mullah from Darvoz. He used to go around the bazaars exhorting people to shun sinful practices and cleave to the lawful path. In those days, men known as *poyaki* would go around the market, somewhat like water-sellers, only instead of a drink of water they would sell puffs at a lighted water-pipe. These *poyakis* usually carried hookahs with silver tops and stands, the better to attract customers.

One Ghijduvon market day, our village imam smashed three of these hookahs in order to prevent people smoking them. He was recounting this exploit to an audience by the bank of the stream, with righteous pride, when my father, who was present, remarked that he had been wrong to do so.

"Why so?" demanded the imam indignantly.

"First," said my father, "because it is not certain that tobacco smoke is forbidden by the *shariat*. In the early days of Islam, pipe-smoking had not yet been invented. All we can say is that it is a dangerous practice, at least for those who smoke. Second, by breaking three hookahs you won't get smokers to give up smoking. But you *will* cause considerable loss to their owners, who are really just beggars with a prop. If smoking in the bazaar were to be officially forbidden, by you or by the government, then the *poyaki* could sell his valuable hookah and support himself and his family for some time on the proceeds."

At this, the mullah riposted angrily: "You're always flaunting your education and jumping on us mullahs—you go too far, for you are hindering us from 'enjoining what is right and forbidding what is wrong."[55]

Everyone expected the two of them to come to blows there and then. But unexpectedly my father rose without a word and went off home, with me running after him. Arriving at the house, he saddled the donkey, then went inside and put on his turban and *joma*. He opened the bread-bin, stuffed everything he found there into a *khurjin*, called to my mother "I'm off to the city," and went out.

"Why are you going to the city without warning me?" my mother complained. "Wait one day, so I can bake a flatcake for the boy"—meaning for him to take to Muhyiddin. But he mounted the donkey without answering and rode off.

Mother asked me what had happened in the bazaar, and I told her about the altercation with the imam. But she did not think this could have been sufficient reason for my father to rush off to Bukhara.

Three days later my father came back from Bukhara, tied up the donkey in its usual place, laid the *khurjin* on the edge of the *sufa*, and without a word to my mother about how Muhyiddin was, went out again. When he returned an hour later, the tension that had clouded his brow ever since his quarrel with the imam was completely gone; his face showed no sign of anger or resentment and, smiling happily, he told my mother all about the dispute. "I've brought a rescript from the *mufti* in Bukhara to prove I was right," he said in conclusion, and brought out from under his arm a sheet of paper, which he read out and explained to us. The text went as follows: "The destruction of property, be it the property

---

[55] A reference to Koran 9:71, "The believers . . . enjoin what is right (*al-ma'ruf*) and forbid what is wrong (*al-munkar*)." This is tantamount to calling Sayid-Murod Khoja an unbeliever.

of the destroyer or of another, is unlawful; and if one destroys another's property, then in addition to his being thereby accounted a sinner, he is obliged to replace the property he has destroyed, or to reimburse its owner a sum equivalent in value." At the foot of the document was the impression of a large seal, fully the diameter of a teacup.

"With this judgment," my father went on, "I showed that what I had said was right, and put the imam to shame before everyone. Our mullahs are ignorant: they listen to fat-turbaned clerics like themselves, but however sensible may be the views of a layman like me, they refuse to accept them. They don't know the wise adage 'Look at what is said, not at who says it'—or if they know it, they pretend not to. The mouths of such as these should be sealed shut with the *mufti*'s seal—in the words of the proverb, 'donkey meat is fit only for dogs.'"

*   *   *

Quick-tempered though he was, my father never hit me hard or raged at me for long. So far as I remember, he only chastised me twice. One such episode took place as follows.

Once he bought a donkey, which turned out to be skittish; whenever anyone touched its mane it would buck and shy away. One summer's morning he took it out to graze in a field where the wheat had recently been reaped, leaving it tethered to feed on the stubble. When the sun was high and the heat intense, he told me, "Go to the field and bring back the donkey—only don't ride it, in case you accidentally grab hold of its mane and it bucks and throws you."

Off I went and untied the donkey, thinking to myself, "If I can find somewhere to use as a mounting-block, and don't hold onto his mane, he won't throw me—what's the point of leading an empty donkey back on foot?" To carry out this scheme I led the donkey into the stream and, slowly and carefully, without touching him anywhere with my hands, I mounted him from the bank. The donkey for his part stood docilely, without making any untoward movement. As he clambered up from the streambed, however, his head was higher than his tail; without a saddle cloth, I was close to sliding off backwards and, to save myself, involuntarily clutched with both hands at the donkey's mane. Immediately he started bucking and rearing, and the tighter I clung to his mane for fear of falling, the more he bucked and reared. Finally I was thrown head over heels onto the ground. My right arm felt as if it had been snapped off at the elbow and began to ache sickeningly; the donkey, still kicking up its heels alternately to left and right, headed for home.

Even more than the pain in my arm, fear of what my father would do threw me into a panic. I had disobeyed him and caused both of us a great deal of trouble, and deserved to be punished severely. After a minute I hauled myself upright, but the pain in my arm increased. It was as if an iron meathook had penetrated my side and was clawing my heart, lungs, and arm all together toward the ground, and I was forced to sit down. At that moment my father appeared, coming from the house, and I steeled myself in readiness for the beating to come.

When he reached me, Father did not beat me or even scold me. He took one look at my injured arm and said simply, "You've disobeyed me and lost the use of your arm. Since it's your right arm, so much the worse for you—now you won't be able to write."

This last observation of my father's hurt me more than a thousand strokes of the switch would have done.

With his kerchief my father fashioned a sling for my arm, then fetched a horse from the village; and, with me sitting behind him, rode off to see the bonesetter in Ghijduvon. The bonesetter determined that my arm was broken in two places, at the elbow and at the wrist, and then proceeded to set it. To do this he pressed so hard that we could hear the creaking as the broken sections of bone came together at the elbow. Setting the arm was a deal more painful than breaking it had been, but out of fear of my father, and of losing face before the bonesetter, I hung on and did not cry out. Father saw my fortitude and said, "Well done, son."

One day some time later, when my arm had set fully and I had completely forgotten the accident, Father called me over to him. He held me by the left wrist, picked up a switch from the felt mat, and hit me once across the legs. "Think yourself lucky," he said, "And listen to me: if you disobey me again, I'll really beat you. Do you understand?"

"I understand."

The other occasion on which my father punished me came about as follows. A mile or so from our village was a small market called Sari Puli Eshon (Sheikh's bridge). One day, Father sent me there to buy salt. On my way back I ran into a friend of my father's, who gave me a message to relay to him. By the time I got home I had forgotten not only the message but even having seen the man at all. When my father asked me if I had seen anyone there whom we knew, I remembered this man, and told Father that I had seen him. "What did he say?" my father asked.

Since I could not remember anything of what he had said, I made up a string of things to tell Father. What I told him, however, must have been obviously illogical and untruthful, for he asked further: "Are you sure he didn't tell you anything else that you might have forgotten?"

"No, that was all he said," I replied, confirming my lies.

A few days later, the man himself turned up at our house. My father showed him into the guest-room and asked him to sit down, then called me in and sat me in front of him, asking him, "What was the message that you gave the boy to pass on to me?" The man repeated what he had told me, which bore no resemblance to what I had told Father. I sat sweating with shame. Father seized hold of my ear and twisted it hard as he said to me: "Next time, pay careful attention to everything you see and listen well to everything anyone tells you! If anyone gives you a message to pass on, or tells you to do something, even if you understand it the first time, ask for it to be repeated and commit it to memory. And don't forget it! But in any case, never lie, for you will be shown up and get a bad reputation into the bargain. At present you have done two things wrong—one, that you forgot the message you had to deliver, and two, that in its stead you came out with stories you had fabricated yourself. If you had admitted then and there that you'd forgotten the message, I would not have put you to shame before our visitor. Now, run off and play!"

This chastisement was a useful lesson to me, and had a lasting effect. It trained me to be observant and attentive, and taught me not to forget messages, events, objects, and people. As for poetry, however hard I try to memorize it, I always forget it quickly—I even forget my own poems the day after I compose them. But anything that was said to me or happened to me that more or less affected my life, I have never forgotten. Even though in the past ten or twelve years my memory ha. deteriorated and I tend quickly to forget what I or others have said or done, nevertheless my early memories are almost all firmly impressed in my mind. This is the result of my father's chastisement on that occasion, which led me thereafter to practice the crafts of memorizing and recall.

After the man had left, I went to see my father with the intention of confessing another lie I had told. But I felt too ashamed, and stood there silent. Father realized that I wanted to tell him something, but that something was preventing me. He asked, "What is it?"

"I want to confess that I told a lie."

"Well, go on!"

"I didn't really fast during Ramadan."

Father laughed. "I knew right then that you weren't fasting, that you were only pretending to, so that you could save up your 'earnings' for the fair. But I didn't say anything at the time, so as not to upset either you or your mother, who was very keen on your fasting. Nevertheless, what you did was a lie and a deception. But you were very young then. I hope you won't do that sort of thing again!"

*   *   *

One year before his death, my father decided to take me to Bukhara, in order to show me the city and leave me to stay with my elder brother at the madrasa for a few days, so that I could learn something of student life and be ready to go back to Bukhara and start school at the beginning of the next academic year. Accordingly, one winter's day he mounted the donkey with me behind him and set off to Bukhara.

As we were passing a place called Yalangi, between Vobkand and Bukhara, the donkey pulled in to the roadside under a hollow tree and stopped. By dint of vigorously applying the stick my father got it to move again, and remarked to me, "Last spring, as I was on my way to Bukhara, I stopped just short of the Yalangi bazaar, under this same tree, to eat lunch and rest the donkey. Even though nearly a year has passed, the donkey still hasn't forgotten, and wants me to let him rest in this same spot. That's why he wouldn't go any farther."

After a moment's silence, my father went on: "A donkey is better than a man who forgets what he has seen and heard. Take care not to forget anything!"

With this very simple, everyday parable, my father underscored by example the precepts he had been teaching me.

22. First Impressions of Bukhara

We arrived in Bukhara after dark, entering the city by the Samarkand gate.[56] My father said that if we had arrived five minutes later we would have been locked out of the city, since the gates were closed at bedtime, an hour and a half after sunset, and the keys would be sent to the captain of the night-watch (*mir shab*).

Inside the city it was dark. At the gatehouse an oil lamp, fueled with linseed oil, gave a dim light. Otherwise there were no candles, lamps, or storm lanterns anywhere to be seen. Since the houses in Bukhara had no windows facing the streets, no light fell on the street from there either. The narrow streets with two- and three-story buildings on either side reminded me of a graveyard.

Somberly we set off through the streets of this "City of Darkness", until we reached the Mir-i Arab madrasa, where my brother and Sayid-Akbar were living. From the west side of this madrasa came a dim light, together with the sound of drums and *surnays*. It was clear that there, between the forecourt of the Mir-i Arab madrasa and the Great Mosque,[57] an open-air feast was being held by the emir. It was a custom in those days that whenever the emir was staying overnight somewhere other than his palace (the *ark*), his hosts would hold a public celebration (*chavki*) in a nearby street.[58]

That night was the first time I witnessed this feast. In a small sunken area only about twenty yards long by ten wide, scores of spectators were gathered. In the middle of the area was a bonfire, before it sat a row of drummers, and in front of these a row of some twenty adolescent dancing-boys with braided hair were dancing and singing. In front of the dancers was a mortar full of oil with old rags blazing in it. The emir's guards carried sticks and were beating back the spectators to prevent them from crowding the performers. I did not much like this entertainment, since it

---

[56] The *Darvozayi Samarqand*, on the north side, was one of eleven gates in the city wall, since demolished.

[57] The *masjidi kalon*, completed in 1514 C.E., is 425 ft. long and 260 ft. wide, and can reputedly accommodate 10,000 worshipers (for the Mir-i Arab madrasa, facing the Great Mosque, see the Glossary).

[58] This emir was Abdul-Ahad, who at this time (1888) was still resident in Bukhara; a few years later he moved his court to Karmina (see Glossary).

reminded me more of the disastrous fireworks display at Dar-veshobod than of a feast.

My father took the saddlebag off the donkey and left it with me, then led away the donkey to be stabled. Together we entered the madrasa. The Mir-i Arab madrasa was one of the best ma-drasas in Bukhara: it had a high portal and a spacious courtyard. Once through the gateway we turned right, and began to climb a staircase. It was dark and winding. My father climbed up the stairs, calling back as he went, and I gingerly followed the sound of his voice, putting my hands on the steps ahead of me as I went up.

It was still dark at the top of the staircase, which led to a narrow enclosed corridor. My father tapped at a door lightly with his fingertips, in accordance with the custom of the madrasa. The door opened and we went in. The room was a tall, domed cell and, except for the door we entered, there were no other doors or windows. In the middle of the cell was a *sandali* and on top of it a single, locally -made, one-ounce candle was burning. This candle barely lit the surface of the *sandali*, while the rest of the room, particularly the high-domed ceiling, was in semi-darkness and very fearsome. When we came in my brother was serving rice near the doorway and Sayid-Akbar, who was nicknamed "Lord Provider" in the village, was sitting at the *sandali*.

After the customary greetings my brother served us a meal consisting of pilau and chicken cooked in butter, which tasted delicious. While we were eating my father asked, "How can you afford chicken?"

My brother did not answer, but "Lord Provider" explained in detail. Apparently the Emir Abdul-Ahad, who was in the third year of his reign, had introduced a custom that whenever he spent the night outside his palace he would order a dish from the closest madrasa after his dinner. One of the emir's kitchen servants would come to the madrasa and announce that anyone who had prepared food should bring it. The young mullahs would then bring their pots and the servant would send them with their pots to the house where the emir was staying. There, the head cook would taste the pilau from each pot, choose one, and send the other pots back with their owners.

The head cook would serve the winning rice to the emir, then the winner's pot would be filled with food from the royal kitchen and returned to the young mullah, who would also be given ten *tangas* (one and a half rubles).

Figure 7. The Mir-i Arab madrasa in Bukhara

Once this custom of the emir's became well known in all the madrasas in Bukhara, everyone in the madrasas near where he lodged would cook pilau in the hope that the emir would accept it. Tonight the emir had stopped at a house near the Mir-i Arab madrasa, and pilau had been cooked in all the one hundred and forty-three cells of this madrasa, despite the fact that many of the people who lived in these cells had not been able to afford pilau even once during the whole winter. These poor students had borrowed money, or bought rice and meat on credit, hoping that the pilau they cooked would be chosen by the emir.

At the end of this account Sayid-Akbar said proundly, "Of the one hundred and forty-three pots of rice cooked tonight, ours was the lucky one, and this rice and chicken comes from the royal kitchen."

At the beginning of Sayid-Akbar's explanation my father had listened to him while he ate. In the middle of the story, when he realized what was coming, he stopped eating and began to look angry. I thought he was going to pick up his switch and beat my brother there and then, but he did not. After the tablecloth was put away he still sat there for a long while, without saying anything to Sayid-Akbar or my brother, or even looking at them. He just sat there like a dervish sheikh in a *khonaqoh* with his eyes closed and head bowed; now and then he raised his head, sighed, and bowed it again.

I do not know if he was able to sleep that night, because I slept soundly. When my brother lit the candle early in the morning I saw that my father was ready and waiting to go back to the village. When daybreak came he got up and said to me, "Come on, son, I'm taking you back to the village, since you won't learn any-thing about madrasa etiquette from these emir-lovers, except how to lick the emir's pots clean."

I begged my father tearfully not to take me back so soon, and asked to stay a few days so we could see the city and visit my uncle, Mullo Dehqon.

He agreed to let me stay a little, adding sternly, "But be careful not to become like these boys, for if you do I'll never so much as look at you again." He then snatched the saddlebag from my brother, who had picked it up to carry it, and left the room. We accompanied him to the stable to see him off; even then he said nothing to my brother. He paid the stable man, mounted his donkey, and rode back to the village.

* * *

The cell where my brother lived was called the "haunted room" and it was even more frightening in the daytime than at night: entering that huge, dark, smoky building on a sunny day really made one feel as if a demon were hiding in every nook and cranny. The awesome dome had a small window covered with alabaster latticework that looked out into the even higher dome of the madrasa mosque. It was terrifying to look out of the window and see only the wide vault of the mosque appear, like a dark bottomless world. The room also had a small skylight. On cloudless days at noon a little spot of light the size of a teacup used to appear on the floor of the room, and this unnatural light seemed as sinister as the white eye of some wild animal in the dark.

Our life in the cell was very simple. Mornings and evenings we would eat dry bread which had been brought from the village, with tea. Every day at one o'clock my brother cooked a hot meal. That too was simple: rice and beans, sometimes kedgeree or leek soup (*pioba*), which tasted very good with dry bread.

The household chores — cooking, washing, sweeping — were all performed by my brother, though I helped him as much as I could. Sayid-Akbar, or "Lord Provider," behaved like a guest, always sitting in the warmth of the *sandali*, looking over his lessons or practicing calligraphy. The only words he ever spoke were to demand of my brother, "When will that food of yours be ready?" or "When are you going to brew some tea?" My brother always answered him civilly, but I was angry and in my heart I felt that his politeness was out of place.

This year I learned a little about the domestic lives of the students at the Mir-i Arab madrasa, and about the arrogance of the senior students and teachers. The Mir-i Arab madrasa was basically a two-story building with cells on both floors set back behind archways. The three- and four-story towers at the corners of the building also had cells built into them; those on the second floor on the inside of the towers were called "hanging cells" (*muallaqa*), and indeed they seemed just like suspended tombs. The main cells on the first floor had one door, and those on the second and fourth floors had two doors, an entrance door and a smaller one opening on the street.

This madrasa had two high porticos facing the north and south ends of the courtyard. Behind these lay a little empty space, and in each a cell had been built that was so short a person could hardly stretch out to sleep there. Since an ordinary door in the middle of a monument would look out of place, the builders had put in a very high door, like a gateway, and the students of the madrasa called these cells "camel stalls." The name was appropriate enough for the doors, but in the case of the rooms, it was an example of ironic humor of a sort very popular in Bukhara at the time. For instance, the Great Mosque boasted a very fat *khatib*, who was so huge that when he went to deliver the *khutba* two men would take him under his arms and carry him up the *minbar* because he could not get there by himself; people used to call him "Skinny Zaid."

Most of the students were poor and in the winter they wore thin, patched coats and only the outer shell of shoes. Even on snowy or rainy nights the younger ones would sit in the open yard on the stones, repeating their lessons, while the older ones sat under the portico preparing theirs.

The seniors, those who had attained the rank of lecturer (*mudarris*) or who had two or three cells to themselves (paid in advance), were always very haughty and supercilious. They usually sat under the portico in the early evening and passed most of their time in backbiting and gossip. As soon as one of them got up and left for any reason, everyone began to carp about him, even though in his presence they would treat him with the greatest respect.

Sometimes they would argue. At the time I did not understand what they were arguing about, but I knew that in the course of the argument they would roundly insult and curse each other, in the coarsest of street language. They routinely called each other ignorant and illiterate. (I later learned that they were telling the truth—they were all complete ignoramuses, with not an educated man among them). But when the argument was over, once again they would treat each other with hypocritical subservience.

*   *   *

We did not live in this "haunted cell" for very long. The owner of the cell, a money-grubbing mullah, had expected my brother and his roommate to feed him, and at the beginning of the school year, when they had brought rice from home, they had fed him twice. But by the time I arrived there was nothing left of their supply, the last of the rice having been used for the emir's supper. Therefore, they could not invite the owner of the room to eat any more, and one snowy day he ordered them to vacate the premises.[59]

My brother and Sayid-Akbar searched for a lodging for three days, until they finally found a place in a quarter called Bozori Khūja. This room was above a grocer who offered his space as "charity" to young mullahs who did not have a place to live. The upstairs was so bad that nobody had lived there that year and it was vacant.

We started to move, and although it was a good mile between the Mir-i Arab madrasa and the room we moved our things easily. We took bedding and mats, pots, plates, and books in one trip, and my brother carried the oil container and kindling on his back. In the end half a sackful of coal remained in the old room; without a sack to put it in we did not know how to transport it. After much deliberation my brother decided that we could carry it in the water pitcher. We emptied the water from the pitcher, loaded it up with coals, and he and I together carried it down the stairs. At the bottom of the staircase Muhyiddin tied a clothesline around the pitcher and hoisted it onto his back. I carried the samovar in my arms, while Sayid-Akbar nonchalantly carried one of his own books under his arm.

We could not go through the crowded bazaar with such an unwieldy load, so we had to go by way of narrow, winding back streets. It was snowing and slippery underfoot, and when we reached the Tanners' Passage, my brother slipped and fell, and the pitcher broke and scattered the coals everywhere.

With his sleeve, Muhyiddin swept an area under the wall clear of snow, and I started to help him gather the scattered coals from the snow and stack them there. "Lord Provider" merely squatted by the wall and with leisurely flicks of his fingers dusted specks of coal dust off his pants as he watched us collect the coals.

This was too much for my brother. Without any warning he rushed at Sayid-Akbar, grabbed him around the waist, threw him down on the snow, sat on his chest, and began pummeling him. "This is what you get for not pulling your weight, and setting yourself above other people," he panted.

---

[59] Aini notes here that he describes some of the conditions involved in renting a madrasa cell in his novella *Margi sūdkhūr* (Death of the Moneylender); see also *Bukhara*, pp. 3-5 and 11-13.

As soon as brother got up from him, Sayid-Akbar rose slowly and, without even shaking the snow off from his clothes, ran away.

I had been surprised by my brother's forbearance towards Sayid-Akbar while sharing the madrasa cell, but I was even more amazed by what he had just done. Well-merited though it was, his sudden assault was totally out of character. I now appreciated the truth of an Arabic proverb that my father once told me: "God protect us from the wrath of a mild-mannered person."

I told my brother how, during my schooldays, I had gotten the lunatic to beat Sayid-Akbar, and how both assailants had attacked him in exactly the same way. As he listened, Muhyiddin's anger subsided, and he laughed and said, "You did well, but don't tell Father about this or he'll punish you."

"This is the first time I've ever mentioned it to anyone, and I don't intend to tell anyone else about it either," I assured him.

*   *   *

In our new living quarters life was very difficult. We had a one-room annex built above the grocery, its walls made of thin wood and not connected to any other building. There was one doorway through which light entered, but more cold than light came in, Since the walls were so thin the room did not heat up very much. As we sat around the *sandali* warming our feet, other parts of us would shiver with the cold. In two days two water pitchers cracked from water freezing in them. We were forced to bring water from the pool, use what we needed immediately, and pour away the rest in the street. There was no place to wash in the room and we were obliged to wash in the street.

Although we had some beans and rice pudding our supply of cooking oil was spent. We bought five ounces of linseed oil from the landlord for eight *pul* (two kopeks), which would last us two or three days. The grocer used a measure made from a hollowed-out pumpkin for the oil. Although he had given us the room free out of "charity," he could not bring himself to give us full measure when selling the oil, and if he did fill it up his hand would shake and spill some into his own basin.

One night it was bitter cold and we went to sleep at my uncle's house. The following morning the grocer told us, "It's not good to leave the room unoccupied at night. It wouldn't surprise me if a thief got in there, dug a hole in the ceiling of the store, and made off with all of my goods."

Then we understood the meaning of the grocer's "charity."

I hardly saw any of the city during this my first stay in Bukhara. I saw the Registan and the Boloi Havz mosque[60] only once, since I could not find my way around on my own and my brother was busy with his lessons. On free days we went to the book bazaar, but on the way there was nothing to see but the shouting and shoving of the carters competing for a way through the narrow streets. I had watched the quarrels between the mullahs at the Mir-i Arab madrasa, but here there was not even that.

The only place I liked to go in Bukhara was the room of my maternal uncle, Mullo Dehqon. He was married and lived in his wife's house. Since this did not have a guest room he rented a cell at the Fathullo madrasa,[61] which was near our place, and taught there. My uncle was a new teacher and had few students. The classes he taught had no more than four or five students in them. He taught mostly from the *Kofiya* and the *Shamsiya*[62] His students yelled as loudly as he did, and I wondered whether they came to him to learn or to argue. I thought that even our village imam taught better than he did; for if most of the imam's pupils understood nothing, at least they all sat quietly and he taught calmly, so there was at least a chance that someone might learn something.

---

[60] Registan (Taj. *registon*, "sandy place, arena"): the public square in front of the emir's palace (*ark*). In the second part of Aini's reminiscences there are descriptions of a public flogging and executions held here (see *Bukhara*, pp. 55-60 and 63-66). There is a more famous registan in Samarkand. *Masjidi boloyi havz*: facing the Registan, opposite the gate of the *ark*. Built in 1712, this mosque is distinguished by a gallery (*aivon*) supported by high wooden pillars with oversize stalactite capitals, which was added to the structure in 1917, and a large ornamental pool (*havz*) in front, from which the mosque takes its name ("the poolside mosque").

[61] The Fathullo-Qushbegi madrasa, built in 1595-96, is on the road leading to the darvozayi mazor (cemetery gate) in the southeast of Bukhara.

[62] The *Kofiya*: i.e., *al-kâfiya fi'l-nahw*, "Comprehensive Grammar," by the Egyptian Jamâl al-dîn ibn al-Hâjib (d. 1249 C.E.), a popular treatise on Arabic grammar used extensively in traditional schools throughout the Middle East in the nineteenth century. The *Shamsiyya*: short for *al-risâla al-shamsiyya fi'l-qawâ'id al-mantiqiyya*, a treatise on logic by Najm al-dîn al-Qazvînî "Dabîrân" (d. 1276 or 1294 C.E.), commissioned by Shams al-dîn Muhammad al-Juvaynî.

Whereas with my uncle's students making as much noise as he did, there seemed no chance that anyone would learn anything.

*   *   *

Sayid-Akbar "Lord Provider" left us to become the servant of an *okhund* named Orif-khon. One day, long after the fight with my brother, he came to see us and tell us about his job. According to Sayid-Akbar, whenever the *okhund* went to a wedding or other feast, a funeral, or the emir's court, he would go before him on foot together with the groom who led the *okhund*'s mount. When they reached their destination the groom would take charge of the horse and Sayid-Akbar would accompany the *okhund* to the door and when the latter took off his shoes upon entering the house, Sayid-Akbar would take charge of them, and clean and polish them. When the *okhund* came out again, Sayid-Akbar would help him on with his shoes and take charge of the presents that the *okhund* had been given, then, together with the groom, escort him home.

He claimed that the work was quite difficult and irksome, but that in return he lived well. He lodged in a room of the *okhund*'s house, which was warm and clean. Every morning he drank tea with cream and ate pilau for dinner every day.

"You," my brother said, "who think you're so high and mighty, who never owned anyone as your equal and were ashamed to make your own bed—what made you stoop to such a menial job?"

"This person whom I have agreed to serve," sniffed Sayid-Akbar, "may be merely my social equal as a *khoja*, but he is more learned than I, so I am not ashamed to work for him. I look down only on people who are inferior to me by birth, or *khojas* who are not as scholarly as I am, as is my right."

*   *   *

When we could no longer bear living in our wretched new quarters we went back to our village, although the school year had not yet ended. My brother took me home and, after two or three days of relaxation, he returned to Bukhara.

In the course of recounting to my father my impressions of Bukhara, I repeated Sayid-Akbar's own justification of his snobbishness. Father laughed, and then said seriously, "As the poet says, 'Don't prate about your father's line and pelf—Be man enough to make a name yourself!' Many people don't heed this advice, but being arrogant because of one's lineage is an idiotic attitude. This wretched *khoja* title often goes to people's heads, and I know some *khojas* who have turned out to be even greater idiots than Sayid-Akbar." And, by way of illustration, he told me the following anecdote.

23. The Mirakoni Khojas' Banquet

According to my father, when he was young he went together with one of the Mirakoni Khojas of his village on a trip to Samarkand. They stayed in the home of one of the Mirakoni Khojas there. During the same period, one of the Khojas of Dahbed[63] held a feast, to which he invited the Mirakoni Khojas. Those khojas who had horses and servants of their own were soon ready, but those without were put to a great deal of inconvenience: they had to hire two horses and a manservant, one horse for themselves and the other as a pack horse for the hired "groom" to manage. My father and his companion were likewise provided with a horse each. "It was actually a good thing that they didn't insist on two horses and a groom *each*," my father said.

The khojas set off from the city of Samarkand for the village of Dahbed with a kingly retinue, and arrived at the banqueting hall. Sundry dishes and appropriate gifts were brought before the khojas, but not a single guest glanced at the food or reached out to take any. The host stood at the foot of the table and, with a bow, besought them politely to partake of the meal. But the khojas disdained to so much as look at the food.

Finally, after much cajoling, the most eminent of the guests—the Khoja in the place of honor—took out his penknife from his purse, picked up a single grain of rice from the platter, cut it in two, put one piece in his mouth and the other on the tablecloth. "We two from Soktaré could see that things were not going well," said my father, "and that for all this abundant fare we would be going back to town hungry. So without waiting a moment longer we set to, and between the point when the khojas

---

[63] A village about ten miles north of Samarkand, a center of pilgrimage to the shrine of a notable sixteenth-century *eshon*, Makhdumi-A'zam.

were vying for established or imagined pecking order with 'Please go ahead,' and 'No, after you,' and the closing prayer, when they were trying to outdo each other in piety, we managed to stuff ourselves."

After the closing recital of the *fotiha*, the host's servants removed the remaining food from the guest table and, in accordance with custom, took it to the guests' servants. After sipping a bowl of tea, the khojas set off back to town with the same kingly retinue When they reached the river bank, the leading khojas conferred together, and finally decided on a spot beneath a willow tree, where they told their servants to spread out the saddle-blankets. The khojas dismounted and squatted in a circle on the dirty horseblankets in their elegant gold-braided robes. The most eminent of them shouted to the servants: "Hey, hurry it up, we're starving!"

The servants, with "Yes sir, coming sir, at once sir," unloaded the horses' feedbags and placed them before the khojas. Each khoja opened his horse's feedbag, scooped out the cooked rice that was inside, and ate his fill. This cooked rice was in fact none other than the dish from which the khojas had eaten half a grain and the rest of which had then been sent to feed their servants—who had stuffed the rest into their mounts' feedbags to save for their masters. Since this had long been the khojas' custom, their servants were by now expert at abetting it.

At that time, I had no inkling that this tale of my father's was distinctly exaggerated. When I was older, I realized that this description of khojas' table manners was not literally true, but I was convinced nevertheless, from my own experience, that it corresponded in large measure to the mindset of the petty aristocracy of that time. At any rate, this fake reminiscence of my father's made such an impression on me that I recognized the hollowness and foolishness of aristocratic pretensions even before I learned of them at first hand. My personal experiences only served to reinforce this conviction.

24. Farming

I was now familiar with some aspects of madrasa life. And now my father was faced with the problem of sending me to Bukhara to study during the next academic year. There was no way he could afford to support two sons at the madrasa. He therefore proposed to me that I should do something myself to earn a sum toward my schooling expenses.

At the far end of our *sufa* was a spare plot of land that my father had planted with apricot saplings. For fear of damaging them we could not use the plow there; but my father told me that I could hoe it over and plant something there, and use whatever I grew toward my savings for school. He bought me a small mattock, and I set to work. I hoed the plot three times over, breaking up the soil to a depth three times that of the mattock head. Now came the problem of raking and harrowing it. For this I planned to use an old door leaf; but since this makeshift harrow had no spikes, I first broke up the clods of earth in my plot with the mattock, plying point and blade alternately. Then the door leaf served to level the soil. Homid Khoja and Ikrom Khoja volunteered to act as the oxen and pull my harrow; but after two or three lengths they were exhausted. So I found another "ox," namely, Khaibar, and harnessed him to the makeshift harrow. The powerful, intelligent dog learned the ropes after a few lengths, and was soon pulling, turning, and stopping on command, while I stood on the door leaf driving him like a regular plowboy.

Once I had harrowed the plot I scattered manure and topsoil over it, hoed and harrowed it once more, and had it ready for planting. I asked my father what I should plant. "People say, 'bumpkins plant pumpkins,'" he replied; "That is, they're better than nothing. But I say, 'beginners plant pumpkins': since you're new to farming, you should sow pumpkins. It's an easy plant that doesn't need much looking-after—especially the 'pilau-pumpkin,' which is not only easy to grow but gives a rich crop."

After allowing a few days for the tilled earth to drink in the sun and for the seeds to soak, Father sowed them for me. Once the seeds had sprouted, I thinned out and weeded the plot, hoed it over three times in two weeks (a process called *kishova* or *kishoba*), and piled more earth around each shoot right up to the top. When the stalk put out tendrils, I watered them for the first time, and when the soil was ready Father showed me where to dig an irrigation channel; I spread the soil from this underneath the stems—this is the method followed in Bukhara, and called *varqoni*.

* * *

This year, my father worked on his land harder than before. He sowed one *tanob* of cotton and one of sorghum. But that year the cotton bushes dried up and my father's labor went to waste; so here I shall be concerned only with the sorghum crop.

In autumn my father watered and hoed the land, in winter he watered it once in early December and again in January, and in spring, after one more hoeing, manured it. There was an old mud wall in our yard that had collapsed and lain in the sun for several years, and this too my father mixed in, clump by clump, with the earth in which he was to sow the sorghum. I helped him with this task: he filled the panier and loaded it on the donkey, and I drove the donkey across the field and scattered the dung and dried earth over it. Next he plowed the field twice over with a hired ox, raked and harrowed it, sowed the seed, then raked and harrowed it once more so that the seed would reach the proper depth.

The shoots came up very thin and about a yard apart. The neighboring farmers advised my father to plow the field over and re-sow it more densely, but he declined, quoting the proverb "mattocks through cotton, camels through sorghum" — meaning that cotton should be planted far enough apart that a mattock can be plied with ease between the shoots, whereas sorghum should be planted with space enough for a camel to canter between the shoots.

Once the shoots had grown a little taller, Father hoed the field three times and piled more soil around the base of the shoots. When the sorghum began to wilt in the heat of the sun, he watered it once. With this single watering, a dozen new ground shoots sprang up from every root. Father left only four shoots in each cluster, chopping off and discarding the rest; he hoped to get a crop of thirty *man* (about 900 pounds) from this one *tanob*.

But that year something intervened that was not only to shatter my father's hopes and our peace of mind, but to disrupt the lives of everyone in Bukhara province.

25. Plague

Early in summer of the year 1306 of the Hijra (corresponding to June 1889), the province of Bukhara was stricken by an epidemic of fever,[64] and the death toll mounted. My elder brother was taken ill in the city and returned home to Soktaré. My oldest maternal uncle Mullo Dehqon caught the plague in the city and died, and his body was brought back for burial to Mahallayi Bolo. My father was not feeling well, and he stayed to mind the house with my younger brothers while I took my mother to pay her last respects to her brother at her father's house. I don't know whether she was infected there, or whether it was due to her grief at her brother's death, but she fell ill while at her parents' house. I put her on a donkey and with difficulty got us both home, where I found that both my father and my two younger brothers, one aged nine and the other four, had fallen ill.

Our house now took on the appearance of a hospital, in which I was doctor, nurse, and orderly all in one. In the large living room five patients were laid out on quilts in a row, and in turn I brought them their drinking water, hot water, or milk, drove the flies away from them and, as far as I could, helped them up when they needed to go outside. Within a week, every house in the village was like ours—and not just in our village, but all over the *tuman* hardly an able-bodied soul was left, and still the death toll mounted. In our village, numbering some three hundred households, every day saw one or two bodies carried to the cemetery.

I did not know at that time—and have been unable to determine since—just what it was my patients suffered from. In those days there were no doctors in the villages. Our village did not even boast the ignorant traditional physician (*tabib*)[65] who would comfort the sick and their relatives by boiling up a potion of weeds and straw; we had only *eshons* and prayer-healers, in whom even our illiterate villagers had no faith, so that they had to ply their trade in remote hamlets.

---

[64] *Vabo* "plague" is the Persian/Tajik term covering an epidemic of one of several communicable diseases which would now be distinguished as bubonic, typhoid, cholera, etc. This one was apparently cholera, which has devastated the region frequently during the last two centuries. At that time its cause (a bacillus) was not recognized even in Europe (there was an epidemic in Hamburg in 1892).

[65] The *tabib* was essentially a herbalist, but his potions also included infusions of the ink from prayers written on scraps of paper; in this respect he played pharmacist to the *duo-khon*'s physician (cf. Appendix II, Section iv, where the village schoolteacher provides "prescriptions" for various ailments in the form of written prayers).

One day I asked Qorī Mahmud—who has been mentioned previously[66]—"Uncle Eshon, how is it you always go to faraway villages to heal people, when there are plenty of sick folks here in Soktaré you could treat?" He replied, "No thief plunders his home village. Am I less honest than a thief, that I should deceive my own neighbors?"

If Qorī Mahmud was right about his practicing deception, he was wrong about its being his honesty that kept him from taking advantage of his neighbors. The villagers had his measure as a prayer-healer, and had no intention of being taken in.

My father was the most seriously ill of my patients. He lay unconscious most of the time and wanted only water to drink. One day he opened his eyes and asked me, "Have you watered the sorghum again?"

"No."

"How long is it since you first watered it?"

"Ten days."

"Fine, it isn't yet time to water it again." And he closed his eyes and relapsed into unconsciousness.

After that, the same scene was repeated several times a day. On the day that I told him it was twenty days since the first watering, he said, "Now is the time to water it again. If you can, go and water it. I mixed in a lot of sun-dried clods—if it doesn't get watered, the crop will be ruined."

I picked up my small mattock and started off for the sorghum field. During this period I came to appreciate Khaibar's intelligence more than ever. He would always follow me wherever I went, and never left my side; ever since I started tending my sick family, he never budged from outside the door of the sickroom. Today when I picked up my mattock and headed outdoors, he looked at me and wagged his tail, then moved closer to the sickroom, put his nose on the threshold and lay watching the patients. He seemed to know that I was going some way away, and had decided to watch over the patients for me.

This year the water was plentiful; moreover, most of the farmers were sick and in no condition to compete for watering rights. Thus I was able with no difficulty to draw water from the main channel, flood the sorghum field, and get straight back to my

---

[66] See Chapter 20, and Glossary.

patients. An hour after my return, Father opened his eyes and asked, "Did you water the sorghum?"

"Yes, I did."

"Well done!" And he closed his eyes again.

On the fortieth day of his illness he broke into a sweat and became wide awake. Be asked for, and drank, some milk. On the next day he sat up, and on the third day, stood up and with the aid of a stick took a walk outside. We were very happy to see him recovered. Ten days later, however, he fell sick again and went back to bed.

Usto Amak, who was also ill, as was his entire family, nevertheless came over once a day from the start of my father's illness to see how he was and to reassure us that he would recover. "All he needs is four cold sweats," he would say. And indeed my father had recovered after sweating; but after his relapse, Usto Amak said nothing and no longer tried to reassure us. To me, however, it seemed that this spell was not so severe as the first one—he slept quietly and did not lose consciousness after he awoke.

On the seventh day of his relapse, when Usto Amak came to see him he told me to fetch him at once if Father's condition worsened. "How do I know if he's better or worse?" I asked him, my eyes filling with tears.

"Don't cry, be a man, be your father's son! Your father's condition is very grave, but he is staying calm so as not to upset the rest of you. You must keep calm, too, so as not to upset him! You will know his condition is worsening if his his breathing becomes labored and wheezing. Now I must go, because my wife was very ill when I left."

Night fell. I lit the oil lamp and kept watch. All except me were sunk in the sleep of sickness. It was still early in the evening when my father started gasping for breath and wheezing. I shouted for Usto Amak. He soaked a wad of cotton and began dribbling water into my father's mouth.[67] The sick man opened his eyes and,

---

[67] Water was squeezed drop by drop into the mouth of a dying person, in accordance with a folk belief, to prevent a demon (*jinn*) from urinating into the open mouth and defiling the soul. This may perhaps stem from Zoroastrian beliefs and usage: consecrated cow's urine (*nirang*) was similarly administered to a dying person, and on death the polluting "corpse demon" is said to settle on the body (see Mary Boyce, *A Stronghold of Zoaroastrianism*, Oxford, 1977, p. 148 and note). An alternative, Islamicized rationale

looking first at me, then at Usto Amak, said, "More water—give it to me with a spoon."

Usto Amak poured two spoonfuls of water down his throat. "Enough," said Father. Then, turning his eyes toward me, he went on: "Study! Whatever problems you meet with, go on studying! Only don't become a kadi, or a *rais*, or an imam! If you like, be a madrasa teacher!" He closed his syes. A minute later he started wheezing again. My uncle began squeezing water into his mouth again. Suddenly my father made as if to sit upright and stared at me, then fell back; his arms twitched once, then he was still, for ever.

Reckoning by the solar calendar, my father was then fifty-seven years old.

After fastening his big toes together, tying a strip of cloth round his head and chin to keep his mouth closed, and closing his eyes, Usto Amak asked me, "You won't be afraid, will you, if I go away and take a look at my own patients?"

"Why should I be?" I answered. "How could I be afraid of my own father?"

"That's my lion," he said, and left. When he came back he laid out the body. My mother and elder brother realized then that Father was dead, and next morning my younger brothers knew too.

*   *   *

In the next village, there was a grocer and hardware merchant called Yūldosh-boi, who used to take raisins, dried apricots, canvas, and cotton clothing made in Ghijduvon to Qazali, Oq-masjid, Orenburg, and other towns of the Kazakhs and Bashkirs, and bring back Russian goods.[68] Once the plague deaths began, he

---

for the practice is that the drops of water represent the spring Kawsar, from which the blessed would drink in Paradise (cf. Koran 108:1).

[68] Qazali, Russianized as Kazalinsk, is near the Syr Darya estuary, east of the Aral Sea. Oq-masjid (Rus. Ak-mechet', "White Mosque," later Kizil Orda, "Red Army") is on the steppe, farther upriver; both were then in the territory of the Khoqand khanate, now part of Kazakhstan (Qazoqiston). Orenburg, an old Cossack settlement midway between Kazan and the Aral Sea, was in the 18th and 19th centuries an important commercial center and ultimately a springboard for Russia's annexation of Kazakhstan and Central

took to selling shrouds. According to him, he did this as a favor to people, otherwise he "would have had nothing to do with such a low trade." When my father died, he likewise did us the "favor" of providing the coffin, shroud, and other funeral paraphernalia on credit, for one hundred *tangas*. According to Usto Amak, if we had had the cash, we could have bought it all in the bazaar for twenty-five or thirty *tangas* less.

For immediate expenses we also needed twenty *tangas* in cash, which Yūldosh-boi also lent us "as a favor," in consideration of five extra to be paid back. We also needed twenty-five *tangas* to pay for the saying of requiem prayers on Sunday and Thursday nights and for the complete reading of the Koran;[69] this sum we collected by dint of taking small loans from different people. In this way I buried my father for a total of one hundred and fifty *tangas*, equivalent to twenty-two rubles and fifty kopeks.

*   *   *

After the mourning for my father was over, our milch cow — whether through my negligence or some other cause — fell sick one night and died.[70] My mother heard about this on her sick bed and observed, "May every misfortune in store for us fall on that cow! If she'd died sooner, maybe your father would have lived! We must offer up her calf too, for your sake and that of your brothers." And she told me to take it and give it to Khoja-khon, a cripple without arms or legs who lived on charity in a corner of the village.

But when I took the calf to him he refused, telling me, "You and your family are worse off now than I am. People give me

---

Asia. The Bashkirs and Kazakhs were Muslim pastoral nomads of mixed Turkish, Mongol and other stocks.

[69] It was popularly believed that on Sunday and Thursday the soul of one recently deceased would return home for a brief visit; these days were thus particularly auspicious for their surviving relatives to have prayers said for them (generally by the imam). The complete recitation of the Koran after a death would generally be undertaken by a *qori* (see Glossary).

[70] The traditional period of mourning is forty days. "Our cow . . . died" (Taj. *harom murd*): i.e., died of disease or natural causes, as distinct from being slaughtered in the ritually prescribed manner (*halol*); the meat of such an animal could not be eaten.

what they can spare, and I get by on that; but you're not used to living on charity. Now that you father's dead, there's no knowing what will become of you." However, my mother made me try again, begging him to take it for the sake of her children's health; and this time I got him to accept the calf in order to please my mother.

I realized then that crippled, bedridden Khoja-khon was a more noble man than our village imam. The latter, officiating at my father's funeral, had taken the ten *tangas* we gave him without demur, though he then had fifty *man* of wheat and twenty-five of barley in his barn, and who knows how much cash and other property. Khoja-khon had nothing but two eyes with which he anxiously watched for his next meal.

My elder and younger brothers, according to the older villagers, were now out of danger; but my mother's condition daily became more serious. At last I could no longer manage to take her outside, and she had to perform her natural functions where she lay, and I would clean up after her. Even though my brothers were better, this improvement was manifested only in their ability to eat a little, and did not mean that they could freely get up and about by themselves. On the advice of the older people in the village I fed them chicken soup, which according to those with experience was the only thing that would build up their strength in their condition. So I killed and salted chickens one after the other, made three or four batches of soup out of each, and administered it to my patients.

*   *   *

Though I watered the sorghum regularly I was unable to protect it from the depredations of the birds: when it ripened, the sparrows picked some of the ears so clean of kernels that they looked like stalks of straw. But the untouched ears were as full and solid as the belly of a polished brass pitcher. The sparrows did not cause too much damage after all, since each one was content with a dozen grains; but then the crows and jackdaws, which were numerous in our village, launched their raids. Now the harvest was in danger of total ruin, and we with it, since our ability to pay off the debts incurred by my father's funeral and to have enough food for the winter depended on that crop; the cotton had long since dried up and died. We had only enough wheat flour stored to last us or month. Still, I could not leave my sick mother in order to go out to the fields and scare the crows away.[71]

Then came a development that enabled me to go off to the fields with an easy mind. During the height of my mother's illness, one of her brothers, Ali-khon, came to see her, accompanied by a man from his village. He told me that after they had buried his elder brother Mullo Dehqon (my uncle), his parents and everyone else in his family had fallen ill. His wife and his brothers' wives had died. He himself had been ill, but had now recovered somewhat, and his parents had therefore sent him to find out how we were.

When he saw how grave my mother's condition was, he decided to take her to be cared for at her family's home. "There, both her parents are alive and I am healthy," he pointed out, "Here, it's too hard for a boy with sick brothers to look after as well." We agreed. He fixed up a traveling litter from two poles with rope strung between them like the rungs of a ladder, and mounted this fore and aft on the backs of two donkeys; then he spread several layers of quilts over the rope rungs and laid the patient on top, covering her with an embroidered sheet. And the party set off.

I don't know how my brothers felt to see my mother go, but I was devastated. I tried not to weep out loud so as not to upset her, ill as she was. But I could not help crying silently. I caught sight of my mother's eyes; they were listless, and two tiny teardrops trickled down her pale yellow cheeks. "May you live a thousand years," she whispered as the donkey-litter moved off.

They disappeared from view, and I consoled myself with the thought that now she would not die, and I would not be deprived of both father and mother at once. My eyes were smarting from the tears, and I wiped them with my sleeve.

* * *

Most of my time was now spent in the field. I stayed at home only long enough to cook for and feed my sick brothers; otherwise I came home from the field at dusk, got up before first light and left for the field again. My chief task was to scare off the birds;

---

[71] The local boys used to scare birds away from the crops by shouting *"Hoi hoi gala gala hoi!"* —A. (*Hoi*: an exclamation of approval or, as here, exhortation: "Shoo!" *Gala* means "flock.")

but no sooner had I shooed the stubborn creatures from one side of the field than they alighted at the other, to peck again at the pearly ears of grain. They paid no attention to the stones or clods of earth that I hurled at them with my sling: they merely flew up at the sound of the stone whizzing over the cornfield, and landed again even before the stone did, to resume their foraging.

Here Ikrom Khoja, Usto Amak's second son, came to my rescue with a trick that eased my labors a little. He told me to bring to the field a stout piece of wood about two feet long and as thick as a man's wrist, together with a saw, ax, file, and auger. He whittled the wood into a cylinder, filed it smooth,then bored a hole lengthwise almost as far as the end, to meet another hole drilled at right angles through one side. This he called his "wooden pistol."

In those days there were many hunters in our village, who used old-fashioned flintlock muskets and home-made gunpowder. Ikrom Khoja obtained a small bag of powder from one of them, filled the cavity in the stick with this, and stopped it up with a wad of cotton; then he aimed it at the birds and lit the touch-hole. As soon as the gunpowder was ignited, the stick burst asunder with a bang. Luckily, neither of us was hurt. But the smell of the powder sent the birds scattering so fast and so far that they did not return for a whole hour.

My ingenious cousin, not content with this experiment, made a second pistol out of a thicker stick than before. This time he poured less gunpowder into it and did not pack it so tight; and this time he achieved the desired result—our pistol went off without bursting, and the birds were put to flight. We waited, and each time the birds returned we fired again. In this way the cornfield was saved from ruin without difficulty. The next day, Ikrom Khoja brought some lead he had obtained from the hunters and made lead shot. The shot he produced was smaller than that made by hunters, being about the size of millet grain. With this in his wooden pistol, Ikrom Khoja shot down sparrows and pigeons, which we spitted on twigs, roasted over a campfire, and ate. One day we succeeded in bagging four pigeons, two of which I cooked for my sick brothers.

The sorghum panicles grains turned white: at last they were fully ripe. By this time Ikrom Khoja's father, Usto Amak, who had fallen ill after my father's death, was up and about again and, walking with the aid of a stick, came out to the field. He ran his eye over my crop and told me: "Go ahead, start harvesting your ripe ears and gather them all in one spot. If you wait around till they're all ripe, or until the fall, it will be harder for you: you won't be able to do everything in that short time." Pointing to the empty wheat field, he added, "That's where you can gather them; it's dry, firm, even ground, where it will be easy to thresh the grain and load it."

From that day forth I buckled down to harvesting the sorghum. Now I needed to stay out in the field day and night. Accordingly 1 cut down the stems from which I had harvested the sorghum heads and built a shelter out of them, next to my pile of grain. The more heads I collected, the more stalks I had to spare, and the more wind- and rain-proof my shelter became. Finally there were so many stalks that half of every day was spent in carrying them to add to my shelter.

Ikrom Khoja would spend the night with me in my shelter; he had no wish to go home to his stepmother. Other village boys who were still healthy, or who had recovered, would also gather together with us in the evening and sit chatting until midnight or later, then disperse to their various homes. Some of them who had stepmothers would sleep out on the sorghum heads or stalks.

$$* \quad * \quad *$$

One night the air was cool, and the keen chill of autumn pierced the body like a cobbler's awl red-hot from the fire. In the moonlight the hoarfrost forming on the standing plants glistened like freshly-fallen snow. Everyone knew that tonight the chill would set in, and tomorrow the harvest would begin in earnest. I could not help thinking that if frost struck tonight, tomorrow I would have to finish my harvesting immediately, even though half my crop was still standing with the husks uncracked. Once the cold had come, it was no good gathering them piecemeal as I had been doing, since for one thing, at the end of autumn the animals were always let loose in the fields to graze, and for another, there was the probability of rain, in which case all my sorghum would be ruined. But how could I harvest all this on my own?

I was racking my brains over this when Ikrom Khoja came up. He was shivering with cold, and complained, "I wanted to bring one of the quilts that were part of my mother's inheritance, but my stepmother wouldn't let me. I asked my father, but he took her side too—'If I took a quilt to give to you,' he told me, 'it would upset her, and since she's only just recovered, it might make her ill again; this sort of cold won't kill you—get out of here!'"

Three other boys came up, and one of them asked me, "Didn't you go to Mahallayi Bolo to mourn for your mama?"

This question struck me like a cauldron of boiling water poured over me, or a millstone turning round on my head and grinding all my limbs into flour. I realized that my mother had died, and that this boy had heard about it somehow and had wanted to break it to me in a way he thought was tactful and indirect. But the tears did not come; it was as if the fire into which those words had plunged me had dried up all the moisture in my body. I wondered what I was to do now: a twelve-year-old with neither father nor mother, my brothers sick, and when my elder brother recovered he would go back to school and I would have to look after my younger brothers. What would become of that studying I wanted for myself, and which my father had urged on me with his dying breath?

One of the insensitive boy's companions whispered to him, "That wasn't necessary—you should be consoling him, not mocking him!" Then, turning to me, he said, "Never mind, you'll manage somehow, you'll see! Ikrom Khoja lost his mother, too."

"Don't worry," Ikrom Khoja chimed in, "I've been living for ten years without my mother, and the wolf hasn't eaten me."

"You may not have a mother," said another boy, who had so far been silent. "But you still have a father and a stepmother. But it's harder for him"—pointing to me—"since he's lost both parents at once. God help him!"

"I wish when I lost my mother I'd lost my father as well," sighed Ikrom Khoja, "so I wouldn't have fallen into the clutches of a stepmother."

When a person is caught in a hopeless situation, he casts about everywhere for solace, and will clutch at any straw. Thus I seized on this remark of Ikrom Khoja to console myself, telling myself that if my father had survived my mother and taken another wife I would have been worse off. A stepmother would not have smiled at me, or given me free run of the house, or let me take any of my mother's quilts—and, even worse, would have turned my kind-hearted father against me. Though I was now fatherless and motherless, at least I was my own master, I had a crop of my own, a donkey of my own, brothers of my own. True, things were hard, but not so hard as being under the thumb of a stepmother! And this reflection greatly consoled me.

My solace lasted until my companions fell asleep and I became aware of my loneliness, especially the absence of my parents, who were the only ones to whom I could turn for sympathy. Once again I was overwhelmed and confused by grief and pain. I wanted to sob, but restrained myself for fear of disturbing my companions, who had gathered round me to sleep out in the frost purely to comfort me. I wished that somehow I could forget all this grief and all these problems, if only for a few minutes, and that I too could rest. With this desire I called to mind the following verse from a *ghazal* of Bedil, which my father often used to recite at moments like this. I started to murmur it to myself softly and sadly:

> Oblivion, where are you? Bring relief!
> Again my memories are filled with grief.

In summertime, the plowmen of the Ghijduvon region used to hitch up their teams and start plowing at ten o'clock at night, so that by sunrise they would have plowed and harrowed the land and still retained the moisture in it, by preserving it from exposure to the parching rays of the sun. During the long autumn nights they set to work after midnight, but still managed to finish before sunup. At such times the one solace enjoyed by these plowmen, who had given up the comforts of sleep for the exigencies of their livelihood, was singing. Most of the villagers in Ghijduvon and Vobkand regions were accomplished singers of both folk and classical songs; despite being illiterate, they had learned the classical *ghazals* and their settings in *shashmaqom* orally from their fathers and fathers' fathers.[72]

The classical songs were in fact very sad, and aptly described the wretched lot of the workers and peasants of that time. Even though each recital included a coda consisting of light-hearted songs set to dance rhythms, these were designed for parties in private houses; the plowmen contented themselves with singing the main body of the melody, which better suited their circumstances.

---

[72] Singers from Ghijduvon and Vobkand have always contributed actively to Bukhara's musical scene; recent representatives include the Tajik folk and classical singer Boboqul Faizulloyev [b. 1897] from Ghijduvon, and the Uzbek singer and instrumentalist Shohnazar Sohibov [b. 1903; graduated from the Moscow Conservatory in 1941] from Vobkand.—A. (See further under *shashmaqom* in the Glossary.)

The plowman who was at work not far from my threshing-floor started to sing a *ghazal* of Bedil in the "Lovers' Melody" (*savti ushshoq*)—also known as the "Great Melody" (*savti kalon*)—and when he reached the climax, another plowman farther off joined in. Listening to that poem in that setting, without even singing it aloud, I was able to weep inwardly and to some degree unburden my distressed heart. Let me then quote here, by way of example, half a dozen lines from that *ghazal* which were peculiarly appropriate to my state of mind on that night:

> Scout for a caravan of tears, the image of a sigh,
>> Creature of torment, like the word of one in pain am I.
> As comrade of my solitude, none but the wounded heart;
>> Banished afar, as lonely as the circling sun am I.
> All Bedil's life his destiny has kept him far from friends;
>> Upon the page of this wide world, a single verse am I.

When the first plowman reached the end of his song, the second started singing, in the melody called "Iraq," a *ghazal* of Hafiz that begins:

> Zephyr, find that dainty deer,
>> Whisper softly in her ear
> That in search of her I roam
>> Hills and deserts far from home . . .[73]

—and, when he reached the climax, the first plowman joined in. In this way the plowmen went on singing in the still fields all the rest of the night. At daybreak they fell silent, and my companions awoke and claimed my attention.

These last few pages are an elegy, a recollection of my life in those days penned sixty years later and dedicated to my mother. If this catalogue of disaster seems excessive and offends my readers, I ask their pardon; I wished only to pay in part the dues of my childhood, and hope they will be indulgent.

---

[73] This celebrated poem is No. 4 in most editions of Hafiz's *divan*; for a translation, see Arberry's *Fifty Poems of Hafiz*, No. 4.

26. Harvest and Aftermath

With the help of neighbors' donkeys and horses and of the village children we threshed and sifted the sorghum and heaped up the grain. The crop turned out to be larger than anything hitherto harvested from similar fields. First of all we sifted out of the heap approximately fifteen *man* (over 4,000 lb.) and gave it to Yūldosh-boi to pay for my father's burial. The assessors fixed the rate at ten *tangas* (one and a half rubles) for each *man* of sorghum. The market rate was twelve *tangas* per *man*, but two *tangas* was deducted because the buyer had to load and transport it from the site himself. Yūldosh-boi took took 125 *tangas'* worth for himself, and gave the remaining twenty-five *tangas'* worth to small creditors.

After paying off Yūldosh-boi and our other creditors, we had about five *man* (1500 lb.) of grain left for our own consumption, which I carried home. The sorghum that was not completely ripe I carried home without weighing.

One week after the harvesting my uncle Ali-khon, who had taken my sick mother away, turned up. He informed me that my mother's funeral had cost them one hundred *tangas*, which he now claimed. I gave him twenty *man* of unripe sorghum at a valuation of five *tangas* (75 kopeks) per *man*; the market rate for this was actually seven *tangas*, but again the sum of two *tangas* was deducted since the buyer picked up the grain himself. What was left served to keep the donkey well fed through that winter.

That harvest was so big that no-one in the village could remember the like of it. Usto Amak had also sown his half-*tanob* of land with sorghum that year, and had harvested three *man* of ripe and two of unripe grain—though admittedly his crop had been fully protected against birds by his own son Ikrom Khoja. People told me that if my crop had been properly looked after, I would have harvested forty *man*. When the village elders saw this bumper crop of mine, they said that such a huge harvest was not natural, and that this was what had shortened my father's life.

Young as I was, I could not swallow this. My reasoning was very simple. I told myself that my father had gone to great lengths to sow one *tanob* of cotton, and that the cotton had failed and brought all his efforts to nothing; yet this failure had not lengthened his life. Why, then, should a successful crop elsewhere have shortened it?

*   *   *

The pumpkins too, the first fruit of my farming, produced an unusually large crop. That fall I picked the ones that had turned orange and stacked them in the porch that had served as my father's workshop: the whole room, five beams long,[74] was soon filled from floor to ceiling with ripe pumpkins. The unripe and half-grown ones I put in the storeroom for fodder.

That winter I devoted systematically to pumpkin-selling. Ghijduvon had two market days per week, Wednesday and Saturday. On each of these days I would load sixteen pumpkins into sacks, take them to market, and sell them retail. Every time, I paid two *pul* (half a kopek) to tether the donkey in the yard, and four *pul* for a pitch to sell my pumpkins. Besides this I would spend four *pul* on a sweet roll and another four on grapes, for my own meal, and would take home two more sweet rolls for my sick brothers. In this way I spent a total of twenty-two *pul*, or five and a half kopeks, every market day. I also took home a *nimcha* (one pound) of meat every week.

When some money had accumulated from the sale of pumpkins, I bought clothing from the bazaar for myself and my younger brothers (my elder brother had sufficient clothes for his needs). With these expenses taken care of, next spring I bought a nursing ewe and her lamb.

27. Head of the Household

That year I was father, mother, and household servant all at the same time. With my older brother still convalescent and my younger brothers only just recovered, they could not help me in any way.

---

[74] The *bolor*, a wooden beam about eight feet long, was the basic unit of construction for Tajik houses, especially wooden ones, where it formed the base for the walls as well as the supports and rooftrees. Consequently it was used as an approximate unit of measurement: a porch or room "five beams long" would be some forty feet long.

Because of her illness, Mother had not been able to make mulberry syrup that year, and had left a small sack of mulberry raisins ready. One of the neighbor women taught me how to prepare a sweet soup from these, so that I made it twice a week and we ate it all week long. We took sorghum to the mill and had flour ground. Every week Ibrohim Khoja's wife baked cornbread for us. Our food that winter consisted mainly of this mulberry-raisin-and-cornmeal soup with cornbread. Once a week we made soup from mashed sorghum kernels. I went to the bazaar, cooked, laundered, and mended our clothes (I had learned to wash clothes when I attended the girls' school in Soktaré, as I described in "The Village School").[75]

*   *   *

In the middle of the winter my elder brother Muhyiddin recovered his strength. But he did not stay long at home, and went to another village to serve as imam and earn money for his next year's studies. We three younger brothers remained at home. The oldest of my younger brothers was Sirojiddin, who was eight and a half years old. Although recovered from his illness, he was still weak. He had always been thin and pale, and the illness had turned him into a dried, faded twig with little appetite. My youngest brother Kiromiddin, however, who was four years old, quickly recovered his strength after the illness.[76]

Kiromiddin had an unusual physique—he was tall for his age, his head was larger than average, and his neck was thick. He had a very broad chest and used to strut about sticking out his chest like a wrestling champion. He laughed little and measured his words seriously before speaking. He was very sharp and quick-witted. He once said something clever that I still remember.

My older brother had gone to serve as imam in the village of Tabariyon, which was ten miles from our village, and after some time there he came back with meat, rice, and oil he had bought,

---

[75] See Appendix II, Section vii.

[76] Kiromiddin died in 1891, only two years after this. Sirojiddin died in the Bukhara prison in 1918 as an enemy of the emir's regime; Aini's elegy for his brother was the first of his revolutionary writings (see Bečka, *Sadriddin Ayni*, pp. 72-3). Muhyiddin was shot at Soktaré in 1922 by a band of Basmachis (counterrevolutionary guerrillas).

and cooked pilau for us. When he had cooked the meal he invited Usto Amak and his son Ikrom Khoja to join us.

We were sitting around the *sandali* eating: Usto Amak in the place of honor opposite the door, my elder brother and Ikrom Khoja on either side, and at the far side we three younger brothers. On top of the pilau lay a large, meaty bone. As a customary courtesy my older brother picked up the bone and offered it to the eldest present, Usto Amak. "I don't have any teeth," said Usto Amak. "Eat it yourselves and enjoy it! The rice will be fine for me."

Since everybody else at the table was younger than Muhyiddin, he began to eat it without offering it around. The bone was big and the sinews were tough, so my brother held the bone in both hands and began gnawing on the meat. All at once he noticed that our little brother Kiromiddin was watching him eat with an indignant scowl on his face. "What are you looking at?" Muhyiddin asked him.

"You're gnawing the bone just like Khaibar the dog!" he said angrily.

Everyone laughed. I was particularly delighted at this repartee of his: he had been longing for that bone, and when his brother had withheld it and started eating it himself he was angry and, prompted by his half-formed sense of injustice, compared Muhyiddin's treatment of the bone to that of a dog. It was a poetic simile in the fullest sense.[77] When I read the works of the poets, I admired their similes more than anything else; but this four-year-old's simile delighted me more than any I had read so far. The fact that it was the spontaneous utterance of a child getting his own back made it all the more enjoyable.

Much as I wanted to become a poet myself, I never really believed it would happen. But in my heart I decided that my youngest brother would eventually be a poet, and after the laughter abated I told him, "You are going to be a poet!" Nobody responded to my comment. Not only the four-year-old, but the others, too, failed to grasp the significance of what I said. I even felt that my older brother was a little offended by the remark,

---

[77] Taj. *tashbehi tom*, i.e., both a material and a metaphorical comparison, since Muhyiddin was behaving somewhat like the proverbial dog in the manger. The Tajik original of Kiromiddin's stricture is also metrically sound, with alliteration and assonance (*khudi Khaibar barin ustukhon mekhoed*).

since instead of correcting the little critic for his impudence I had praised him.

By that time I had put aside all thoughts of going to study in Bukhara. Though I wanted this more than ever, particularly after my father's last words, this hope seemed to he an impossible dream. Since my older brother was determined to continued his studies at all costs, I had no choice but to care for my younger brothers like a parent. If I went off to Bukhara, these two children would surely perish. My conscience charged me with their upbringing above all my desires to study.

I also put aside studying with the village imam and absorbed myself in domestic affairs. That spring I bought a nursing ewe and lamb with the money left over from the pumpkins I had sold and put them to graze. I thought to myself, "These sheep will both be big and fat by autumn. If I sell one we'll have money to see us through the winter, and we can slaughter, salt and eat the other."

I grazed the sheep by our family burial plot in the overgrown cemetery, which was nobody's private property. Since everyone else was afraid of the "wrath of the saints" and of "*jinn* and dragons" and did not graze their animals there, the pasture was better, too. It was pleasant to go up to the top of this hill and to gaze at the surrounding fields and farmyards; and I especially liked to trace out with charcoal the epitaphs carved in the tombstones and read them.[78] On one stone this folk verse was written in a fine *nasta'liq* script:

> Of this world's cruelty there's no end,
> Alas! It sunders friend from friend;
> The friend who's ours for but a day
> It violently tears away.

On another stone were written these four lines by Sa'di:

---

[78] I have described how I used to graze my sheep in the cemetery in my essay *Kolkhozi "Kommunizm"* [The Collective Farm "Communism"] — A. This was first published in the journal *Baroyi adabiyoti sotsialisti*, 1934, Nos. 3-4, and in Russian translation under the title *Cherez dvadsat' let* (Twenty Years After) in the periodical *Nashi dostizheniia*), 1934, No. 5.

> I heard that Jamshid, that auspicious king,
> Wrote this upon a stone beside a spring:
> Many, like me, have tarried here to drink,
> And then departed, quicker than a wink.[79]

With the passing of spring and the withering of the grass at the cemetery, I moved my sheep to the river bank (known in those days as the *odogh*, from *ob-dogh*, "high-water mark"). The water of the Zarafshon periodically overflowed, making the pasturage along its hanks very lush. All of the cowherds and shepherds from our village brought their animals there too. We would leave our animals to graze while we sat in the shade of the willows and played all sorts of games. Whenever we felt hungry we picked green beans from the edges of the fields and irrigation ditches, boiled them with salt and made a fine stew (I described these activities in my novel *Ghulomon*). Sometimes we would tie fishing lines along the edge of the water and manage to catch small fish. We would grill these immediately over the fire and salt them, and they tasted delicious.

*   *   *

As autumn approached we could no longer graze our animals by the river bank. This came about as follows. The *odogh*, the land on the river bank up to the limit of flooding, was considered crown land. Every villager who cultivated land there gave four tenths, i.e. forty percent, of his crop to the emirate of Bukhara. In those years the *amlokdor* of the Ghijduvon region was a man named Qarabek. He was an unmitigated tyrant, who collected this tax punctiliously, with the utmost vigor and regular recourse to force and guile; on top of this he would even find ways to put the villagers in debt to the emir.[80]

During those years, therefore, the peasants ceased cultivating these lands and the fields grew thick with briars. Still the *amlokdor*

---

[79] *Būstân*, end of Tale No. 1 (see Wickens' translation, p. 30; cf. the similar sentiments—likewise attributed to Jamshid—in Tale No. 154, p. 226). The verse involves a play on the words *chashma* "spring, fountain" and *chashm* "eye." For Jamshid and Sa'di, see Glossary.

[80] These methods are protrayed in the novel *Ghulomon*—A. (See also the following chapter.)

managed to collect money, in the form of a "briar tax." Eventually the fields on the floodplain deteriorated into wasteland.

Qarabek came in person to the land by the river to collect his briar tax, and saw all the cows and sheep grazing there. He decided to impose pasturage dues as well, and summoned all the cowherds and shepherds before him. But the herdsmen, secretly warned by the other villagers that he was up to no good, drove their animals away and dispersed in all directions.

And so because of this we no longer took our animals to the river bank, but grazed them on cultivated land after the harvest (which in those days was called *angor*).

* * *

That year we were not able to get any yield from the two *tanob* of land my father had left us. There was no way I could have worked the land by my own strength alone, but after the death of my father one of the Tajiks in our village, Mirzo Mū'min, who had been a friend of my father's, came to my aid. He plowed up his own cotton field, the crop of which had withered, for winter wheat, and his sorghum field for spring barley, telling me, "Take care of this yourself. Its yield will be all yours, and you need only leave me the stalks for my oxen to graze on." But the seed merchant I got the barley seeds from gave me winter barley instead of spring barley. Thus, after the barley had sprouted a little way, it collapsed on the ground and stopped growing.

When the wheat came up it flowered, then was stricken with blight and withered away; and the seeds that it dropped did not grow either.

Since I had enjoyed such success with the pilau-pumpkin that I had planted the year before on the plot of land at the end of our *sufa*, I planted it again this year, not realizing that one should not plant the same crop—especially vegetables—two years in a row on the same land. When the vine flowered and began to sprout pumpkins, parasitical weeds flowered at their roots (what the poets call "flowers of ill omen"), and the pumpkins yellowed and fell off. That year not a single one was worth eating.

So it came about that I was not able to produce any crops the whole year. To cap it all, we had a cold spring, so the apricots and mulberries were frostbitten, and our orchard produce was also worthless.

28. Soktaré in the 1870s and 1880s

Up to the year 1868, when the emir of Bukhara went to war with
the tsar and had to sue for peace, the *amlokdors* of Ghijduvon—including those of our village, and in common with the
other *raions* of Bukhara—took forty percent of all produce in
taxes for the emir's government. After the treaty with Russia, this
practice was officially abolished; nevertheless the Emir Muzaffar,
under the pretext of having to pay war reparations to Russia,
unofficially rescinded this provision and issued oral instructions to
his officials to extract the maximum possible taxes from the
farmers. The government officials, of whom it was said that if the
emir ordered them to bring him a turban they would bring him a
whole head, took not only the peasants' turbans, heads and all, but
the very skins from off their backs.

The next emir, Abdul-Ahad, continued to ignore the treaty
provisions, and each year demanded even more taxes from every
raion, to secure which he appointed "experienced and efficient"
men as *amlokdors*. On his accession one Qarabek, who had
previously served as secretary to several *amlokdors*, by reason of
his "experience" was appointed *amlokdor* of Ghijduvon, the most
fertile and productive spot in the whole land of Bukhara. Qarabek
came from the village of Tahti-Qūrghon, near Soktaré, from a
community known as Burquts.[81] This savage tyrant, being well
acquainted with the *raion* of Ghijduvon and in particular the
villages around Soktaré, carried out his exactions chiefly in this
region.

In Tahti-Qūrghon there was a large lake. Qarabek forced the
inhabitants, unpaid, to fill it in with earth dug from a nearby hill,
level it off, and build him a mansion and garden. He kept them at
this forced labor even through the year of the plague. Qarabek
was also the first to impose a levy on land left untilled, by the
name of "briar tax" (*khorpuli*). When farmers plowed over such
land in order to prevent weeds and briars growing, yet left it
unsown, he imposed yet another tax by the name of "fallow field

---

[81] Burqut: Turkicized Mongols who emigrated westward with Chingiz
Khan's hordes in the 13th century and settled at various spots in the Zarafshon valley, including Ghijduvon.

tax." Qarabek's example was subsequently emulated in every *raion* of Bukhara.

There was in the village of Tahti-Qūrghon an eighty-year-old former army officer, a Burqut like Qarabek, known popularly as Bek-Bobo (I forget his real name). He owned forty *tanob* of land to the north of Sari Mazor in the Soktaré area, a government fief given him in reward for his past services (*tankhoh*). He was a simple and kindhearted fellow, who never overworked the peasants who farmed his land and neither supervised the harvest in person nor sent overseers. His tenants were two brothers, Tajiks of Soktaré called Mirzo Yūldosh and Mirzo Mū'min, who were close friends of my father. They always told him how they had been working hard year by year to increase the yield of this land, but how Bek-Bobo never asked for any extra and was always content to receive just as much as they took him.

When Qarabek became *amlokdor* of Ghijduvon, his eye lighted on this forty *tanob* of prime land. He went in person to Bek-Bobo and asked him how much his forty *tanob* yielded annually. On the basis of Bek-Bobo's reply he calculated his income as four thousand *tangas*, and applied to the emir for leave to pay Bek-Bobo four thousand *tangas* cash per year from the royal revenues and incorporate his forty *tanob* into the crown lands and tax it accordingly. The emir naturally acceded to this request and issued a commission in his name to effect the transfer. As a result, the crop of this forty *tanob* was taxed out of existence and the land reduced to untilled and fallow fields in the space of three years, with Mirzo Yūldosh and Mirzo Mū'min still obliged to pay the requisite taxes.[82]

---

[82] *Tankhoh* (Pers. *tankhwâh*): this kind of subinfeudation (similar to the *tiyul*: see *Encyclopedia of Islam*) was a common practice in the Bukhara emirate. Officials and ex-offficials of the court would be assigned land in lieu of a salary or pension, which they would turn over to working tenants in return for a fixed proportion of the yield. If, as here, the fiefholder did not reassess the yield each year, as the government *amlokdor* would have done, the tenants could increase their margin of subsistence. In this case, the *amlokdor* obtained an arbitrary resumption of the property and reassessed the yield; it was not then worth the tenants' while to continue farming it, but since they were in effect fined for not working it (Qarabek's novel "briar tax" and "fallow field tax"), they were totally ruined.

*   *   *

Early in the year of the plague, Qarabek was promoted on account
of his "efficiency" and appointed *amlokdor* of Ziyo-uddin
raion,[83] which produced cotton and rice. Nevertheless, the forced
labor on his mansion at Tahti-Qūrghon continued, on his instructions, under the supervision of his successor as *amlokdor* of
Ghijduvon.

We village boys used to go when we were at a loose end to
watch the construction. Inside the rooms, plasterers would be
carving designs in the alabaster. At the end of the second summer
of the epidemic, news came that Qarabek's son had died, and he
sent orders to the builders to construct a tomb of baked bricks
faced with white alabaster. While they were working on this, one of
the plasterers said to another, "I wish to God we'd heard that he
himself had died, and we could build a black tomb for him!"

Hardly a month elapsed before news came that he had died. At
that time the plasterers were working on the panels round the walls
of the rooms, and for the lower part of this they mixed coal dust
in with the plaster to color it gray. And although with the death of
Qarabek no-one forced them to go on with his commission, the
builders of their own free will carried out their earlier pipe-dream
of building him a tomb and plastering it over in black. Popular
opinion had it that God had commenced Qarabek's eternal
torment from the very day of his death; his tomb was blackened
like the smoke-blackened walls of a room, because of the fires of
Hell burning in his grave.

After Qarabek's death, work on his mansion came to a halt;
builders and laborers went their separate ways, and the yard and
rooms were strewn with bricks, plaster, paint, and all sorts of
construction materials. The *amlokdor* of Ghijduvon locked it up
and took possession of it for the emirate. The ruins of this building remained until the time of the revolution in Bukhara, after
which the people demolished it and carted off the bricks and
woodwork to put to their own use, declaring that at last each had
gotten his due.

---

[83] Ziyouddin, now called Pakhtakor (cotton-farmer), in the Zarafshon valley
between Bukhara and Samarkand, is still a major cotton-growing district; the
rail station is still called Ziyadin.

Figure 8. Mirzo Abdul-Vohid Munzim

29. Off To Bukhara

Although I had abandoned my hopes of going to study in Bukhara, something suddenly happened to make this dream come true. At the end of the summer of 1889, my seventy-year-old maternal grandmother sent word to me to bring my younger brothers to her so she could see us all before she died. I left Ikrom Khoja in charge of my sheep, locked the door of the house, and mounted my donkey, placing the older of my younger brothers behind me and the younger one in front of me, and off we rode to the village of Mahallayi Bolo.

During our stay there, a visitor came from Bukhara to the village of Mahalla, which was near Mahallayi Bolo. This was Sharifjon Makhdum, the son of the late chief kadi and noted scholar Abdushukur; his host was the local imam Mullo Abdusalom, who was my elder brother's tutor. Mullo Abdusalom summoned Muhyiddin over to his residence to help entertain the guests, and on hearing from him that I was at my grandmother's house in Mahallayi Bolo, he invited me to help too.

Sharifjon Makhdum had arrived with his entourage, and additional guests had been invited in his honor. My brother was in the guestroom laying the tablecloth and arranging seats,[84] and I busied myself with lighting the samovar on the *sufa*. When it boiled I made pots of tea and kept them warm for others to take in to the guestroom.

I was sitting by the samovar cleaning teapots when a boy came out of the guestroom who was my height, although thinner. He sat on the edge of the *sufa*, looking bored, and said to himself, "Mavlono Jaloliddin Rumi[85] said:

---

[84] For a Tajik banquet, the *dastarkhon*, or tablecloth, is spread out on the floor in the center of the room, and quilts and cushions are arranged around the outside of it against the wall. It is set with innumerable dishes of fruit, nuts, bread, yoghurt, salad, cold meat, etc., and the guests are plied with tea as they work through this. In due course the rice and cooked meat (pilau) is served, on a large communal platter. In modern times, vodka and brandy are virtually indispensable additions to the table.

[85] Pers. Mawlânâ Jalâl al-dîn Rûmî (1207-1273): the greatest Persian mystical poet, author of the *Masnavî*, a long mystical-didactic epic, and a series of *ghazals* dedicated to his mentor Shams-i Tabrîzî. Born in Balkh,

'Avoid the country, it makes a man a fool;
It dims the mind and tarnishes the soul.'

I ignored Mavlono's advice and came to the country, and now I'm sick and tired of it. I can't even find anyone to pass the time here with a game of verse-capping (*bayt-barak*)."

I asked him, "What's verse-capping?"

With a look of surprise, he asked me, "Are you literate?"

"I can read a little."

"Do you know any verses by heart?"

"A few."

"Verse-capping goes like this," he began to explain. "I quote a verse of poetry, and you answer it with a verse whose first letter is the same letter as the last letter of mine. Then I answer you with a verse whose first letter is the same as the last letter of yours, and we go on 'capping' each other's verses in this way. Whoever can't cap a verse loses, and once a verse has been recited it can't be used again. Would you like to try it?"

"Why not," I said.

He recited a verse and I capped it, and he capped that, and I capped his verse, and so on for about fifteen minutes. Then I began to flag: even though I had not exhausted all the verses I knew by heart, those that started with the last letter of my opponent's previous verse came to me more and more slowly. My opponent came up with the necessary verses faster than I, and I could see he was quite experienced at this game. For every letter he knew many appropriate verses, and memorable ones at that. Yet from his intonation it was obvious that he did not fully understand most of them. I took advantage of his weakness and began to cheat: sometimes I substituted a spurious word or phrase for the beginning of a verse that did not begin with the right letter, and other times I changed the word order of the verse so it would start with the necessary letter. To be sure, this destroyed the meaning of the verse, but my opponent didn't notice the difference.

---

some 300 miles southeast of Bukhara, he fled westward from the Mongol invasions and settled at Konya (Iconium) in Asia Minor, known to the Muslims as Rûm—hence his name.

Rûmî also wrote: "That Bukhara is a mine of knowledge;/So whoever possesses wisdom is a Bukharan" (quoted by Frye, p. 50).

All at once my opponent recited a verse that ended in the sound *zh*. In my whole life I had never come across a verse beginning with *zh*. I only knew two words that began with the letter *zh*: one was *zhola* (dew, or hail), the other was *zhozh* or *zhozh-khoi*—literally "to chew camel-thorn," i.e., to talk non-sense. I tried to place one of these words at the beginning of a verse, but I could not think of one quickly enough, and my opponent said impatiently, "Hurry up and answer, or forfeit the game!" At that moment, sheer necessity provided inspiration, and I recited:

> "*Zhozh* and *mozh*, and *zhozh* and *mozh*, and *zhozh* and *mozh*;
> This is all *zhozh*, from beginning to end, pure *zhozh*!"[86]

If this verse can be called poetry, it was my first poetical creation.

My opponent objected: "That verse begins with *j*, not *zh*!"

Since I knew very well that the first letter was *zh* and not *j*, I stood my ground. Inside, I was bursting with laughter, since the entire "verse" was sheer nonsense and my own fabrication. Fortunately my opponent did not realize this. As we were arguing, a middle-aged man with one eye, likewise from Bukhara and evidently one of Sharifjon's servants, came out. After listening to our argument for a while, he suggested, "You should go and ask Makhdumjon[87] which of you is correct."

---

[86] *Zhozhu mozh*: *zhozh* alone means "camel-thorn" or "nonsense"; *mozh* is a nonsensical echo-word serving to intensify it. The couplet is slyly self-referential, its comic effect clinched by Aini's opponent's trivial and unfounded objection. The fricative *zh* is an original Persian/Tajik phoneme, as is the affricate *j*, each being represented by a distinct letter of the alpha-bet; but *zh*, apart from French and Russian loans such as *zhândârm* and *gârâzh*, occurs infrequently. In most Uzbek dialects there is a single pho-neme (represented in the modern written language by *zh*) to which words of Persian provenance that include *j* are assimilated.

[87] The Tajik/Persian word *jon* (life, soul, dear one) is conventionally added to most given names of Tajik and Uzbek men, and may betoken affection, respect, or an element of cultural solidarity. Sharifjon Makhdum (*q.v.* in the Glossary) has the given name "Sharif," to which *jon* is usually attached; here his title *Makhdum* (applied to the sons of religious dignitaries) is used in referring to him respectfully, but the *jon* is transferred to it.

My opponent wrote down the verse with his pencil on a piece of paper, in a fine hand, and trotted off confidently to the guest-room. Two minutes later he emerged looking like a bedraggled hen, sweating with embarrassment, and said sulkily, "Makh-dumjon wants to see you."

"Well, were you right or not?" I asked him, as though I still did not know how the issue stood.

Without answering me, he repeated, "Makhdumjon wants to see you—hurry up."

But I did not go. How could I appear before some highborn man from the city, whom everyone treated with deference and whose servants even wore neat city attire, in my torn and dirty country clothes? A few minutes later my brother came out of the guestroom and called to me, "Come, don't be embarrassed. 'Decree supersedes decorum,' as the saying goes."

I went up, stood deferentially just at the threshold, and greeted the company. The room was full of people. Most of them were white-turbaned mullahs, and some of the elders of the village seemed to be there, too. In the place of honor sat a young man of about twenty-five with a fair complexion and dark brown hair. This was evidently Sharifjon Makhdum.

Sharifjon looked at me keenly and asked, "What's your name?"

"Sadriddin," I answered.

"Very good. Were you the one playing *bayt-barak* with Mirzo Abdul-Vohid?"

I nodded my head, but could not speak.

"You're right, *zhozh* is written with a *zh*, not a *j*," he said; then, "How would you like to come to Bukhara to study?"

I hung my head and said nothing. But my heart ached at being robbed of the chance to study, and my eyes filled with tears.

My brother spoke up: "Our parents have passed away. We have younger brothers, and he is the only one left to care for them. It is because of this that he cannot go to college."

"Well, however we can manage it," said Sharifjon Makhdum, "we must send this one to school. He seems to be a gifted boy. It's not easy to trip up our know-it-all in verse-cap-ping"—pointing to my opponent, Mirzo Abdul-Vohid.

My brother's tutor, Mullo Abdusalom, the host, put in a word: "I will also try to ensure he can go to school in Bukhara." Turning to me, he added, "Go back and keep your samovar boiling!"

I left the guestroom bursting with joy, not only because Sharifjon had confirmed that *zhozh* was spelled with a *zh* — since even if he had not, I knew very well that it was so — but first because the secret of my home-made verse had not come out, for if Sharifjon had recognized its origin he had not embarrassed me by publicizing it; and secondly, as a result of this meeting, I determined once more to surmount all obstacles and at all costs to go to school in Bukhara.

Two days later the guests left, and I went to see my brother and his teacher to settle the matter of my going to Bukhara. Ultimately it was decided that we would leave my younger brothers with my grandmother and I would go with Muhyiddin to the madrasa. Mullo Abdusalom said, "Somehow or other he'll get through life at the madrasa, with God's help. Since we have made a promise to a great man" — meaning Sharifjon Makhdum[88] — "we must send him to Bukhara."

*   *   *

In accordance with the customs of that time there were important duties to attend to before we could leave. We would have to give a feast to observe the first anniversary of our parents' death, and have our two younger brothers circumcised.[89] If we did not perform these obligations, we would be ostracized from the community. But performing them required a lot of money and, much as we two elder brothers racked our brains, we could not solve the problem.

Then it suddenly occurred to me that if we sold the house and garden left to us by our father in Mahallayi Bolo we could raise the necessary funds. I told my brother, "We don't need this house at all, we won't ever be living in Mahallayi Bolo again. Whereas if

---

[88] Sharifjon Makhdum was also a poet under the pen-name Sadri-Ziyo, who compiled a literary memoir in verse [see Glossary]. The boy I played *bayt-barak* with, Abdul-Vohid Munzim, became my close friend from that day forth, and died of a chill at Stalinabad in March of 1934. — A. (See further in the Glossary, under Munzim.) Of note here is that in the 1990 edition of *Yoddoshtho* (Dushanbe: Adib, 2 vols.) Aini's "Stalinobod" is corrected to "Dushanbe."

[89] Commemoration of the first anniversary of a death is not mandated in Islam, but it is a feature of both Zoroastrian and Hindu practice. For circumcision, see Chapter 1, note 2.

we don't sell the property while our grandparents are still alive, it wouldn't surprise me if some scoundrel like Mullo Navruz eventually got it for nothing."[90]

My brother thought this a good idea. We immediately sold the property and returned to Soktaré, where we gave a dinner in observance of the anniversary of our pbvh arents' death, and the next day prepared a small celebration and had our brothers circumcised.

* * *

When my brothers were recovered, I sold my sheep and had a suit of winter clothes made for each of us. I tied what little money was left (five *tangas*, worth seventy-five kopeks) around my waist to save for later. I also put aside the greater part of the mulberry raisins and dried apricots for my brothers, and saved a little for Bukhara. I picked out as many of the quilts and pillows as we would need, and left the rest, together with the plates, pots and washbasin, in the house, locking the door after me. My father had left a small cooking-pot and a clay pot of oil that he had used when he stayed at the madrasa; these I also packed to take to Bukhara. Muhyiddin sold the donkey, to help defray our joint expenses at the madrasa. We sent our dog Khaibar back to the shepherd uncle who had given him to us when he was six months old.

I took my younger brothers and their belongings back to the village of Mahallayi Bolo, and was finally all set to go to Bukhara.

End of Book One

---

[90] The machinations of Mullo Navrūz are described in my novel Ghulomon, and also in an article I wrote in 1947 on the occasion of elections to the Supreme Soviets of Tajikistan and Uzbekistan—A. This was *"Intikhobot va javonon"* (Elections and Young People), first published in the newspaper *Tojikistoni surkh* of 11 February 1947; reproduced in *Aknun navbati qalamast*, Vol. 1, pp. 388-92. Mullo Navrūz falsely claimed kinship with the deceased father of two youths, had them declared legally incompetent, appropriated their inheritance, and sold them to the emir for his slave corps, in which they died of exposure that same winter.

Appendix I

Ahmad the Exorcist

Figure 9. Ruined mausoleum in Soktaré

FOREWORD

According to his sister, Aini borrowed the name "Ahmad" for his protagonist from that of a particularly superstitious youth who happened to be staying at the author's house in Samarkand during 1928, when he wrote the story.[1] But the real hero of this didactic tale is the young Ayni himself, seen in a series of set-pieces based on episodes from his boyhood in Soktaré during the 1880s and his early student days at a Bukhara madrasa during the 1890s. Some of the characters and events depicted here—"Ahmad"'s father, his dog Khaibar, the fireworks contest, Bobo Niyoz-Gūppon—have their analogues in the first volume of Aini's reminiscences (chiefly Chapter 9), which was not written until some twenty years after *Ahmadi devband*.

The supernatural beings variously referred to here are the *dev*, *pari*, *jinn* (q.v. individually in the Glossary) and *ajina*, a fearsome shape-changing demon. The *dev*, or demon, is generally hostile to man and often solitary, inhabiting a particular cave. The *pari* is gregarious and mischievous. both are native Iranian spirits, corresponding respectively to the ogres and fairies of European folklore. The *jinn* or genie (a collective noun in Arabic; the singular is *jinnî*)—familiar from the *Arabian Nights*—were in origin *genii loci* of the Arabian desert, accepted in the Koran as actual beings created "of smokeless fire" (Surah 15:27 and 55:15), who evidently came to Iran and Central Asia with the Arab conquerors and were partially assimilated to the indigenous

---

[1] Kholida Aini, p. 72.

demons. They inhabit a different perceptual plane from human-kind, but can be conjured up by means of a talisman or a spell.

In western Christian folklore there is a distinction between ex-orcism, which is sanctioned by the Church and restricted to banishing parasitical spirits from a person or place, and sorcery, which is one of the black (i.e., pagan) arts, enabling the exponent to enlist the active aid of evil spirits for good or ill. In Iranian folklore, the *devband* ("demon-binder") is more than an exor-cist, but less than the complete sorcerer: he can "bind" demons by oath (taken on religiously-sanctioned names or talismans) to refrain from molesting humans and even to help in actions for good. Rustam, the principal hero of the Iranian national legend, is dignified with the epithet *devband* in Firdawsi's *Shahnameh* (Book of Kings); he overcame demons by physical prowess and literally bound them in chains, or tied their thumbs together, which rendered them helpless. This more literal meaning of *devband* appeared in the Russian translation of the tale as *povelitel' divov*, i.e., "commander of demons"; Kholida Aini maintains that it should be translated as *zaklinatel' divov*, "conju-ror" or "exorcist" of demons.[2] In English, too, "exorcist" seems preferable as a translation of *devband*, since in terms of Aini's allegory the scientifically-educated reformist is no sorcerer, battening on the superstitions of the past like the village *eshon*, but a priest of the new ideology sent to exorcize the demons of superstition and blind tradition that hold his people back.

Ahmadi devband appeared first in serial form in 1928, in the organ of the People's Commissariat for Education, *Rahbari donish* (Guide to Knowledge; Nos. 8-9 and 11-12), then in a revised version in the journal *Baroi adabiyoti sotsialistî* (For a Socialist Literature; 1936, No. 6), and in book form in 1939. It was included, after further minor revisions, in an anthology of Aini's works in 1949, and in this version was published in Vol. 1 of his collected works (*Kulliyot*) in 1963. It was reprinted in the anthology *Aknun navbati qalamast* (Dushanbe, 1978; Vol. 2, 79-106), from which this translation was made. An Uzbek version appeared in 1937 (in *Mushtum*, No. 12) and a Russian translation in 1937 and 1973 (S. Aini, *Sobranie sochinenii v shesti tomakh*, Moscow 1973, III, 133-53).

---

[2] Ibid.

i

In the Ghijduvon district of Bukhara there is a village called Khoja
Soktaré, where the khojas have been famous as exorcists and
sorcerers for generations. From the outskirts of Bukhara city as far
as Miyonkolot, people afflicted with madness—that is, possessed
of devils—flocked there to be cured; and not only the insane, but
cases of everything from typhoid and malaria to cuts and
scratches found their way to Soktaré.

To the north of the village is a high hill, on top of which lie
buried the fathers and forefathers of these khojas. This cemetery
is called Haftalam, for the seven yak's-tail banners—the sign of
the seven perfect sages—that always stood over it.[3] The center of
the cemetery was at the very summit of the hill, where the mausoleum of the khojas of old lay enclosed within a private wall.
Outside this wall, all the way round the hillside down to the very
foot, were clustered the graves of the masses of mankind.

All around this cemetery was rich farming land, legendary for
its fertility: an array of gardens, orchards, plantations, each more
flourishing than the last, met the unbelieving eye. If you were to
climb to the top of the hill very early in the morning when the sun
was just rising, or late one afternoon as it was setting, you would
see a sight of indescribable beauty. Sit on a marble tombstone at
the eastern tip of the hilltop and look down: an endless sea of
alfalfa, waist high and not yet in flower, will meet your gaze. In
these meadows six-months old lambs, free to graze at will, wander
like ducklings swimming in a limpid pool, each nibbling daintily
with pure white teeth on the particular clump of greenery that has
caught its fancy; and pert kids, never still for an instant, ignoring
all that tempting fodder and—maybe to browse on the undergrowth among the trees, maybe just to show off—go bounding up
the hill. If you could tear your eyes away from the lush emerald-

---

[3] Persian *haft 'alam* 'seven banners.' The setting up of prayer flags and
other insignia over tombs is a custom from pagan times adopted by
Buddhists and Muslims in parts of Central Asia. The yak's-tail banner,
properly called *tugh*, is a token of precedence and a processional standard still
used in Tibet; it was adopted by the Mongols and Turks and has appeared in
subtle variants from the Balkans to Korea, notably as a battle standard (with
horse tails) in the Ottoman empire, and one of the standards known as *'alam*
(with silk streamers) that lead the Moharram mourning procession in Iran.

green meadows and look a little way beyond, you would be dazzled by beds of newly-ripened musk melons, fields of freshly blooming cottonflowers, acres of tall, ripe corn. The shouts of the village boys driving the crows, jackdaws and starlings away from the corn and millet with their slings and clapper-sticks would recall the war cries of some medieval army. A dense flock of the birds, scared into flight by the swish of the slings, would rush off cawing over your head in search of an unguarded field, like a black spring storm cloud.

If you were to gaze a little farther still, you would notice that right on the banks of the Mazrangon stream, at the edge of the village, a profusion of trees—willow, elms, silver poplars and others—had spread out their lush foliage and intertwined their branches so that the walls and roofs of the villagers' houses were almost completely hidden. On the far side of the Mazrangon, next to the village, a broad flat plain stretches away down to the river's edge. This is crisscrossed from end to end by irrigation canals from the Mazrangon, mill streams for overshot and undershot wheels, branch channels and drainage channels large and small, dug by the villagers around their plots. The trickling of these various streams, the rushing of the mill races and the roar of the River Zarafshon blend into one melodious symphony.

This pleasant vista is augmented by fields of sesame, peas, vetch, musk melons, watermelons and, above all, rice. Even the uncultivable land on this plain is not empty: here, licorice plants grow waist-high. Among their dense stalks pheasants, which are nowhere safe from man's depredations, build their nests, lay eggs, hatch the chicks and rear their brood in blissful confidence. The Zarafshon, skirting this verdant meadowland from northeast to southwest, seems a sparking liquid semicircle of quicksilver.

Turning your gaze aside from the Zarafshon toward the purple shadow of Qarnab Mountain, you would decide you had seen enough of this side of the hill and want to view the other side. There your attention would be drawn first to the northwest side of the cemetery, where the ground was prettily covered with vine-yards and plantations of young fruit trees. Going into the enclosure by the south gate and out through the north gate, just before you came within sight of the plantations, you would be startled to find the mouth of a dark cave looming before you.

ii

Yes, the cave of the Khoja Soktaré cemetery was frightening. Not merely because of its narrow entrance and broad, deep and dark interior, but more especially because it was popularly supposed to be the lair of demons, fairy folk, evil spirits, and a dragon guarding an enchanted treasure. The upper façade of the cave had weathered and crumbled over the years and collapsed halfway down the hill, and a column of baked bricks had been built to hold up the roof, so that the entrance looked like a lopsided oven doorway. There was a local tale to the effect that when the roof partly collapsed, the demons who lived there had entreated the exorcist of those days to do something to prevent their home falling in; they in turn would obey him and his descendants for all time. And this was why the exorcist had built the brick column.

Opposite the cave entrance is an alcove in the wall, where anyone who wishes to gain power over the spirits should sit and recite spells and invocations for forty days.

To the west of the hill is a garden with a pond and trees where the devs and paris were said to gather for nightly relaxation and revelry. People would hear the sound of poetry being recited and music coming from there at night. A whole range of tales arose in connection with that cave: if anyone disturbed the paris there at night they would beat him to death, or at least until his mouth was left permanently crooked. Some nights the devs would howl so horribly that anyone within earshot would fall in a faint.

One of the weird creatures that had taken up residence in that cave was the guardian dragon. A sorcerer of old is said to have hidden a treasure hoard deep inside, protected by a spell, and by his magic arts to have summoned the dragon from beyond Mount Qof, at the end of the world, to stand guard over it. The noise of this dragon's breathing could be heard at night—and sometimes during the day—by anyone who cared to listen. Every so often the dragon would come out at night and go down to the Zarafshon to drink. Its mouth was so huge that it would lay its lower lip flat on the riverbed, raise its upper lip straight into the air like a drawbridge, and with a single gulp suck up all the water in the river. It would go on drinking like this for an hour or two then, having slaked its thirst, it would return to its lair. And woe betide anyone this dragon might happen to encounter on its way to or from the river, for it would swallow him whole. But it would not molest anyone who did not come near it; such was the contract it had made with the sorcerer.

Those who kept vigil for forty days in the alcove opposite the cave with the intention of gaining magic powers could not withstand the devs and paris at night and would fall into a swoon; some of them became paralyzed or their mouths twisted and they eventually died. Those who saw their devotions through to the end and attained the rank of devband told how, while they were praying aloud, such a terrible demonic roaring and draconian snorting would issue from the cave that fainter hearts than theirs would have died of fright. But those who had studied at the feet of a true spiritual master, whose faith was firm and who sedulously completed their vigil, would gain complete mastery over demons and compel their absolute obedience. They also told how sometimes a sort of flame would appear near the cave, the work of the paris who wished to burn the would-be sorcerer. At such times, too, the watcher must conquer his fear and invoke the aid of his master, or else he would be destroyed before attaining his goal.

Although during the daytime any pilgrim or sightseer could come to the cemetery and pass close by the cave, nobody dared approach the vicinity by night.

The insane, the possessed and the generally sick would come from afar and sleep at the houses of the khojas of Soktaré. And since the present-day khojas were the descendants of the sorcerers of old, they cured their patients, presumably with the aid of the subjugated devs and paris in the cemetery of their ancestors. If the patient or his friends were at all skeptical, however, the cure was not effective.

Such were the popular beliefs attaching to the old cemetery, the cave, and the khojas of Soktaré.

iii

It was winter, the season of snow and rain. Ponds and streams froze over, tree branches shriveled and snapped off, the cattle and donkeys huddled in a corner of the stable or at the back of the barn, the cats crouched shivering under the *sandali* like mice that had seen a cat. At this time of year only the bull camel, of all four-footed creatures, roars and rampages around in rut, foaming at the mouth as if demented; and of all the birds, only the crow seems all the happier the more it snows, jumping and dancing about in the snow and deafening winter's frostbitten ears with his raucous cries.

During this three-month spell of cold weather, the villagers' days passed none too pleasantly. Their sandali braziers, filled with hot coals at daybreak, were reduced by mid-morning to a pile of wet ashes by reason of the dampness of the ground. Farming being impossible, the men's activities were confined to separating the cotton bolls from the pods, ginning it, and weaving, and those of the women to spinning thread and winding it onto spools.[4] The little boys, however, did not have such a bad time of it in winter. On sunny days they would go out into the fields under the wintry sun and romp about madly until they were exhausted, or have snowball fights on the frozen ponds and streams. Thus they quickly whiled away the short winter days, and when night came they fell asleep at once, oblivious until the next day's sunrise of any new happening or fresh snowfall. Doting mothers tucked them in and kept their sleeping forms warm until morning, so that they hadn't a care in the whole wintry world.

The grownups of all ages had no recourse to keep winter's blues at bay but to gather once a week in order to talk, sing songs, recite verses and tell stories and jokes. Such sessions took one of three forms. In the *gashtak*, each one of a group of people in turn would entertain the others in his house; in the *dangona*, a group would pool their money to pay for a weekly party; and in the *harifona*, a group would get together and cook up a communal rice dish. The younger ones preferred the *dangona*, while the middle-aged would more often arrange a *gashtak*. The *harifona* generally took place in teahouses, millhouses or stores.

iv

One winter's night, when the roofs of the village houses were covered with snow, some twenty young men of Soktaré gathered in the guestroom of one of their number for a dangona. The guestroom was well furnished by frugal village standards: straw had been strewn over the floor against the damp, and on top of this reed mats had been laid, and over all was spread good, thick Kazakh felt. Even the quilts were not as dirty as usual. At the far

---

[4] The women of the Bukhara villages continued to make most of their own clothing up until collectivization [early 1930s] -- A.

end of the room was a warm sandali, and just inside the door was a cast-iron brazier, nicely ablaze. Ranged round the brazier were six teapot-stands, each with a pot of hot green tea. Outside the guestroom was an open fire in an alcove, over which hung a large black kettle of boiling water to replenish the teapots. The fire was kept blazing with branches of apricot, apple, mulberry and other fruit trees that had been broken off and brought especially for the party. The sandali and the brazier inside were periodically fed with glowing coals from the fire.

From the sandali to the front of the room were ranged four large candles, locally made, each weighing about one pound. The candle flames, the blazing brazier, the sandali, the steaming teapots, the smoke of the water-pipe as the guests each took a puff and passed it round, all combined to make the guestroom as hot as a bathhouse. Indeed, it even looked like a bathhouse, with the steam and smoke curling up to the ceiling so as to completely obscure the beams and wattle. Were it not for two open windows set opposite one another in the north and south sides, just under the eaves, the guests would have fainted in such a suffocating atmosphere.

The table was spread generously with bread and raisins, candies and *pechak* (a sort of candy made in twisted strands), pistachios and almonds, dried apricots and rowanberries, soup, rice, melons and grapes. The host was one Niyoz-Gūppon, who was the *bobo*, the senior and acknowledged leader of the young men of Soktaré. Niyoz-Gūppon had attained this unofficial rank not by virtue of his years, but by dint of the fights and wagers he had won and a variety of other impressive exploits.

The soiree began with some solo singing, a recital by anyone with a good voice who knew an arrangement of a ghazal, interspersed with appreciative plaudits of "Bravo!" (*ofarin*) and "Long life!" (*namuri*; *zinda bosh*). When this ended, several voices took up a chorus of ruba'is, quatrains and folksongs; whenever the singers stopped for breath, the jokesters of the assembly would mimic them, extemporize comic verses, and interject various wisecracks.

Some time after midnight, one of the company went outside to relieve himself. Barely two seconds later he uttered a piercing shriek: "Help! Murder!" The rest of the company, thinking he had surprised a thief or other rogue, snatched up knives and sticks and rushed outside. They found their companion sprawled by a lean-to cattle shed on a pile of manure, with a large black bull that had broken out of the shed snuffling and snorting at his motion-less form.

They checked the path to the outer gate, the barn, the roofs, but found no trace of an intruder. There were no footprints on the freshly fallen snow to indicate that a thief had come and gone. Finally they picked up the unconscious man and carried him indoors. They doused him with cold water, and after a while he came to and opened his eyes.

"Who brought me here?" he asked the people bending over him.

"We did."

"Did you see it too?"

"See what?"

"The dev!"

"What dev? Where?" asked one of the company, a youth of sixteen or seventeen named Ahmad.

"When I came out of the guestroom and was heading for the shed," the patient explained, "A dev in the form of a black bull suddenly appeared and charged at me—I don't know whether it got me or not, I only remember that I yelled and then blacked out."

Ahmad couldn't help laughing at this. "Bravo, you big tough fellow!" he said. "A bull breaks out of the cowshed, you take it for a dev, and are scared out of your wits!"

The man made to protest that he really had seen a dev, but the others confirmed Ahmad's explanation. "Sure it was a bull, we saw it too—and after we carried you inside, Mukhtor led it back into the shed and tied it up."

The episode had in fact happened as follows. The man had been in a great hurry to get to the midden, and had lifted the hem of his shirt to undo his pants in readiness. The bull, which as the result of his master's absence at the dangona that night had not received his usual ration of fodder and was very hungry, mistook the man with his raised shirtfront for his master bringing him his evening hay. The man, who had heard tale after tale of devs and paris and jinn from his mother and grandmother, and firmly be-lieved that when a dev intended to attack someone it would invariably assume the form of a bull, took the real bull for a demon in disguise and nearly died of fright.

The youths all laughed at his misadventure and made great sport of him. One asked him how he would get home on his own that night, and another suggested he exchange his long knife and haversack for scissors and a spindle. A third yelled sarcastically, "Hurrah for such a brave fellow! If we had four more like you, our donkeys would bray in the streets of Khiyobon in Bukhara!"[5] Then one of the company, Shokir by name, spat out a stream of snuff-brown saliva and addressed the rest.[6] "You're all big tough men at someone else's expense—but you don't know a thing about devs and jinn. Now who knows if that really was the bull that had been in the shed, or a dev in the form of a bull?" Shokir spat a quid of snuff underneath the mat and went on, "It's often happened to me that a dev has taken on the form even of my own bull and tried to attack me."

"Tried to, nothing—the dev must really have taken possession of you," Ahmad interrupted, "or you wouldn't be raving like this."

Shokir glowered. "The dev tried to get me, but I was saved by the power of this bracelet"—he rolled up his sleeve and revealed a large bracelet—"that was given to me by Eshon Barakat-Khoja, rest his soul."

"Eshon Barakat-Khoja was a great exorcist," joined in Ashur. "My mother, God rest her, told me that when she was a child an evil spirit began to torment her, appearing in her dreams every night and frightening her. Barakat-Khoja, who was her neighbor, heard about this and performed an exorcism, reading the *Fotiha* over her. After that, the spirits left her alone and never frightened her again. My mother even drove out demons from others. The sick would come to our house, and Mother would tie an old rag round the end of a stick, light it, and wave it round above the patient's head while reciting in a loud voice: '*Alas-alas*, all

---

[5] This comment refers to the following piece of local lore: The inhabitants of the Bukhara city quarter known as Khiyobon [Garden Walk] were noted for breeding huge, fierce donkeys; other donkey-breeders who fancied themselves as tough guys would drive their animals in herds to the streets of this quarter to challenge the Khiyobon donkeys. If the challengers brayed louder, the Khiyobon donkeys would be intimidated and fall silent, and conversely if the Khiyobon donkeys brayed louder, the outsiders would be silenced and their owners considered defeated.—A.

[6] The "snuff" (Taj. *nos*, in Afghanistan *naswâr*) is a mildly narcotic mixture of tobacco, lime, powdered charcoal and linseed oil, which is placed under the tongue or between the cheek and gums; Aini habitually used it. (Becka, *Sadriddin Aini*, 98)

sickness cease, in the name of the Forty Saints, the Eleven Saints, the Seven Saints and Khizru-Ilyos!'[7] If the patient believed in her, he was cured."

"—And if he didn't believe, of course, he'd grow even sicker and eventually die!" Ahmad interjected scathingly. "All this nonsense comes of people's fear and cowardice. Nothing 'supernatural' can harm a person who isn't afraid."

"Devs and jinn are cunning fiends," Bobo Niyoz-Gūppon broke in. "If your enemy is human and challenges you openly, you can tackle him man to man, and may the best man win. But the evil demon is a treacherous scoundrel, an enemy who strikes from behind and fells you once and for all. Being tough is no use against devs and jinn. They're the only thing any of us here is afraid of."

V

Niyoz-Gūppon picked up the mouthpiece of the water-pipe, took a few puffs, and went on: "First I'll tell you what happened to me. You see, when we men of Ghijduvon had a fireworks contest with the men of Vobkand, I was the captain of the Ghijduvon team.[8] The firework I was holding hadn't been properly packed, and when I lit it the whole thing caught fire all the way down to the bottom and blew the plug out. My arm was badly burned up to the elbow, my clothes caught on fire, and if my teammates hadn't grabbed me immediately and thrown me into the Darveshobod

---

[7]*Alas-alas*, a contraction of Arabic *a-lastu bi-rabbikum* 'Am I not your lord?' (Koran 7:171), a phrase evocative of the Last Judgment, is a formula found in Persian mysticism and popular magic. Khizru-Ilyos (i.e., Khizr and Elias) is one form of the name of a widespread Eastern tutelary spirit, traditionally identified by Muslims (under the name Khizr) with Moses' unnamed guide in Koran 18:65, by Christians with St. Elias or St. George, and by Jews with the prophet Elijah; he has in his possession the Water of Life, and is often invoked for the guidance of travelers or of those psychically astray.

[8] For a description of fireworks being made, see Chapter 19. The autobiographical antecedent to this episode is not the fireworks contest witnessed by young Aini at the Darveshobod fair, but one he watched as an adult at Ghijduvon during the Ramadan night fair (see Chapter 19, third footnote).

pond, I'd have burned to death." Niyoz-Gūppon showed them the scars on his arm, and continued his tale.

"This was enough—a single firework's backfiring—for the men of Vobkand to start crowing that we had lost the game. We just packed it in without arguing, and left it till the next year to get even."

Niyoz-Gūppon took another puff at the water-pipe and resumed: "The following year, as it came time to go to Darveshobod, we ordered a huge firework-cylinder from Usto Ravshan the ironfounder. The mold for this was fashioned by Mullo Fayzi, one of the top craftsmen of his time. Mullo Fayzi prepared the powder, too: he put copper and iron filings and God knows what other minerals in with the gunpowder, so that when we set it off this firework blazed like a rainbow and shot sky-high a pillar of flame that looked as if convolvulus and morning glories were twining up it and bursting into bloom, while all around it flared a real peacock's tail of colors. . ."

Perhaps the smoke he had been puffing constantly had not brought Niyoz-Gūppon to the same pitch of euphoria as the adventure he was reliving, for in mid-narrative he reached out and took a handful of snuff from Shokir's snuffbox, sucked it up between teeth and cheeks and went on: "This firework was so big, one man—nay, two men!—couldn't hold it at arm's length. So we set it up on an elm plank seven foot long by three foot wide. . ."

Probably as a result of his non-stop talking, Niyoz-Gūppon's snuff dissolved in his mouth sooner than he expected and stopped him in mid-sentence. He spat his quid against the wall and resumed: "The day of the festivities arrived, and the night of the contest. Four fireworks experts, including me, picked up the platform by its four corners and stood on the space that had been cleared for us. Rockets and hand-held fireworks kept going off all around. When the display was at its liveliest and the competition at its fiercest, we set off our custom-made giant. Sprays and starbursts shot skyward, and shouts of amazement went up from friend and foe alike. The men of Vobkand stared openmouthed; we four yelled and roared like fighting camels lunging and foaming at the mouth in the arena, and all the time the firework was flaring we pranced round and round carrying the plank, like horses harnessed to a mill wheel. . ."

Niyoz-Gūppon, who in the course of recounting his adventure seemed to be setting off the "Ghijduvon Special" all over again,

wiped away the snuff-stained spittle from his mouth and moustache and continued in a more subdued tone. "Alas, when the
powder was still only half-consumed, the firework exploded and
blew up the platform in all directions—eight people were killed,
including the three who had been carrying the firework with me. I
escaped with only a broken arm."

"Were many spectators hurt?" asked Ahmad anxiously.

"Of course they were," Niyoz-Gūppon rejoined. "Lots of
people were injured by flying debris from the firework and the
plank, everyone was running off in a panic in all directions and
many were trampled underfoot—luckily, just then Qalandar
Zarangarigi and Hamro Gavboz, who were at that time hiding in
the hills, suddenly showed up out of nowhere, carried the injured
out of harm's way and took the children and old people out of
the melee into the shelter of a barn."[9]

"How was it that the Qalandar and Hamro-Gavboz were in
hiding?" Ahmad asked.

Niyoz-Gūppon exchanged his hitherto subdued accents for a
more heroic tone: "The Qalandar and Hamro-Gavboz are real
men, they're not afraid of anyone!" The reason they were fugitives turned out to be as follows. One day fifteen or twenty of the
amlokdor's men rode out to assess the tax due on a peasant's
wheat harvest. They took off their horses' bridles and bits and, on
the pretext of surveying the size of the crop, waded out into the
wheat field and fed their horses on the ripe golden grain—and of
course a good deal of the wheat was also trampled flat under their
hooves. The peasant cried out: "Tyrants! If you feed my crop to
your horses and trample it into the ground, how do you expect me
to produce taxes on it?"

The amlokdor's men took exception to the peasant's outburst,
and one of them hit him over the head with his riding whip. The
peasant began weeping and wailing. At this juncture, Hamro-
Gavboz and the Qalandar, who happened to be passing, arrived on
the scene and took the peasant's part, cursing at the amlokdor's
servants. The latter then laid into them with their riding whips; but
they found they had a couple of lions by the tail. Grabbing the
peasant's cattle-goad and hoe, the infuriated newcomers counter-
attacked the amlokdor's men and split open the head of one. The

---

[9] A *qalandar* is a wandering dervish. Hamro-Gavboz appears frequently in
Aini's *Jallodoni Bukhoro* (Butchers of Bukhara).

amlokdor's men took to their heels and reported to their master, who sent an armed party to arrest the Qalandar and Hamro-Gavboz. But these two had already gone into hiding. And even two years later, they dared not show themselves in public. On the night of the fireworks they had come secretly to watch, and thereby saved a great many lives. When the authorities learned that they had showed up, they set the wheels in motion to capture them, and the fugitives went underground again.

"That's demons and ghosts for you," said Ahmad, archly. Then he asked, "Didn't the authorities say anything to the ones who had caused so many deaths and injuries?"

"No," said Niyoz-Gūppon. "That same night, we famous pyrotechnicians went into hiding. Jaloliddin the *amin* stepped in and collected three thousand tangas from all those who had been involved in the fireworks display, kept some of it for himself, and distributed the rest among the four district governors of Ghijduvon, to turn a blind eye to our part in the affair. Still, the governors for appearance's sake arrested and expelled eight poor devils who'd never held a firework in their lives. We were safe to ply our skills as usual."

Ahmad asked: "Is your arm still up to holding a firework?"

"Not my right arm, though I can still handle any kind of firework with my left. But. . ."

"But what?"

"Even though my right arm was crippled, I can still do anything with my left—but something else happened to scare me off. In fact, I was about to tell you about it, but somehow I got going with the fireworks story. . ."

"Go on, tell us, tell us about it!" The youths all around him hung eagerly on the older man's words. Taking a puff of his freshly filled water pipe, he resumed the tale of his adventures.

"Once I stayed late at Ghishti bazaar and left after sundown. By the time I reached the cemetery two hours later it was pitch dark. There was no moon, and black clouds covered the stars. Thinking of devs and paris, I couldn't tear my eyes away from the cemetery. All at once I saw flames flickering in one corner of it. And I, who wasn't afraid of those fireworks contests, felt a bit jittery at the sight of this fire. . ."

"What was the fire?" Ashur interrupted him tensely.

"Evil spirits," replied Gūppon. "If it weren't for the bracelet on my arm, those jinn would have burned me up. And even

though I was protected by the power of the bracelet, ever since that day I've been afraid of all fire, since I can't help connecting it with evil spirits. I don't know if I'll be able to compete in this year's fireworks contest. So you see, it isn't fair to blame poor Rūzimurod for fainting. There's good reason to fear demons, fairy folk and evil spirits."

"Bobo," said Ahmad, "don't think I'm boasting—but I'm not afraid of spirits and suchlike!"

"Don't put on airs, junior!" said Shokir. "You haven't been bitten yet. You can talk that way in front of a score of your friends—but go alone one night to the cemetery and you'll find you've bitten off more than you can chew. You play the skeptic there, and the spirits'll knock you off before you can yelp!"

Ahmad bristled, and retorted hotly: "Big brother Shokir, what makes you so tough and bold? I'll not be cut down to size by a lanky beanstalk like you!" He paused for a moment, then looked at Shokir again. "Bet you I can go right now to the cemetery!"

"Bet you can't," scoffed Shokir, and the others chorused, "Bet you can't! Bet you daren't!"

"Ahmad, my lad, don't be hasty," cautioned Bobo Niyoz-Gūppon. "Don't get all riled up at someone who's a size taller—and a mite wiser—than you. The man who isn't afraid of evil spirits hasn't been born. You haven't seen a dev yet."

"Whether I have or I haven't is my business," said Ahmad. "The bet stands, just as I said."

"All right, what are the conditions?" asked Shokir in the same scornful tone.

"You're the older, you set them," said Ahmad.

"Ahmad, don't be childish!" said Bobo Niyoz-Gūppon, still trying to chivvy some sense into him.

"Who's being childish?" Ahmad replied, even more hotly; and, pointing his finger at Shokir, added: "Better to be cut down in my prime than end up as lanky as that!"

"No need to fight, just fix the bet," said Rūzimurod.

"It's Ahmad's bet," said Shokir.

"It's your bet, or for all of you," said Ahmad.

"If it's for all of us, then I'll make it," said Rūzimurod, and in solemn tones announced the conditions: "If you go to the cemetery and return safe and sound, we undertake to feed and entertain you for free at every future dangona, harifona or gashtak, as long as you live; if you are killed, God have mercy on you; and if you turn back, you must give a feast for all of us."

All clamored their consent. "What do you say, Ahmad?" asked Bobo Niyoz-Gūppon, turning to the youth.

"Whatever you decide, friends, I accept."

Ahmad and Bobo Niyoz-Gūppon shook hands solemnly, as if concluding a business deal, and Bobo gave Ahmad his knife, saying: "Walk around the cemetery from east to west and you'll reach an alcove in the wall opposite the cave. Carve a mark in the alcove with this knife. Then go through the courtyard and out the far gate, where you'll find yourself in a wooded area. Cut a sprig from a bush, leave the knife under that bush, and come back with the sprig. All right?"

"All right," said Ahmad. "But I'm taking my dog along with me."

"What for?"

"There are jackals in the cemetery; without a dog they might attack me."

"How come someone who isn't afraid of evil spirits is scared of jackals?" Shokir asked scornfully.

"It makes sense to be scared of jackals," said Ahmad. "If a pack of jackals attacks an unarmed man they're certain to win. But to be scared of ghosts is for women."

"Watch your mouth!" said Shokir hotly.

"Cut it out, you two," Bobo interposed. "Least said, soonest mended. We'll soon know the men from the women, and the lions from the foxes."

Ahmd stood up and went out, taking Bobo's knife with him. Outside his own house, which was next door, he called, "Khaibar! Khaibar!" and, joined by his dog, set off toward the cemetery.

* * *

One of the company gave Ahmad up for lost. "Such a pity that a lad not yet in his prime should throw his life away for a silly prank!"

Another demurred. "To blazes with him, it's his own funeral. Nobody forced him to go shooting his mouth off. What can you do with an ill-mannered kid like that? Sooner or later he was bound to come to a bad end."

A third said, "Think about tomorrow—if anything happens, what can we say to Ahmad's family? It's Bobo's fault for not looking after him. If Ahmad was being childish, Bobo should have talked some sense into him."

"Why me?" Bobo protested. "I argued with him more than once, but he wouldn't listen. No use banging your head against a brick wall—let him learn the hard way, I say."

Ahmad must have been dreaming, to think of going to the cementery at this time of night," said Rūzimurod incredulously. "He'll be back before he's halfway there, no question about it, you'll see."

"He won't dare show his face here," proclaimed Shokir with a self-satisfied air. "He went off in a huff, without thinking what he was saying. Sooner than come back, he'll sneak straight off home to bed—the first we'll see of him will be at the feast he'll give for us."

"What feast?" Ashur asked Shokir. "He doesn't have any money to throw a dinner for all of us—he'll be up by first light tomorrow and on his way to Bukhara, and never come back to the village!"

*   *   *

The discussion was still going on when Ahmad came in. There were no signs of fear in his face or demeanor. In his hand was a sprig of foliage, which he swung nonchalantly as if it were a spray of basil he had just plucked in the garden.

"What did you do?" asked Bobo.

"Everything that was agreed," replied Ahmad, laying the sprig of greenery in front of Bobo.

"What about the knife?"

"I placed it at the foot of the bush I cut this sprig from."

"Bravo! I take my hat off to you," said Bobo resignedly.

"We don't know for sure yet," said Shokir skeptically. "How do we know whether this sprig was cut at the cemetery, or from his own private plot, where there's also an overgrown ruin?"

"Ahmad doesn't lie," said Bobo. "Anyway, we'll find out for sure tomorrow."

"Well, was there a fairy banquet going on?" Rūzimurod asked shyly.

"Huh!" Ahmad answered. "If you call the howling of jackals a fairy banquet, then it was quite a celebration. Unfortunately, as soon as Khaibar barked they shut up; the 'spirits' fled, and I didn't get a chance to join their revels."

"You mean the demons in the cave stopped roaring and the dragon stopped snorting when your dog barked?" Rūzimurod scoffed.

"No," said Ahmad with a smile. "It was windy, and I suppose the demons and the dragon didn't hear my dog bark because of the wind, since they didn't stop roaring and snorting. . ." Ahmad was silent for a moment, then continued in serious tones: "You're right, people, every time there's a wind, noises come from inside the cave. You think the noises are devs roaring and dragons snorting. Now how on earth can a huge dragon, which can drink the River Zarafshon dry with one gulp,fit inside a cave so narrow that it wouldn't even admit a donkey without paniers? Be reasonable! Without reason, the head is nothing but a hollow gourd, the mouth is a useless jug, and the eyes are empty glasses!"

All the village bravos were now defeated, and so were obliged to swallow Ahmad's sarcasm with a good grace. Only Shokir was still skeptical, but thought it best to keep his counsel until daylight revealed the truth of the matter.

The sun rose, and it became abundantly clear to all that Ahmad had fulfilled all the conditions of the bet. But they still could not believe that he had done it unaided by other than his own personal resources of courage. Instead, they maintained that he had learned magic arts, and from that day forth they took to calling him "Ahmad the Exorcist"

vi

There was lively speculation as to whether Ahmad had really acquired power over the devs and paris at such a tender age, or whether he had a powerful talisman that kept him safe from all harm, or if there was some other secret he was keeping from his friends.

The answer actually lay in Ahmad's upbringing and the events of his earlier childhood. He was born and brought up in a family of Soktaré khojas, and had been fed with legends of devs and paris, the tale of the dragon in the cave, and the dangers of the cemetery, no less than anyone else. As a result, by the age of eight or nine, Ahmad was thoroughly scared, so that his heart leapt into his mouth whenever he saw the seasonal dust devils, which he thought were real devils on the move. The old women especially used to spice all the tales they told to children like Ahmad with incidents involving demons and evil spirits.[10]

This sort of entertainment had a very bad effect on Ahmad. He believed that under the earth, in the air, beneath various fruit trees—especially the towan tree—on piles of ash and manure, lived countless malignant little folk and evil spirits. Accordingly he was unable to go out alone to relieve himself after supper; if he had to go out in the dark, his mother had to go with him. His father, however, was unaware of this. Once he had heard Ahmad say that he was scared to go out alone, and had severely scolded him, and his mother too, for bringing the boy up to be a coward. As a result neither Ahmad nor his mother dared breathe a word to the head of the house about being afraid of demons and spirits.

*   *   *

One night Ahmad's mother was not at home. It was summer, when people generally slept out on the roof. Ahmad's father had just watered the half-acre or so of wheat he had planted at the back of the house, counting on the wind to blow the chaff and debris to one side of the plot. But before the water had spread evenly, the wind dropped and left the debris floating among the wheat. Ahmad's father was a meticulous man, and was not about to let his crop be ruined for lack of a breeze. So he cut himself a leafy elm branch, waded into the freshly-watered plot and swished the water so that the chaff piled up at one end.

While his father was busy doing this, Ahmad was left alone on the *sufa*. He was very frightened, but was even more afraid of admitting his fear of being alone to his father. The evening passed and it began to grow dark. Then Ahmad started to imagine the devs and paris and evil spirits all around him. Ahmad closed his eyes, praying that he wouldn't see anything. A moment later his heart skipped a beat, as the fancies became even more real: something seemed to be trying to clamber onto the back of his neck to strangle him.

Ahmad was forced to open his eyes. At the far end of the sufa he saw a host of little animals such as foals, lambs, puppies, kids,

---

[10] A reference to Sulton-posho and Tūti-posho: see Chapters 6-8.

and the like. The foals had little red donkey saddles and red blankets on their backs, and red silk ribbons with little bells tied around their necks; and the other animals were likewise wearing silk ribbons round their necks and ankles with bells that tinkled with their every movement. These little creatures were frolicking together, jumping up on one another, nibbling one another's neck, now and then tussling over some morsel they had rooted out from among the garden rubbish.

Ahmad wanted to tell his father, but stayed silent for fear of the scolding he knew he would get. He was so scared he couldn't move. He trembled from head to foot as if with a fever, and teeth chattered so fast that it sounded like a virtuoso performance on the *rubob*. He could not tear his eyes away from these strange animals. Suddenly he saw them all line up and advance toward him. Terrified, he rose to flee for his life, but his feet were rooted to the spot. "Daddy!" he screamed, and collapsed.

Ahmad's father responded quickly. "Don't be afraid! I'm coming!" he called in surprise. At the sound of his father's voice Ahmad plucked up courage and opened his eyes—to see that the animals were all running away, some of them jumping onto the roof, some into the mulberry bush at the far end of the sufa, others along the pathway to the outer gate. In a twinkling, all had disappeared.

Ahmad's father reached him and took him in his arms, comforted him and asked what the matter was. Weeping and sobbing convulsively, Ahmad told him in detail everything he had seen.

"You're right, the things you saw were jinn," his father told him. "But there's something else you didn't know, and that's why you were afraid of them." Once the boy had calmed down, his father sat him in front of him and began as follows.

"Listen to this. My father once went on a journey to the shrine at Nurato, riding a very fine horse. As he was about to go up Ghazghon Mountain, he noticed that the horse's crupper looked bowed. Now my father thought to himself, 'This isn't the sort of horse to let a single rider strain his back, let alone his crupper—there's more here than meets the eye.' So he made a quick grab behind him, just above the horse's crupper—and felt in his fist a handful of long hair. At once he twisted this around his wrist and held on tight. 'Show yourself, I conjure you, or I shall slay you!' he commanded, just like a sorcerer.

The owner of the hair manifested himself, and my father saw that it was the king of the jinn, who holds court at our cemetery.

My father stormed at him: "How dare you take advantage of me like this! Did you not know that I am a conjuror of demons?" The king of the jinn apologized profusely and humbly promised never to do it again. 'When you set out on pilgrimage to Nurato,' he explained, 'I decided to accompany you, so that by your grace my pilgrimage would be acceptable. As far as here, I ran alongside your stirrup, and to all the lesser jinn we encountered on the way I proclaimed what a great man you were. But here I forgot myself and mounted your horse for a lark; forgive me this discourtesy!'

'For such impertinence, you deserve to die,' my father told him. 'But if you swear an oath never to harm my children and children's children, and not to let other jinn and paris harm them, I'll forgive you and let you go.' The king of the jinn swore not to harm my father, his children, or his children's children, nor to let other jinn harm them, till kingdom come.

"And that's the reason," said Ahmad's father, "why demons, jinn and paris cannot harm anyone of our family. Since you didn't know about this, you were afraid, and they showed themselves to you; don't be afraid from now on, and they won't even show themselves."

After this, Ahmad was no longer afraid, and nothing supernatural appeared to him. He would go out alone at night, and deliberately seek out those places the old women said were inhabited by jinn. He was hoping, in fact, to see one of the spirit people again, to catch him and remind him of the covenant that his grandfather had concluded, and to give him a sound thrashing in revenge for the many years of torment he had suffered through his fear of the jinn. But he never saw any again.

vii

When Ahmad was twelve, he could read and write fluently. He loved to read the works of the classical poets, and one day in the divan of Sa'di he came upon the verse:

> Devs have no dealings with men, fear them not
> —Fear rather devilish men![11]

---

[11] In Chapter 9 of *Reminiscences*, this verse is quoted to young Aini by his father. The appeal to Sa'di (q.v., Glossary) is particularly appropriate in

Ahmad pondered the meaning of this verse, and came to the conclusion that devs, far from concluding non-aggression pacts, were incapable of harming people anyway. As soon as he got the chance, he read this verse out to his father and asked him what it meant. His father replied: "My dear son! Your mother and the other women had scared you out of your wits with their fantasies of demons and fairies. I realized that if I simply told you not to be afraid, it wouldn't work. So I decided to apply a hair of the dog that bit you, and I made up a fairy tale to drive out once and for all the fear that had been instilled in you for so many years. Since they had made you ill with their lies, I cured you with another lie. That tale of my father's pilgrimage to Nurato and the oath sworn by the king of the jinn—it was all a lie, that I made up for the best. Sa'di is quite right, men are more powerful than anything—devs, paris, jinn, none of them can harm a human being. All the harm that people imagine is done to them by evil spirits is nothing more than the product of their own silly brains that have been addled with listening to foolish stories. The imagination is a powerful creative force, and for these people all sorts of things real and nonexistent are dubbed 'demons'; they paralyze themselves with fear, give themselves spasms, even die of heart attacks brought on by their fantasies. Rest assured, son, that demons and fairies cannot harm humans. The only thing that harms them is their own fear."

Ahmad's father was silent for a moment, while he gauged the effect his words had produced. The he went on to explain the second part of the verse: "By 'fear rather devilish men' Sa'di doesn't intend you to be scared of them and run away, or to meekly accept anything they do and say. No, he means you should beware of evil men and try to oppose their evildoing. As Sa'di himself amply clarifies in the very next verse: 'Requite evil with evil, good with good; with roses, be a rose; 'midst thorns, a thorn.'"

Ahmad's father believed in the existence of jinn and paris. The only difference between him and his contemporaries was his conviction that such beings could not harm humans. He was determined to educate his son likewise, and accordingly amplified

---

view of Ahmad's father's salutary tall tale, since Sa'di is famous as the proponent of the white lie ("A well-intentioned falsehood is better than a mischief-making truth," *Golestân* Book 1, Story No. 1).

his explanation: "Sometimes at night, in places like cemeteries, people see flickering lights like flames. And that's all there is to the jinn. What could a single dying flame possibly produce that could send a man mad or kill him? The embers in our own hearth are more powerful!"

This is how Ahmad's father brought him up; and so it was that he was able to play the hero and win the bet by going alone at dead of night to the cemetery, a thing that bold Bobo Niyoz-Gūppon for all his reputation was unable to do.

viii

Ahmad continued with his studies. For some twenty-five years he lived at the madrasas of Bukhara, studying and teaching. Of all the mullahs and theology students, he was the only one who was not afraid of paris and jinn.

One summer night in Bukhara, Ahmad was sitting with a few fellow students by the rosebed of the Badalbek madrasa. One of them went out to ease himself. A few seconds later, a scream was heard from the vicinity of the outhouse. Ahmad and the others whirled round and set off at a run in the direction of the cry. They found the student lying on the ground, foam visible on his lips. When they had calmed him down, they elicited the explanation that he had seen a jinni.

Ahmad laughed and asked, "Where is it?"

The student pointed to the foot of a wall and replied, "I saw it there, in the form of a flame."

They all looked where he was pointing, and indeed there was a flame flickering there. Everyone started in alarm; but Ahmad walked casually up to it and scuffed earth over it. The flame vanished. Everyone acclaimed Ahmad as a devband.

This episode occurred in Ahmad's early student days. Up until then, like his father, he believed in the existence of fairy folk, while maintaining that they could not harm humans. The proof of the existence of such creatures was precisely the appearance of these strange lights at night.

A few years after this incident, Bukhara was on the brink of an intellectual revolution. Newspapers, periodicas and scientific-technical works of all kinds began to pour in from all over the civilized world. One of the readers of this new literature was Ahmad the Exorcist.

In one of these scientific books, Ahmad read that one of the components of bone is a chemical substance called phosphorus, which at night—especially in warm weather—can appear like a flickering light. This "phosphorescence" can occur whenever bones decompose. The lights that appear at night in graveyards, old mosques, dunghills and the like are a result of this, since such places are full of rotting bones. Ahmad had read in history books that the Badalbek madrasa was built on the site of a former cemetery; he realized that the Will o' the wisp that had scared all his colleagues was nothing more than phosphorescence.

Once he had learned this from his reading, Ahmad was convinced that there were no such things as devs, paris and jinn. All the supernatural beings that people feared were either pure figments of the imagination or things that could be explained by physicists and chemists.[12]

Even though he never completed a regular technical education, Ahmad became through his own experience and studies a leading educator. He never let slip an opportunity to warn parents and teachers not to bring up their children on a diet of demons, fairies, evil spirits and similar superstitious fancies, or they would jeopardize their future health and happiness.

---

[12] The effects of Aini's precepts were still evident in Tajik educational policy and practice until shortly before perestroika. In an article titled "Atheistic Education of the Young" in the newspaper *Tojikistoni soveti* (28 July 1983, p. 3) a Ministry of Education official uses the examples of dust devils (cf. section vi above) and phosphorescence as suitable topics for scientific debunking of superstition, keyed to atheistic indoctrination in secondary schools.

Appendix I

The Village School

Figure 10. Mosque in Soktaré, which housed the *maktab*
attended by young Sadriddin

FOREWORD

Written in Samarkand in October 1934, *Maktabi kūhna* was first published in 1935 in book form. It was reprinted several times and included in the syllabus of high schools in Tajikistan. A Russian translation in 1935 appeared in an Aini anthology, *Iz proshlogo* (From the Past), and was used in the Russian high school syllabus; there is an abridged English translation of this by Margaret Wettlin, "Memoirs of the Past," in *Soviet Literature*, 1967, No. 9, pp. 5-20. Aini himself produced an Uzbek version which was published in 1938, and the work has been further translated into at least eleven languages of the former Soviet Union and into Czech, Polish, and Chinese. The present translation was made from the anthology *Aknun navbati qalamast* (Dushanbe, 1978), Vol. 2, pp. 107-144.

Maktabi kūhna is literally "the old(-fashioned) school," and is intended as a contrast with the modern type of school introduced by the Jadids, adherents of the *usuli jadid* (Tajik *usuli nav*), the "New Method" of education as espoused by Aini and other enlightened Tajiks and Uzbeks of Bukhara in the early years of this century. Like *Ahmadi devband* (1928), it is a novella-length thematic compilation of autobiographical materials that were later to form part of *Yoddoshtho*. In contrast with that earlier work, its episodes are all taken from the same period of Aini's childhood (age six to eleven) and form a consecutive narrative rather than a mosaic of discrete anecdotes. However, *Maktabi kūhna* is less polished in style, and occasional lapses in continuity (cf. note 4) point to a lack of revision. In the corresponding chapters in the first volume of Aini's reminiscences (15-16), he purposely omits the episodes recounted in *Maktabi kūhna* (see Chapter 15, first paragraph); as a result, the two works are fully complementary, whereas the relationship of *Ahmadi devband* to chapter 9 is more that of a finished painting to a pencil sketch.

Aini's main purpose is to furnish eyewitness documentation of the stagnant state of the nineteenth-century *maktab*, as he was to do for the madrasa in the later volumes of his Reminiscences (see Bečka, "Traditional Schools," respectively I and II; Medlin, p. 29ff.). To this end he illustrates clinically—with his boyhood self as guinea pig—the crippling combination of a cramped, dark, chaotic schoolroom, irrelevant subjects, ineffectual teaching techniques, and ignorant, selfish teachers that he, as a bearer of the "New Method," was pledged to thwart.

We are reminded of Thomas Hughes' *Tom Brown's School-days* (1856), a quasi-autobiographical description of an English boy's progress through a public school, Rugby, during the "enlightened" headship of Dr. Arnold and his muscular brand of Christianity. The dominance of ideology and tradition over practical pedagogy, the caning and hazing and bullying and snobbery, the numbing inculcation of "grammar"—not of the vernacular, but of Latin or Arabic—were intuitively resented by both Tom and Sadriddin; yet the experience did indeed make men of them, if not entirely for the reasons cited or in ways anticipated by their mentors. Hughes joined the Christian Socialists' movement and helped to found the Working Men's College, of which he became the principal. Aini went on to found the first Tajik Jadid school in Bukhara and the first Soviet school in Samarkand. The principal textbooks he wrote were both intended for primary schools: *Tahzib us-sibyon* (Education of Boys) in 1909, revised and expanded in 1917, and—perhaps in tribute to the girls' school where he learned more than he had from the boys'—*Qizbola yoki Kholida* (The Little Girl, or Kholida) in 1922, the first Uzbek reader for girls. As he proudly asserts in the closing lines of *Ahmad the Exorcist*, Aini became and remained a leading educator, in theory and practice.

i

I must have been six years old when my father took me to the
school next to the village mosque. My mother told me, "You were
four years, four months, four weeks, and four days old when we
first took you to school, following the normal custom, with a plate
of cookies wrapped in a napkin as a gift for the teacher. You were
very young then, and my heart ached at the thought of you
suffering there, so we decided to allow you to stay home for a
couple of years and play instead. Now work hard, and try to catch
up with your classmates, who started school when they were four
years old."

My mother's parting injunction made a strong impression on
me. I determined to heed it and catch up with my classmates as
soon as I could, and even surpass them.

The school building was not so spacious as our house, which
had two doors on each side,[1] nor was it as well-lighted and
peaceful. The school consisted of one narrow room, with a single
door that was kept closed during cold weather, and a small
window, about two feet high by one foot wide. This our teacher
had covered with a sheet of paper, rubbed with linseed oil so that it
would not tear in the rain and snow. This paper had picked up the
dirt and dust from the street, and looked like a dirty black *damgir*.
If my memory serves me right, that paper was the same color as
the teacher's wrinkled face. No real light entered the room
through this window. Two small skylights were set into the walls
below the roof, but the light that entered through these fell on the
upper walls, rather than on the floor, of the schoolroom.

The floor of this room, measuring about ten feet square, was
divided by four beams laid crosswise into nine sections, or low
stalls. The teacher sat in one corner section at the front of the
room, to one side of the doorway, where the window was; the stall
immediately in front of the door served as a shoerack; and the
children squatted in the other stalls.

I don't remember how many students were in the school then,
but this much I recall: all the boys between the ages of four and

---

[1] A house with two doors in the southern wall and two in the northern is
called *dubahra*, "dual-purpose," i.e. suited for both summer and winter
residence. — A. (Cf. the description of the two buildings facing the inner
yard of Aini's house in Soktaré in Chapter 1.)

twelve from our village, which was said to have a population of about three hundred families, were there. In addition, since our village was one of *khojas*, esteemed for their special piety and learning, some of the more conscientious Muslims in the neighboring villages sent their boys to our school instead of their own. I distinctly remember that the school resembled our small chicken coop at home. The only difference was that the chickens in our coop usually clucked contentedly, whereas the children in the schoolhouse made an ear-splitting din.

I entered the school together with my father, who carried a plate of cookies and raisins wrapped in a napkin, as the traditional "sweetener." The teacher opened the napkin, broke one of the cookies, ate a piece, and offered some to my father, who also ate. Then, the teacher broke up another cookie into tiny bits, as though to feed chickens, and scattered them all around the schoolroom and over the boys. All the boys immediately started fighting, tearing at each other's clothes, pulling ears, scratching, and poking eyes—all this accompanied by a shrieking, yelling, weeping, and wailing loud enough to raise the roof; and all for the crumbs that the teacher tossed to them from my "sweetener."

The teacher did not sit idly by during this uproar. Several canes of various lengths rested against the wall behind him; one of these, a good nine feet long, stood in the far corner. This he seized and began beating the boys over the head. The boys, without retaliating, stopped their fighting, and started crying and shouting to high heaven: "Please, sir, we won't do it again!"

I could stand it no longer, and began wailing along with the others. My father tried to comfort me, promising that if I stopped crying and stayed at the school he would give me a baby donkey. The teacher joined in, "And I'll bring you a lump of sugar candy every bazaar day."

My father's promise could not persuade me to stay in that place, which appeared to have been built specifically as a children's torture chamber, but the teacher's promise of candy, in spite of his cruel treatment of my classmates, convinced me that he would not hit me. But I still could not tear my eyes away from those canes, particularly the long one that reached from one end of the room to the other and from which no boy could escape, no matter how he might huddle in the farthest corner of the schoolroom . . .

The boys quieted down a bit. The teacher picked up a wooden board, wrote a lot of things on it, and showed it to my father. But my father, who was literate, objected to something or other. At first, the teacher protested heatedly, but my father held his ground. Finally the teacher capitulated and handed the board to my father, saying, "Set the price yourself." My father took out a small knife from his pocket, scratched out some of what the teacher had written, and carved his own version.

From that day forth my father was a very great man in my eyes; I considered him even wiser and more powerful than the teacher, whom I had thought of as the wisest and most powerful man in the village. I took heart and thought that if the teacher hit me I could complain to my father, who would come and beat the teacher. The teacher had a cane, but my father had a goad that not even the strongest ox could resist. The teacher, who was a small, thin-faced, withered man, would surely die from a beating with my father's ox-goad.

The teacher made me kneel in front of him, placed a writing board for me on the edge of the dividing beam, and told me to say *auzu billoh* and *bismilloh*. It had been a long time since my father had taught me this, but I managed to repeat it without getting tongue—tied. The teacher was very pleased, The other boys appeared to be watching me with envy, but they did not raise their heads, because they were afraid of the teacher's cane. Instead, they looked out of the corner of their eyes and, with their hands in front of their faces, pointed at me with sidelong looks at each other. I was afraid that if they got me alone they would poke my eyes out with those same fingers.

The teacher recited the *Fotiha* and the boys said "amen," and in this way my induction into school was completed. My father went home, leaving me there in the chaotic schoolroom.

ii

After my father left, the teacher gave me a place close to him and assigned one of the older boys to teach me. The boy told me to look at the board and said, "*Alif, be, te, se.*" I repeated the names of these four letters, and when I was able to say them myself the boy went to teach other boys. He was the monitor, whom the other boys called *Khalifa*.

Then the teacher left the room. Now, pure bedlam broke out. First the boys got up and began wrestling with each other, the stronger boys throwing down and beating the weaker ones. After half an hour of this fighting, Khalifa got up from his place, took the teacher's long cane, and started hitting them all. I was scared and wanted to run away, but could not: the door to the school was barred on the inside with a wooden beam that a six-year-old like myself could not have budged. Khalifa's threat, "Sit in your place or I'll hit you," forced me to my seat, where I kept my head down and peered at him furtively.

After Khalifa had beaten all the boys back to their seats, he stood up, still clutching the cane, and said, "All right, kids! It's time for bows and arrows!"

All the boys started shouting, "Bows and arrows, bows and arrows!" and once again there was a great uproar. At the same time, the preparations for archery began. The boys pulled reeds out from under the mats upon which they sat, which constituted the school's only carpeting, and took sewing thread out of their pockets. They fashioned simple bows by attaching a piece of thread to both ends of a reed. Then each archer held his reed bow in his hand and, using another reed as an arrow, shot some other boy. Full-scale fighting broke out again, each boy aiming for another one's face, nose, forehead or eyes. After some minutes of this melee, Khalifa grabbed his cane again, and began beating the boys indiscriminately, shouting, "Come on, form ranks, we're going to have a battle!"

The boys joined in: "Form ranks! Form ranks!"

Khalifa divided the class into two groups, each containing both big and little boys, and placed them at opposite ends of the room. He formed two rows on each side, with the small boys at the rear and the big ones at the front.

In the middle of all this an arrow struck a boy in the eye, and with cries of "Oh, my eye!" he dropped out of the ranks. His teammates became incensed; they took their torn-up mats from under their feet and hurled them directly at the enemy. The other side did not take this lying down; they too pulled up their mats and threw them at their opponents. The school was full of fighting and reeds were strewn everywhere. I was afraid I would be crushed beneath the boys' feet, so I went over to the section where the teacher would have sat and stood flat against the wall. . .

The battle raged on. Suddenly, someone began pounding at the school door from the outside and then kicking it angrily. I thought the door was going to break. Hearing this, the boys scurried to their places and hid behind the beams of the stalls like little mice fleeing from an approaching cat. The beam was not high enough to hide them, so they covered their faces and put their heads down; their backs, however, remained conspicuously exposed.

The pounding at the door continued, but no one dared to open it. When the boys had finally settled into their stalls, Khalifa opened the door. The face of the person who entered the schoolroom was contorted with rage, his eyebrows and whiskers bristling like the fur of a cornered cat, and his eyes bulging almost out of their sockets. It was the teacher.

The teacher strode into the room, snatched the long cane that was still in Khalifa's hand when he came to open the door, and first beat Khalifa a dozen hefty whacks over the head. Khalifa, caught red-handed, looked like a dog that the gardener had found stealing grapes: he cried out and tried to dodge, but the long cane reached every corner of the room and cracked him repeatedly on the head.

When the teacher had sated his fury somewhat on Khalifa, he sat down. I was still cowering against the wall in his section, and he sent me back to my own place, but did not hit me. Then he raised his long cane again and began thrashing the boys, who were still crouching behind the beams with their heads down and backs sticking up. With each blow he hit fifteen or twenty boys, who all chorused, "We promise not to do it again!"

Then the teacher ordered: "Read!"

The boys began to rub their beaten backs and, without taking their eyes off the teacher, they turned their heads to their books and writing boards and began reading something very loudly. I imitated them and bent over my board, with one eye fixed on the teacher, and repeated loudly, "*alif, be, te, se.*"

Then the teacher summoned Khalifa, who stepped up before him without any apparent trepidation, despite his having just been thoroughly beaten. I was amazed at Khalifa's courage, and wished I could be as fearless. I daydreamed that if I were Khalifa and the teacher went for me with his cane, I would not try to escape, but rather I would take the cane and give the teacher a beating. What a pity I was then so small and timid!

The teacher asked Khalifa, "Tell me, which of these boys started all that commotion?"

Khalifa named ten or twelve boys, The boys stopped reading and listened so they could hear who Khalifa was naming. But the teacher put a stop to this, again taking up his long cane to remind the boys to keep on reading. After listening to the names of the accused, the teacher shouted, "Silence!"

The boys all held their breath.

The teacher called out the boys implicated by Khalifa. When the teacher called the wrong boy, Khalifa would correct him: "No, not that one, this one," and pointed out a different boy. When a dozen of the older boys were thus assembled in front of the teacher, he ordered Khalifa to lock the door. Khalifa did. "Get the *falloq*!" the teacher ordered.

I had heard of a *falloq* before, but I had never seen this terrible device. Khalifa walked behind the teacher and took down a stick that was hanging on the wall. This stick was about three and a half feet long and had a rope loosely tied to it at each end.

"Ahmad, are you still playing games?" the teacher asked one of the boys standing in the row of offenders before him.

"Please sir, I didn't mean it, I wasn't playing any games, it was Muhammad!" he cried out. But the teacher ignored the boy's whimpering and pleading, and looked at the boys standing on either side of him. "On the floor!" he said.

The other boys grabbed him and laid him flat on his back: then, without waiting for any further orders, they wrapped the *falloq* rope around his ankles. Two boys grabbed the ends of the *falloq* and began turning it. The rope tightened around the boy's ankles until it seemed as if his feet might be cut off, and he yelled, "Oh! I'm dying! Oh, my legs!"

The other boys stopped reading and in terror listened to the trembling in his voice. But the teacher plied his long cane and made them, too, cry out. They resumed their reading aloud. The teacher handed Khalifa a four-foot cane from the collection leaning against the wall and ordered, "Beat him!"

Khalifa started beating the soles of Ahmad's feet as the other boys held his legs twisted in the *falloq*. Ahmad's cries and screams became unbearable, but they were mingled with the noise of the boys reading out loud so that the two sounds were indistinguishable. Anyone passing by in the street would have assumed that the boys were simply reading very loudly . . .

Khalifa beat the soles of Ahmad's feet so hard that they started to bleed, and the cane was stained red. The teacher, perhaps seeing the bloody cane, ordered: "Enough!"

The beating stopped. The *falloq* was taken off, and Ahmad glared at Khalifa with hatred.

"Get Muhammad"' the teacher ordered. The boys laid Muhammad down in the same way, tied his legs in the *falloq*, and twisted it. Khalifa beat the soles of his feet until they, too, were bleeding. This continued until all the boys who had been called out had been beaten.

I felt sorry for these boys, because none of them was a ring-leader—it was Khalifa, who had then falsely denounced them into the bargain. I wanted to tell the teacher about this, but I was afraid of Khalifa. But my sympathy for the beaten boys and my outrage at Khalifa did not last long. The teacher turned to Khalifa and said, "I know that *you* are the chief instigator of horseplay like this." The teacher then looked at the boys still lined up before him who, unable to stand for long on both feet because of the pain, were hopping alternately from one foot to the other, and said, "On the floor with him!"

The boys, as if they had been waiting for this very command, threw Khalifa down, trapped his ankles in the *falloq*, and began twisting it tight. Khalifa cried out, "You're cutting of my legs, don't twist so hard!" But nobody paid any attention.

The teacher gave one of the boys a fresh cane and told him to start beating. He did. The boys holding the *falloq* twisted it still further, and Khalifa cried, "Go ahead and beat me as much as you want, but don't twist the *falloq* so hard!"

So the boys twisted it even harder.

After the boy with the cane had beaten Khalifa's feet a few more times, the teacher turned to another and said, "Now it's your turn. No need to wait till doomsday to pay him back!"

The next boy took the stick from the first boy and began beating the soles of Khalifa's feet even more savagely . . .

In this way, some of the boys who had been beaten on account of Khalifa got to pay him back with interest.

"Enough for now!" the teacher said. The beating stopped, but the *falloq*-holders did not release Khalifa's feet. The teacher asked them, "Well, aren't you satisfied yet?"

"Salt!" demanded one of the boys.

"Very well, salt it is," agreed the teacher. He searched through his purse, which was under the quilt, and then said, "I don't have any salt. Who does?"

The boys who had been beaten looked through their pockets, and one or two of them found some salt wrapped in cloth. "Sprinkle it on!" said the teacher. A generous amount of salt was sprinkled onto the cuts on Khalifa's feet, and then the boys rubbed it in with their hands. Khalifa began bellowing like a bull.

"Let him go!" the teacher ordered.

The boys untwisted the *falloq* and released his feet from the rope. Khalifa wiped his tear-filled eyes on his sleeve, limped over to his place, and sat down. The boys were now all "reading" aloud, or rather shouting in unison. The teacher picked up his long cane, whacked a few more heads, and shouted, "Silence!"

The boys quietened down, and the teacher resumed, "Tomorrow, each of you bring in eight *pul* for the mats you destroyed today."

The boys chorused, "Yes sir, we'll bring it!"

"Class dismissed!" said the teacher.

Like a flock of sparrows that have just escaped from an eagle, the boys leapt up from their places and ran to the door. The door was still locked. Khalifa slowly got up, limped over to the door, opened it, and went out first. The other boys crushed through behind him, pushing past one another as they left. I went out last.

All the boys crowded in front of the schoolhouse. Khalifa turned to them and said, "*Salom!*"

All the boys answered him in unison, "*Assalomu alaykum!*"

The boys headed off in different directions. Those who had been beaten, however, went with Khalifa into the back street behind the school, which led to my home. Khalifa announced to them, "Tomorrow we'll play marbles and have quail-fights. Come prepared!" The boys assented, then they too went home.

We were free from school for the day. In my life I have been truly liberated twice: once was in 1917 when I was forty-two years old and was rescued from the emir's prison after suffering seventy-five lashes,[2] and the other time was that day when I was six years old and was released from my first day at school. I have never been able to decide which of the two was more welcome.

---

[2] Aini and several other suspected liberals and Jadids were jailed and flogged in April 1917 after pressure from the provisional government in Tashkent forced the emir to proclaim reforms: see Bečka, *Sadriddin Aini*, p. 35. Aini gives his age as forty-two according to the Muslim lunar calendar; reckoning in solar years, his release came a few days before his thirty-ninth birthday. Aini's own account of his liberation is to be found in his Concise Autobiography: see *Aknun navbati qalamast*, Vol. 1, p. 84, or the Persian *Yâddâshthâ*, p. 822.

iii

I went home, and no sooner did I see my mother than I burst into tears. My mother kept asking, "What happened to you? Why are you crying?" But I couldn't answer her. My father appeared from nowhere and asked me more sternly what was wrong. "Speak up! What happened to you? If you don't tell me, I'll cut off your ear."

I was so choked up from crying that I was gasping for breath, and could only manage to say, "The boys fought with each other."

"What's it to you if the boys fight?" my father said, "You didn't fight with anybody and nobody fought with you, so what are you crying about?"

"*Domullo* hit them." I was using the boys' term for their teacher for the first time.

"He did right. Fighting boys deserve to be beaten."

"I'm not going to school any more."

"You're being silly," said Father sternly. He was silent for a moment, then went on more gently, "Why aren't you going to go to school?"

"Domullo will hit me."

"He can't hit you. If he hits you I'll cut off his ear," my father said. He took his knife from his pocket and showed it to me, saying, "This is my knife;" and repeated, "If Domullo hits you I'll cut off his ear with this very knife!"

I began to relish the thought of seeing the bloody, severed ear of the teacher I hated so much, and thought to myself, "Fine, if Domullo hits me I'll tell Father and he'll come and cut off his ear while I watch."

Yet I was still afraid, since I had not yet had a caning; when Domullo's cane came to rest near my feet I could feel my soles itching and burning, my heart sank, and my breath grew short. I decided I could do without seeing the teacher lose his ear. Then again, I remembered that a neighbor of ours had a donkey with one ear missing and whenever he rode out on it the boys would sing out, "His ass has only got one ear!" and they would clap and cheer. I always enjoyed that, and thought that if the boys saw Domullo missing an ear they wouldn't have to fight one another to have fun—everyone would enjoy laughing at the one-eared Domullo instead. That was a sight I really wanted to see! Then I thought of a plan that would enable me to see Domullo lose his ear without my being caned. With this in mind I told my father, "If you don't go and cut off Domullo's ear first, I won't go to school." He replied "Then I won't get the baby donkey for you."

Oh, the baby donkey! . . What a lovely thing that will be. And if I put a red collar with pompoms and jingle-bells on him, how much prettier he will be! When I ride him he will prick up his ears and lash his tail and kick up his heels, and it won't be like riding a donkey, but floating along on a cloud! Such fantasies dispelled all my nightmares of school, and I gave in to my father, though I decided to press my luck just a little: "If you give me a donkey with a collar and pompoms, then I'll go to school."

"Good for you, my boy!" he said. "Go to school without crying, and I'll give you everything."

I wiped my eyes, picked up a piece of bread, and went out into the garden. I broke a branch off a willow tree, sat astride a low mud wall that my father had built round the kitchen garden, and pretended that the wall was a donkey. "Giddy-up!" I yelled, as I whacked it with my willow switch. Of course the wall didn't budge, but pretending it was the donkey foal I so greatly desired cheered me enormously.

iv

On the second day I went to school early, and when I arrived no one was there but the teacher. I greeted him and was about to go and sit in my assigned place when he stopped me and asked, "Did you bring the money for the mats?"

"No, I forgot it,"

"What kind of mullah are you going to make? Run home quick, and fetch eight *pul* from your father to pay for the mats."

I put my writing board on the ledge in front of me and set off. I had not gone far when Domullo called to me, "Sadriddin!" I went back and stood in front of him.

" Cross your arms on your chest!"[3] he ordered irritably.

I obeyed somewhat suspiciously with a wary glance at the canes behind him. And indeed he reached toward them. Fearing

---

[3] The traditional attitude of servitude or respect.

that he was going to hit me, I shouted with involuntary defiance, "If you hit me my father will cut your ear off!"

He laughed and said, "Don't worry, I'm not going to hit you. So long as you don't play games I won't hit you."

His laugh reassured me, and I waited for his next instructions. He took some of the shorter canes, handed them to me, and told me, "Take these and drop them in the pool by the mosque. Then go home, get the money from your father and bring it back."

I ran so fast that my feet barely touched the ground. I was so happy—the teacher had laughed, and had told me to throw away his canes! First I threw the canes in the pool, then I went home and asked my father, who was working on a mill wheel, for the money.

"How much is it?" he asked.

"Eight *pul.*"

He searched his pockets, pulled out eight copper coins, and gave them to me. I left my father's workbench, hut then turned back and told him, "Domullo smiled at me, he said he wouldn't hit me, and he gave me his canes to throw in the pool!"

"Good, good. Hurry along now, get back to your lessons," he said.

I ran all the way back to school. By now some of the boys had arrived and Domullo was busy collecting his mat money. I too came forward to give him the money I had received from my father. I crossed my arms on my chest and, without holding out my hand, I cupped it and showed Domullo the money. He laughed again, and said, "Bravo, now you're being well-behaved! But you needn't cross your arms on your chest when you're giving someone money."

Emboldened by this dispensation, but without taking my left hand from my chest, I held out the money with my right hand. The teacher took it, and even offered up a prayer: "God grant you grow up to be a mullah!"

I decided that maybe Domullo really wasn't so bad after all, since he had gotten rid of his canes, and had prayed for me when I gave him the money for the school mats.

The teacher went on collecting the money. Any boy who had not brought it he sent hack home for it; some boys came back a second time empty-handed, saying that their fathers promised to give them the money on market day. To which he replied, "Then I won't buy new mats until you've all brought your money, and I'll send these old, torn mats to the bathhouse of the mosque to be used as firewood. You can sit on the ground, and there won't be any reeds to play with, either."

At this, the boys who had brought in the money pestered and prodded those who had not: "Eight *pul* won't kill your father. Come on, bring it in!" They for their part protested, "Look, I said on market day!" And some started crying.

I thought privately that the fathers of these boys must be very mean and tight-fisted. I did not realize then how much eight *pul* (equivalent to two kopeks) was worth to them, and how hard it could be for a poor man to find that much money. I recall that around that time we had visitors, and my father gave me one *tanga* (64 *pul*), and a sack, and sent me to the house of Sharif-boi, the rice merchant, who lived in our village. Father had said, "Give him this money, and he'll give you two *choriks* of rice. But don't tell him we're going to make rice pudding, or he'll give us poor quality rice. If he asks what we're cooking, tell him *osh*, but don't tell him what kind of *osh*."[4] When I think that two *choriks*, that is, nine pounds, of good rice cost sixty-four *pul*, eight would buy more than a pound of rice. This really was a lot of money.

With all the arguing about mat money, the first period of class time was soon over. "Go home, tea-break!" Domullo said.

As yesterday, the boys got up shouting and pushing, said goodbye to each other, and went to their various homes. I also went home, ate, played with my cat for a while, and returned to school. The teacher was already there, and the boys began filing in.

When all the boys were inside, the teacher said, "Read!" and picked up his long cane. Everyone, including myself, shouted out "*alif, be, te, se.*"

Domullo turned to Khalifa and said, "Teach the lesson!"

Khalifa, who was still sore from the previous day's beating, got up and limped from boy to boy, sitting down and writing out the day's lesson on his board.

Domullo himself took charge of my lesson. He sat me across from him and put my board in front of me. "Read your lesson!"

"*Alif, be, te, se,*" I recited, without looking at the board.

---

[4] *Osh* is the general term for a cooked meal, though it normally implies pilau (*oshi pilav*), which requires long-grain rice. A variation of this anecdote is repeated below, at the beginning of Section vi.

"Correct, well done!" Domullo said. He busied himself with writing something of his own, and told me, "Read the next line, '*jim, he, khe.*'"

I repeated Domullo's words while looking at his dirty, sallow face, his dull, bleary eyes, and his goat-like beard, which moved up and down as he spoke. After prompting me in this manner and hearing me repeat it after him, he said, "Now you read."

"*Alif, be, te, se,*" I said.

"No, no, read the next line," he said.

But I did not know what was written on which line, so I went on watching Domullo's expression, and waited.

"I said read the next line," Domullo insisted. He was still busy writing, and when he had filled the piece of paper he was working on, he slipped it into his wallet on top of a pile of other pages he had been writing since early morning. He looked at me, waited silently for a while, and then said, "You are a very stupid boy. I've taught you so much and you haven't learned a thing."

"What did you teach me?" I asked.

"*Jim, he, khe,*" he said.

"I know that," I said, and repeated, "*jim, he, khe,*" and then added, "But I don't know what comes next."

"That *is* the next line, well done! Go back to your place and continue reading."

I went back to my place and started repeating "*jim, he, khe,*" but I could not take my eyes off Domullo's face, especially his goat-like beard. When he half-closed his eyes and sat writing in silence, his beard fascinated me and reminded me of the beard of a goat we once had at home.

We used to have a goat which I had looked after myself and fattened up. One very hard winter all the streams froze, the mills were closed, and nobody bought the mill wheels that my father made. My father could not find enough money to buy meat for nearly two months, so our goat had to be slaughtered. I yelled and cried, but my father ignored my pleas. He sharpened the knife, laid the goat down, tied its legs together, and while my mother held its legs my father cut its throat.

I cried and cried as I looked at the goat. Each time the goat jerked convulsively as it died, its beard moved up and down just like Domullo's beard when he talked. When the goat was dead my father severed its head from its body and tossed the head aside; I picked up the head and looked at it fondly. Its eyes were half-closed and its beard jutted out. Domullo's beard, as he sat still, reminded me of my dead goat, and I felt sad. Despite this, I kept repeating *"jim, he, khe"* . . .

Then there was a knock at the window, next to where the teacher was sitting.

"Who's there?" said Domullo, as he pulled the paper window aside. It was a woman, wearing a face-veil and *faranji*. She held out a *tanga*, saying, "Take this offering, and please give me a prayer for a headache, a prayer for a toothache, a prayer for a sore eye, and a prayer to speed the delivery of a child, and let the boys go, for charity's sake."

"You want me to give you four prayers and let the boys go, for one *tanga*? Oh no, that will cost you at least another *tanga*," the teacher replied.

"I've come all the way from Obkena," the woman said. "My neighbor, Sharof-boi's wife, can't deliver her baby and is in great pain. He gave me a *tanga* and sent me for a childbirth prayer. My other neighbors' wives all have various pains and asked me to bring prayers for them too, and said they'd send you the money as soon as they could. I've come all this way on foot to do a good deed, and I'll come back with the rest of the money when they find it. Now for charity's sake, let the boys go."

Domullo took the *tanga* and put it in his purse. He took four slips of paper from among the pile in his wallet, which he had been writing all morning, and gave them to the woman.

"Which prayer is for which pain?" she asked.

"These are all-purpose prayers," Domullo said, "whichever one the patient takes will cure her."[5]

The woman took the prayers and left. Domullo dismissed the boys for charity's sake.

Next morning at school, before the mid-morning tea-break, we heard a horse passing outside and a voice called out at the school door, "Domullo, Domullo!"

Without leaving the room, or even opening the window, the teacher shouted back, "Yes, what do you want?"

"There's a funeral at Obkena. Sharof-boi's wife has died!" the man answered as he spurred his horse away.

---

[5] Written prayers might be placed on the affected part of the anatomy in order to effect a cure, but more usually they would be immersed in water for the writing, i.e. the ink, to dissolve, and then given to the patient to drink; cf. Chapter 25, second note.

Domullo was disconcerted; he took off his turban and set it on the floor, then, perhaps in order to perform his ablutions, made to go outside.

"Your prayers didn't work very well, Domullo, did they? Sharof-boi's wife died after all!" Khalifa taunted him.

"Don't be so skeptical!" Domullo told him, "It's not that the prayer didn't work—she died because of her own lack of faith. If she had had faith she would have delivered. 'Faith heals all,' as they say." Then, turning to the boys as he left the school, "Tea-break, you lot!"

An hour later we were all back at school, except for the teacher.

" Lads, let's make a deal," said Khalifa.

"What deal?" they all asked in unison.

"When we play games, no one tells Domullo, and no one tells on anyone else."

"You first!" said one of the boys who had been beaten on Khalifa's account.

"From now on, if you don't tell, then I won't either," Khalifa said to the big boys; then, turning to me, "And don't tell your father, either. Your father's a trouble-maker. One day I was stealing apricots from one of your trees and he told Domullo and my father about it, and both of them beat me."

"No, I won't tell." I said.

"If you do, I'll get the other boys to *kharmurd* you."

"No, I won't tell!" I assured him. The first time I had only said it, but this time I meant it, because I was terrified of being *kharmurded*.

Qnce, a *maddoh* came to our village to tell his stories. All the grownups had gone to a neighboring village for a celebration, and only teenagers and children gathered to hear him. The *maddoh* began his story. When he reached the climax, he stopped and announced: "Everybody bring me whatever they can spare—bread, money, watermelon, dried apricots, raisins—and then I'll tell you the rest of the story."

All the children ran to their homes and brought something for the storyteller. I brought a handful of dried apricots from my mother. The *maddoh* collected all the things, put them in his saddlebag, and loaded it onto his donkey. Then he said, "I'll tell you the rest of my story when I come back next week," and mounted his donkey. The boys begged and pleaded with him to finish the story, even offering to bring more gifts, but he would not give in. Then one of the older boys cried, "Let's *kharmurd* him!"

Everybody took up the cry: "*Kharmurd, kharmurd, kharmurd!*" They all grabbed him, pulled him off his donkey onto the ground, and proceeded to beat him. The *maddoh* cried out, "Ow, you're killing me, let me go and I'll finish my story!"

"It's much more fun to beat you than to listen to your story," they said, and went on hitting him. Eventually, the *maddoh* was too weak even to shout any more. "Come on, let's dump him in the water!" one of the older boys suggested. So they picked up the half-dead storyteller and carried him to the Mazrangon stream, which passes through our village. They dumped him in the water, then dragged him out again. His turban had fallen off his head into the water, and one of the boys held onto a tree and leaned out over the stream to fish it out.

They put the soggy turban into his *khurjin* and sat him, soaking wet, on his donkey, which they sent on its way with a blow from a stick, "Get out of here!" they called, "and take your stupid story with you!"

Ever since that incident, I had been thoroughly scared of *kharmurding*, and so from the bottom of my heart I promised Khalifa, "I won't tell my father about any games."

"Now let's play marbles," Khalifa said.

The boys must have played this game in the school several times before, since they immediately got up from their places, pulled the torn mats to one side, and started digging hollows in the ground. The game began. Lots of "marbles," or rather, peach and apricot pits, changed hands: The skillful boys outmaneuvered the simple ones, and the stronger ones simply hit the weaker ones and took their marbles. Once again, they all began fighting, crying, screaming, and tearing at each other's clothes. One of the boys latched on to me, and ordered, "Either play the game or we'll put you in the middle and peck your head."

I didn't have any marbles or apricot pits, and I didn't know how to play. My mother never made pockets in my coat or tunic, because, she maintained, "boys with pockets become thieves." So to keep me honest, I was never given the chance to carry legitimate paraphernalia for games, and did not know how to play any either. However, I was even more afraid of being subjected to a "head-pecking": this was a nasty form of hazing where several boys would put one in the middle, take off his cap, and peck at his head with their fingernails like woodpeckers at a tree. I was

desperately trying to figure out how to escape this fate, when
Khalifa came to my rescue: "Let him be," he said "His father is a
tattle-tale."

Although I was hurt by this insult, it was clearly one way out of
this kind of danger. From then on, whenever someone threatened
me, I called out to Khalifa: "Call these boys off me, or I'll tell my
father about the games you play!" And Khalifa would comply
forthwith.

Khalifa next picked up Domulla's long cane, whacked a few
heads, and stopped the mayhem that had been a game of marbles.
"Time for quail-fighting!" he announced.

No one really wanted to play this game, since only Khalifa and
one other boy had quails. Khalifa, however, came up with a
solution: "The two of us will make our birds fight and everybody
else can bet," he said.

But few of the boys had money for bets, either, and their
"marbles" had been won by the experts. They said they would
have to go home and get some more fruit pits. Khalifa agreed, and
most of the boys ran off home. Meanwhile, Khalifa and the
remaining boys straightened up the room from the previous
game: they filled in the hollows and spread the mats over them,
but left a circle of earth exposed in the middle of the room.

The rest of the boys returned, and the quail fight began.

Khalifa sat across the ring from the other boy who had a bird.
The other boys sat next to them, and those who could not find a
place in the circle stood behind. Khalifa and the other boy untied
their waistbands and took their quails out from under their tunics
where they had been hidden. First they licked the birds' beaks,
then exposed their claws and rubbed spittle on these, then under
their wings . . .

Khalifa challenged his opponent: "How much do you want to
lay on it?

"Twenty," came the reply.

"Raise you ten!"

"Raise you twenty!"

In the end the fight was set at a hundred each, that is whoever's
bird turned tail first would have to give a hundred fruit pits to his
opponent.

"You kids place your bets too!" Khalifa ordered the other
boys.

The other boys in turn placed bets with each other, either on
Khalifa's quail or on his opponent's, likewise staking ten, fifty, or

up to a hundred, depending on how much they could afford. When all the bets had been made, Khalifa and the other boy released their quails. The birds stretched their claws, arched their necks, and began to fight. One would peck at the other's head, the other would feint sideways, the first would scratch at the other's eye, the other would bite its neck, and both would go rolling over the arena. In a little while the poor birds were both bleeding, but neither had run away. The boys picked up their birds, groomed them again, and set them on each other again. After a couple of rounds, the other boy's bird ran away squeaking, with Khalifa's bird chasing it round the ring. What an uproar there was! All the boys began shouting, clapping, and whistling . . .

At that very moment Domullo suddenly reappeared. When the boys had returned from home with their extra fruit-pits, they must have forgotten to lock the door from the inside, so that the teacher was able to walk right into the school without knocking. The boys were so busy cheering and jeering that they did not even notice Domullo until he had taken up his long cane and commenced whacking heads. I alone had been standing on the fringe of the arena, with one eye glued to the fight and the other on the door, so as soon as Domullo's goat-like beard came into view, I quietly got up and went over to my place.

After Domullo was tired of caning people, he sat down in his stall and said to me, "You're a smart boy."

The other boys also settled down in their places. Khalifa stood in front of Domullo. Perhaps he hoped that the teacher would ask him to name the guilty ones again; but in this he was disappointed, for Domullo, without asking him anything, told him: "Go fetch the canes that I ordered to be put in the pool yesterday. They should be well soaked by now and will be fit to teach you boys some manners!"

Khalifa went. All the boys were shaking like leaves. But Domullo had told me that I was a smart boy, so I alone remained calm. Khalifa brought the canes and tossed them down before Domullo. Without more ado, the latter ordered the other boys, "First lay him down!"

Some of the older boys came forward, laid Khalifa face-up on the ground, bound his feet in the *falloq*, and lined up his soles for the beating. I could see the wounds from yesterday's beating on his feet.

"Beat!" ordered Domullo.

One of the boys picked up a cane that Khalifa had brought and hit the soles of his feet. But the first blow splintered the cane. The boy picked up another cane and it, too, broke at the first blow. This continued until all of the canes that Khalifa had brought had broken without hurting him.

Domullo was furious. He picked up the broken sticks and, after carefully inspecting them, declared, "The canes I sent to be put in the pool were mulberry, which shouldn't break at all, especially after soaking overnight. This rascal didn't fetch my canes, he dipped some dried willow sticks in the water and brought those." Then he said to the boy holding the last broken stick, "Fetch my canes from the pool!"

The boy went and Khalifa remained with his feet in the *falloq*. The boy returned empty-handed and announced, "There are no canes in the pool!"

Domullo said, "Evidently this rascal hid them somewhere. Very well, from now on instead of using mulberry switches I'll use sticks from pomegranate trees. For the moment I can discipline this miscreant another way. Lay him face down!"

The boys released Khalifa's feet from the *falloq*, laid him face down, and Domullo took his long cane and started beating him on the back. But Khalifa crouched on all fours and squirmed back and forth, managing to dodge most of the blows. So they spreadeagled him, holding his arms and legs, and one boy put his foot on the small of his back for good measure. Khalifa cried out involuntarily, "Not so hard, or you'll kill the quail!"

"Oh! So he has a quail, does he?" Domullo exclaimed. "Find the bird and give it to me!"

The boys quickly stuck their hands inside Khalifa's tunic and took out his quail, which they handed to the teacher. Without a second thought Domullo wrung the neck of the bird, which was still bleeding from the fight, and tossed it aside.

Khalifa cried, "Ahmad has a quail too, why don't you kill that as well?"

"Bring me his bird too!" Domullo responded.

The boys left Khalifa and grabbed Ahmad. Khalifa himself got up and stuck his hand down Ahmad's tunic, took out the bird, and gave it to Domullo. Domullo wrung this bird's neck, too, and threw it away. "Enough for today, you're dismissed; I'll cane you tomorrow." Then, as an afterthought: "Remember, tomorrow is Thursday—don't forget the Thursday bread."[6]

The boys crushed past one another to get out of the school. But today after the formal *salom* there was no immediate rush homeward. The boys stood in the street to settle the matter of their bets on the quail fight. The winners wanted the losers to pay up, but the losers protested, "The birds are both dead, the fight doesn't count!" Fighting broke out. Khalifa and Ahmad took off their coats, laid them aside, and squared off against each other. I ran home.

V

I continued at school; so did the confusion and excitement. Despite this, in a few weeks I had learned the names of the Arabic letters. Sometimes Khalifa taught me and sometimes Domullo. Next we started to learn the vowel diacritics. I found these lessons more interesting than simply learning the names of the letters. In these lessons I learned to repeat "*alif zabar—a, zer—i, pesh—u.*"[7] I found saying these words quite pleasant. I learned this rule by heart for all the letters of the Arabic alphabet. After this I began to learn "double *zabar, zer*, and *pesh*": I was taught to say "*alif* and double *zabar—an*, double *zer—in*, double *pesh—un.*"[8] This rule, too, we learned by heart up to the end of the alphahet: "*be* and

---

[6]*Noni panjshanbegi*: pupils were expected to bring the teacher a loaf of bread every Thursday [the last day of the school week] as payment in kind. — A. (See Bečka, "Traditional Schools, I," pp, 291-3, esp. note 8.)

[7] The Arabic letters in which Persian is written (as was Tajik, up until the 1920s) represent consonants; short vowels following these may be written as diacritics above or below the letter, these signs being called *zabar* ("above"), *zer* ("below") and *pesh* ("before"). Reciting this rule in the form Aini quotes here, once for each of the twenty-eight letters of the alphabet, without demonstrating its application, is pointless.

[8] In Tajik, *alif du zabar — andu, du zer — indu, du pesh — un*: this rule describes an orthographic convention (*tanwin*, nunation) peculiar to Arabic. At this stage of their education the phrase would be incomprehensible to the children (especially with the intrusive *d*), and even for those who at a later stage might learn Arabic it offers no grammatical justification. Aini's appreciation of the musical qualities of these phrases is intended ironically.

double *zabar—ban*, double *zer—bin*, double *pesh—bun* . . . "
This lesson was not bad either, and the words sounded even more melodious. If the former phrase is likened to the statement of a melody in a classical music recital, the latter may be compared to its rhythmic development and recapitulation.

For each lesson I worked from a different copy-board which my father, not the teacher, had written out for me, because Domullo had said, "Your father is very particular. He doesn't like my handwriting, so tell him to write it himself."[9]

At the end of the year I began learning the *abjad* but I did not enjoy it at all. In these lessons I was made to repeat, "*Alif* with *be* and *zabar—ab*, *jim* with *dol* and *zabar—jad*: *abjad*," and so on.[10] For one thing, saying these words was difficult, and for another, the words sounded unmusical and unpleasant . . .

One day my father said to me, "Now that you've learned the alphabet, I'll teach you how to count with it." He put my alphabet board in front of me and pointed to some of the letters one at a time, asking me, "What's this?" and "What's this?" I could not answer any of his questions, because I did not know what those things were and nobody had taught me.

"So what have you been reading in school all these days?" he asked angrily.

"*Alif* with *be* and *zabar—ab*, *jim* with *dol* and *zabar—jad*: *abjad* . . ." I repeated by heart my lessons from the alphabet.

"Oh, so you're a parrot! You can say anything, but you don't understand what you're saying."

I imagined then that a parrot must be a very bad thing. Only later did I learn that a parrot is a very pretty and reputedly smart bird, which can learn and repeat whatever it is taught but, not being human, does not know the meaning of what it says. For this reason, people who repeat things without understanding them are compared to parrots.

Then my father searched through my pile of copy-boards and took out those that had letters or letters and vowels written on them in charcoal. He pointed to individual letters on each of them

---

[9] Pupils wrote in charcoal on an individual wooden board (*takhtacha*), copying whatever the teacher had written at the top of it.

[10] *Abjad* (see Glossary) is the first of seven mnemonic nonsense words made up of all the letters of the Arabic alphabet in their "numerical" as distinct from their "literary" sequence. As Sadriddin's father demonstrates below, the form taken by these lessons is useless for practical purposes.

and asked me to identify them. Again I could not. But when he showed me each board and asked me to read the whole, I recited from memory everything that was written there—and a few things that were not. "You're a parrot," my father repeated, adding, "It's not your fault, it's Domullo's and Khalifa's fault. They've taught you to repeat everything like a parrot, but they haven't really taught you anything."

He was silent for some time, then said, "He's a blind semi-literate, and I expect him to teach reading and writing! I'm a fool. Don't go to school today."

This made me very happy, since I was heartily sick of reciting the *abjad*.

vi

My father invited the *khatib*, the *mutavalli*, the muezzin, and a couple of the village elders for supper one evening, We spread the tablecloth and served *shir-birinj*.

I should mention here that on market nights or when guests came over we generally made *shir-birinj*. My father used to tell my mother, "You need a lot of oil to cook pilau, and meat too; but *shir-birinj* is cheap because all we have to do is buy rice, and we can get the milk and butter from our cow." But whenever he sent me to buy rice he would say, "Don't tell him we're making *shir birinj* or he'll give us poor-quality rice."

One time I asked him, "Should I tell him we're cooking pilau?"

"No!" my father answered, "that would be a lie, and you shouldn't get used to lying! Don't tell him how we're going to cook the rice."

But to get back to my story: after the guests had finished the *shir-birinj* and were drinking tea, my father said, addressing the *khatib*: "I invited you over, my friends, to talk about our village teacher."

"What's the matter with the teacher?" asked the *khatib* point-edly.

"Nothing's the matter, except that he's illiterate," my father replied. "He can't even teach the alphabet; I had to teach my son myself."

The *mutavalli*, taking the side of the *khatib*, said, "It's enough for him to teach the boys of our village as much as he knows.

Nobody in this village is going to make his son a madrasa professor."

My father countered, "This teacher can't even teach what he knows. My son has been at the school for one winter and he can now recite the *abjad*, but so far as reading is concerned, he can't distinguish *alif* from *be*. On top of this, the teacher doesn't supervise the boys at all, and they've all become quail-fighters and gamblers."

When I heard this and realized that my father was aware of the boys' quail-fighting, I was very scared. If Khalifa found out about this he would say that I had told my father about the games, and would *kharmurd* me.

The *khatib* said, "You're obviously more literate yourself, and know better how to teach. Why don't you teach your son yourself, instead of sending him to school and having to send Thursday bread and sweets? Leave the poor teacher alone to earn his bread."

My father replied, "I have a piece of land that I have to till in order to feed my family. It doesn't yield enough for all our needs, so when my hands are free I make mill wheels. On top of that I have to weave clothes for my children in the winter. If I teach my son myself, who will do my work?"

My father made a sour face, then suddenly he laughed and, addressing the *khatib*, said, "My ulterior motive in inviting you here was to get the teacher replaced by someone better. Since you don't agree to this, do something else so that I won't have wasted my *shir-birinj*."

My father had an odd habit that some people found offensive. When he was bothered by something, he would freely and unabashedly speak his mind. Here he had openly admitted the purpose of his hospitality, except he smiled as he spoke in order not to make his guests feel uncomfortable. The *knatib* asked, "What should I do to deserve your *shir-birinj*?"

"Let my son study with the girls in your house with your wife Bibi Khalifa."

"How can I allow a boy to study with girls?" the *khatib* asked.

"Let's not be more pious than we have to," my father said. "My son is only seven years old, and according to the *shariat* it is permissible for him to be with girls until he is twelve."

The *khatib* agreed. "Fine, send him to the girls' school and let him learn to read. But from time to time you should invite us over for some of your *shir-birinj*," he finished, with a smile . . .

The supper ended, and I was relieved to have escaped the risk of being *kharmurded* by Khalifa.

vii

The next day my mother took me to Bibi Khalifa's school. For the "sweetener," she took raisins and cookies on a tray covered with a napkin and the cap that she had embroidered for my circumcision feast.

Bibi Khalifa was from Sari-mazori Ghijduvon, and was the wife of the *khatib* of our village, who was from Darvoz province. She was a pale, middleaged woman, fat and pauchy. She was so fat that when she was sitting, her knees underneath her skirts looked as big as one of the mill wheels my father made. When we came in she was sitting on a pile of quilts at the far end of the room. The girls were sitting on felt mats around the edge of the room. In front of the girls were folded pillows on which they put their books, instead of on wooden ledges as in the boys' school.

Bibi Khalifa welcomed my mother nicely and laughingly referred to her having been forced to take me on by virtue of my father's rice pudding. She added, "Bring me a plate of *shir-birinj* when your son reaches the *tabbat*."[11]

"Should God grant that day, I'll bring you a plate of pilau," my mother answered her.

Bibi Khalifa untied the napkin, broke up the cookies, and shared them with the girls. Here the offering was distributed quite differently from the way it had been flung around in the boys' school. The teacher handed it to her *khalifa*, who was one of the older girls, and she in turn gave a piece to each girl, and ate the largest piece herself.

---

[11] *Tabaq . . . tabbat*: it was customary to present the teacher with a gift, the name of which resembled the words of the Koranic passage the student had just mastered: thus the beginning of Surah no. 111, *tabbat* [*yadâ abî lahab*] "Perish [the hands of Abu Lahab]" called for a plate (*tabaq*) of food, and the beginning of Surah no. 110, *idhâ jâ'a* [*nasru'llâhi wa'l-fath*] "When comes [the help of God, and victory]" — pronounced *izo jo'a* by Tajiks — evoked *ezor-joma*, a suit of clothes (cf. Bečka, "Traditional Schools, I," p. 302).

Grace was said, then Bibi Khalifa had me repeat *bismilloh* and *auzu billoh*. Thus my second formal induction to schooling commenced. My mother left and I stayed at the girls' school.

Bibi Khalifa began to teach me from the middle of the *abjad* alphabet, where I had left off at the boys' school. Her method of teaching was a little different. She pointed out each letter with a little stick as she got me to say its name. But she too was not very interested in whether I knew the letter or not. Bibi Khalifa was always busy teaching. She would call up students and teach them one by one, so that the whole day was spent in repeating lessons.

Bibi Khalifa's class ran from after breakfast until noon. When noon arrived the children did not go home for lunch, but ate what they had brought in the school. They all gave half of their lunches to Bibi Khalifa.

The first day I had not brought any lunch, so Bibi Khalifa gave me a piece of bread from one of the girls and told me, "Today I'm treating you to lunch. Tomorrow you can bring extra bread with you and give me a big piece of it."

After eating, the children cleaned up and swept the room and garden. Some days she gave the girls clothes to wash, and-made me join in too, saying, "You should learn how to wash clothes, because it will come in useful if you go to Bukhara to study at the madrasa."

Bibi Khalifa also kept a long stick against the wall behind her, but I never saw her use it. If she was teaching and a child could not give the correct answer, Bibi Khalifa would slap her across the face with the long, wide sleeve of her dress, which was made of linen or printed cotton. But this slap was no harder than a puff of wind.

Her students—all girls, except for me—did not play rough games or hit each other. When they had any spare time in between sweeping the yard or washing clothes, they played with dolls. They prepared mud pies and served them on pieces of pottery, giving parties for their dolls.

They made a little boy doll for me. At their weddings my doll had to be the groom for all their dolls. Since mine was the only boy doll, sometimes he had to suffice for ten or twelve girl dolls. I must admit that I liked this game very much.

But sometimes the girls, whose poor dolls were all married to the same husband, would make them fight, and my doll would have to make peace among them. I still remember that I felt a little put out by this, and I promised myself that when I grew up I would not take two wives. Even so, I felt proud that all these girl dolls needed my boy doll.

Later another boy came to the school, but he never attained the status of father-in-law; the girls considered him too rough, and did not make a doll for him.[12]

viii

I continued at Bibi Khalifa's school. I finished the *Haftyak* and memorized some of the short surahs in it; I read the Koran right through, the "Four Books," and some Khoja Hafiz.[13] But other than those things I had actually read with Bibi Khalifa, I could not read anything. For example, I could read a poem by Hafiz that I had read in school, no matter in whose handwriting, but I could not read a poem of his that I had not read in school even from my own book. In other words, I still did not know how to read; and I could not write at all. Despite this my father withdrew me from the school and sent me to study under the *khatib*. He in turn set about teaching me from a book called *Avvali ilm*. I was then ten years old.

However, I had learned the Arabic alphabet well, and could read some surahs of the Koran, though very slowly. The reason for this was my father's determination to teach me to read and reckon with the *abiad* system, while I was still at Bibi Khalifa's school. We spent a good hour every evening, from after the sunset prayer until bedtime, working on this.

First he acquainted me with the sounds of the alphabet: "*a, be, je, de...*" Then he taught me how to read the letters in combination. After that he taught me how to count the letters: "*alif* one, *be* two, *jim* three, *dol* four..."

---

[12] This boy was Abdullo, who is mentioned briefly at the beginning of Chapter 15, and whom the young Aini was surprised to see again taking part in the fireworks contest at Darveshobod (Chapter 19).

[13] *Haftyak*, lit. "one-seventh (of the Koran)" is a selection of shorter surahs for school use; the "Four Books" (*chor kitob*) is a manual of instructions on ablution and prayer. Both these books included some translation and instruction in Tajik; "reading" the rest of the Koran, however, was a matter of repeating the words after the teacher without any appreciation of the orthography, phonology, or meaning of the original.

In this way my father succeeded in teaching me the whole writing system and its numerical applications. After about a month I was able to read the Arabic alphabet and use it for counting; the first nine letters for the units, the next nine for the tens, then the hundreds, up to one thousand.

After I had learned all this my father said, "Now I'll teach you something else very interesting. There are also nine figures and one zero, which were invented by the mathematicians of India. With these numbers we can count everything in the world."

I was very excited to learn what sort of magic this might be. To be able to count everything in the world with those ten things was really something worth knowing; I thought of how many times I, even with my ten fingers, had miscounted the days of the week. . . I begged my father to teach me as quickly as possible, and he consented.

First he wrote out all nine figures. Every day he taught me a different number, and then he wrote and explained the zero as well. Next he showed me how one and zero could be written together to make ten, and so on for the rest of the numbers. I did not find it too hard to learn, because I had already learned to compound tens and hundreds with the *abjad* system.

After I had learned this my father told me, "You have now learned something that nobody else in our village knows. The *maktab* teacher, your former *domullo*, doesn't even know how to count with letters, let alone with figures."[14]

---

[14] As Aini's father mentions, the figures we know as Arabic numerals (and which in the Islamic world are called Indian numerals) and the symbolic use of zero that goes with them were developed in India; they were introduced into Central Asia and the Middle East, as tradition has it, by the mathematician Muhammad al-Khwârazmi (from Khiva) as early as the ninth century, and spread rapidly via Muslim Spain to Europe. However, they were not generally used in Islam, even by scientists, much before the eighteenth century. Translations into Arabic from Greek mathematical works, and original treatises such as Omar Khayyam's solution of quadratic equations (ca. 1100 C.E.), continued to be written longhand, in words. Arithmetical notation for purposes of bookkeeping, etc., was in various quasi-literary codes, including that of *abjad* (which was also used in the Greek and Hebrew alphabets). It was thus possible up until the present century in many parts of the Muslim east — even, and especially, in al-Khwârazmi's homeland! — for otherwise quite literate persons such as Aini's *domullo* to be barely numerate.

I felt very proud of my rare skills, and an incident followed that made me even prouder. Here is how the story goes:

In Sari-mazor the New Year's fair was under way.[15] It was attended by many visitors from neighboring villages. As part of the celebration games there were wrestling matches, for which the men were divided into two teams which faced each other across the arena. My father sat in front of the men of our team, with me in front of him. Champions came out from both sides and wrestled. Initially the men from our village were winning every contest.

A young mullah, a madrasa student from Bukhara, stood up to challenge a young man from our side who had just thrown one of their champions. Without a moment's hesitation our young man came to grips with the mullah, but after a short struggle took a fall.

Another boy from our side challenged the mullah. This boy must have appeared stronger to the mullah, because he said, " I won't wrestle with him." His excuse, however, was not that his challenger was stronger; instead, he protested: "He's a shepherd and I'm a mullah. It would be beneath my dignity as a doctor of the law to grapple with him."

Upon hearing this my father became very angry. He jumped up from where he sat and, dragging me along with him, strode out to the middle of the arena and called out to the mullah.

"What do you want?" said the latter.

"Are you a mullah or a wrestler?" my father asked him.

---

[15] New Year: *navrūz*, lit. "new day," the beginning of the Iranian solar (and agricultural) year, is celebrated at the time of the vernal equinox, on or about 21 March. It is of great antiquity, and remains the most important and joyful holiday of all Iranian peoples (including Kurds, Afghans and Baluch) and many of their Turk neighbors, notably in Azerbaijan and Uzbekistan. It is marked by open-air fairs and picnics, the exchange of visits and gifts, spring cleaning, new clothes, egg-painting and other practices, many of which are common to spring and Easter festivals the world over (cf. *Bukhara*, p. 22). In pre-Islamic times the holiday was more or less assimilated into Zoroastrianism; it continued to flourish through the Islamic period, but—partly owing to the different calendars—has never acquired an Islamic sanction or coloration. Nevertheless, it was discouraged throughout most of the Soviet period as a religious relict. Since independence it has been confirmed as a national holiday in Tajikistan and Uzbekistan. (For a relict of the corresponding autumn festival, see Chapter 18, note 1.)

"I'm a wrestling mullah!" he answered.

"If you're a mullah," my father said, "Forget that he's smaller than you, and compete with my eight-year-old son here in scholarship. We'll see whether you're a mullah or not. If you're a wrestler, then wrestle with that youth, who is your age and size, so we can see who is stronger."

Having issued his challenge, my father looked at me and said, "Son, ask this man something from the *abjad*."

Coolly, I asked him, "How much is *te*?"

He stood open-mouthed, unable to answer.

"You tell him how much *te* is," said Father.

"It's four hundred!" I said.

Then my father asked the mullah the values of various letters, none of which he knew. In each case my father next asked me, and I answered.

Our side jeered at the mullah, who turned beet-red with shame.

My father said to him, "Now that we've seen the extent of your scholarship, go and wrestle with that young man like a shepherd!" And the mullah did.

No sooner did they come to grips than the mullah fell. A great cheer went up, and the match was over.

The young men on our side said to my father, "It was your son who really threw that mullah: he was so humiliated in the quiz that he couldn't regain his strength for the wrestling match!"

This made me feel even prouder, and I told myself that I must learn every science. Though in fact I still could not read properly . . .

*   *   *

Here ends the story of my elementary education. How I studied and became literate and involved in literature I will tell another time.

Samarkand, October 26, 1934

GLOSSARY

This glossary comprises Tajik and other foreign words (in italics), specialized English terms, and names of people and places occurring more than once in the text. The following conventions are also valid for the footnotes.

Tajik names and terms are generally transliterated from the forms used in Cyrillic editions of Aini's works: *yo* stands for the letter *ë*, a reverse apostrophe for the hard sign (and/or Arabic *'ayn*, which it usually represents), and *gh*, *q*, *ū*, *h*, and *j* for the "additional" letters of the Tajik Cyrillic alphabet. The accent on final *-ī*, an orthographic device of Tajik to avoid confusion with the unstressed final *-i* of *ezâfeh*, will not normally be added in single words. Similarly, Tajik *ĭ*, representing consonantal *y*, will normally be transliterated in diphthongs as a simple *i* (e.g., the second letter of "Aini"). Terms transliterated as from Persian or Arabic are distinguished by use of *â* instead of *o* and a few other self-evident variants.

As regards pronunciation, *gh* resembles the Parisian uvular *r*, and *q* is pronounced as in Arabic, farther back on the palate than *k*; these two sounds are quite distinct in Tajik, unlike their status in standard Persian. *Kh* represents a strong uvular fricative as in Persian or German. The vowel *ū* (originating in the vowel *o* of the earlier Persian *vâv-e majhul*) resembles a rounded version of the vowel heard in the mid-western American pronunciation of *book*. Tajik *e* (corresponding to the historical *yâ-ye majhul*) approximates to French *é*, and *o* to the vowel heard in English *corn* or *saw* but without the final glide. The other sounds of Tajik are similar to the corresponding sounds of Russian (especially the vowels and *zh*, as also heard in French *Georges*) and English (notably the consonants *ch*, *sh*, *h* and *j*). Before vowels, Tajik *e* and *i* represent the complex sounds *ye* and *yi*; hence transcriptions here such as *Sayid* and *Mahallayi Bolo*.

Tajik prefers to spell complex names as single words, and to write the connecting syllable of *ezâfeh* (*-i*) as part of the preceding word. For the sake of clarity, such units have sometimes been hyphenated (e.g., the first entry below appears in the original as

Abdulvohid Sadri Sarir). In the case of Aini's birthplace Soktaré and a few other place names, an accent has been added to indicate that the final syllable is pronounced.

For well-known people and places an established English form is used (Hafiz, Bukhara). Where a Tajik (Taj.) form differs appreciably from a Persian (Pers.) cognate or an Arabic (Arab.), Russian (Rus.), or Uzbek (Uz.) original, this is identified in parenthesis. We have generally preferred Tajik forms of place names to Russianized ones (e.g., Zarafshon, not Zeravshan; Shofirkom, not Shafrikan). In some cases there is a widely-used Uzbek form corresponding to neither of the others (Uz. Vobkent, Rus. Vabkent, Taj. Vobkand), and occasionally Tajik or Russian usage is not internally consistent ("Ghizhduvon" in some editions of *Yoddosht'ho*—as also in Uzbek usage—is Ghijduvon, the form chosen for this translation, in *Ahmadi devband*; cf. Rus. Gizhduvan or Gidzhduvan).

Abdul-Vohid Sadr-i Sarir, Qozi: (1810-1886), a minor official of the Bukhara emirate, an acquaintance of Aini's family. He began his career as a court poet, and in his fifties accepted appointments as kadi in various districts, including Ghijduvon. Examples of his poetry, of a conventional mystical kind, are quoted by Aini in his *Namuna-yi adabiyoti tojik*, pp. 385-91.

abjad: a term coined from the first four letters of the Arabic alphabet, in the sequence of the early Semitic alphabet, in which the letters have numerical equivalents on a decimal scale from 1 to 1,000. The system was earlier used for numerical notation and—particularly in Persian verse—for puzzles such as chronograms (*ta'rikh*), in which a memorable date is encoded in the letters used to spell a name, word, or phrase (for an example, see Chapter 16, p. 126).

Abu Muslim: the leader of the successful Abbasid revolt against the Umayyad caliphate in 747-750 C.E. For some years he governed the eastern province of Khurasan (including most of present-day Uzbekistan and Tajikistan), and put down a Shi'i insurrection in Bukhara. He was assassinated on the orders of his distrustful overlord, the caliph al-Mansur, in 755. Immensely popular then and since, he has become the hero of a folk epic (*dâstân*) still transmitted orally in Afghanistan and

Central Asia (see *Encyclopædia Iranica* Vol. 1, "Abu Moslem Ḵorâsânī").

Ahmad[-i] Donish: also known as Ahmad Makhdum and Ahmad Kalla (1826-97), a brilliant polymath of Bukhara. He excelled in the traditional arts of painting, calligraphy and poetry, and was versed in traditional philosophy and science, but became an advocate and theorist of social and political reform. He visited St. Petersburg three times as an envoy of the emir (in 1856, 1868 and 1870) and left an account of his travels, the *Navodir ul-vaqoye'* (Remarkable Events). He is portrayed in the second volume of Aini's Reminiscences (see *Bukhara*, pp. 31-37), and more extensively in the third and fourth volumes; see also Allworth, *Central Asia*, pp. 172-4; Rypka, pp. 529-32.

amin: lit. "trusty, trustee," village headman; governor of a small rural district within a *tuman*, subordinate to the *amlokdor* (cf. *arbob*), responsible for collecting taxes and distributing government-owned land and water.

amlokdor: provincial or district assessor of government taxes (on all property except *vaqf*); in practice the most powerful provincial executive of the emirate.

arbob: landowner, landlord; village headman; in Bukhara especially, a rural district official, in theory elected by the community, in practice usually appointed by the *amlokdor*.

ark, arg: fortress, citadel; the fortified residence of the emir of Bukhara in the city, containing also offices, dungeons, etc.

assalomu alaikum: (Arab.) "Peace be upon you," formal greeting or farewell among Muslims (short, less formal version: *salom*, "peace").

auzu billoh: see *bismilloh*.

Avvali ilm: "Principles of Knowledge," the second textbook used in elementary classes of Bukhara madrasas (the first being *Bidon*: see Chapter 16, where, however, the *khatib* teaches from these in reverse order). The Arabic loanword *ilm* denotes any kind of formal learning or science, but in this context connotes the legal requirements of Islam. The book, in Tajik, inculcates religious precepts in a catechismal (question-and-answer) format.

aivon: alcove, porch, portico; any space enclosed on three sides and on top, and open in front. In Central Asia there are two principal types of *aivon:* (1) the portico or gallery of a *mehmonkhona* or a small mosque, with a raised walkway and flat roof supported by one or more wooden pillars; (2) a tall, arched niche in the center of one or more of the four sides of the courtyard of a large mosque or madrasa.

Bedil (Pers. Bidel), Abdul-Qodir):   Indo-Persian poet (1644-1720). Born at Azimabad (now Patna) of a Central Asian immigrant to Mughal India, he learned Persian at school and became a nonconformist philosopher-poet, a master of the involved and fanciful "Indian Style" of Persian verse and of the mystical lyric (*ghazal*). Almost unknown in Iran, his work was greatly admired and widely imitated in Central Asia, where it was further popularized by special reciter-interpreters (*Bedilkhon;* see Rypka, Chapter X, and pp. 515-20). During the purges of the late 1930s, two Tajik intellectuals were sentenced to twenty-five years' exile for attending such a recital (R. M. Qobâdiyânî, "Adabiyât-e moqâvemat-e tâjik," *Âshnâ* 6/31 (1375/1996), p. 27). Aini wrote a monograph on Bedil (Stalinabad, 1954).

Bibi Khalifa: "schoolma'am." Appearing here as a name, the term was used generically in Tajik (the Uzbek equivalent was *otin*) to denote an educated woman (often the relative of a mulla) who ran an elementary school for girls, usually in her home.

bismilloh: "in the name of God [the Compassionate, the Merciful]," Arabic phrase used to invoke divine favor for the undertaking of a ritual or important task (e.g. sacrifice); pronounced before reading the Koran, and written at the head of official documents and formal letters.

bobo (Pers. *bâbâ*): (1) grandfather (after the name, as Amak Bobo; (2) affectionate and/or respectful form of address to a senior or social superior (preceding the name, as Bobo Niyoz-Gûppon).

boi (Uz.): a rich man, esp. a landowner; used as a title after a personal name (as Botur-boi; cf. Turkish *bey*). In contemporary Tajik usage, an adjective, "rich."

chorik, choryak: unit of weight, approximately 2 kg. or $4^1/2$ lb.

choryakkor: sharecropper, who worked a landowner's fields in return for one quarter of the yield (occupation: *choryakkorī*).

chronogram (*ta'rikh*): see *abjad*.

damgir: a cloth placed over cooking rice to absorb the moisture and excess oil.

Darvoz (Pers. Darvâz): a region in Mountain Tajikistan, northwest of the confluence of the Vanj and Panj rivers. At this time it was a dependency of the Bukhara emirate. In 1895 western Darvoz, on the left bank of the Panj, was ceded to Afghanistan.

dev (Pers. div): demon, ogre. A monster of superhuman size and strength, generally solitary and hostile to man; it may appear in the form of an animal, esp. a bull.

devband: exorcist, sorcerer; see Appendix I, Introduction.

divan (Taj. *devon*): the collected works of a poet (other than longer compositions independently titled).

domullo: teacher at a traditional-style primary school (*maktab*); respectful term of address for any teacher or scholar (see Bečka, "Traditional Schools, I," p. 291).

duo-khon: lit. "prayer-reciter," prayer-healer; one who, having acquired a reputation for piety, treats the sick by reciting Koranic verses or other invocations over them.

Emir of Bukhara: the title of emir (from Arab. *amir*, "commander") was adopted by the ruling khans of Bukhara only with the Manghit dynasty (1753-1920). The two emirs mentioned in this volume of Aini's reminiscences are (1) Muzaffar ud-din (r. 1860-85): his expansionist ambitions in Central Asia clashed with those of imperial Russia, and ended in the Russian defeat of the emirate and imposition of a protectorate in 1868 (see Allworth, *Central Asia,* Chapter 4; Wheeler, Chapter 4). (2) Abdul-Ahad (r. 1885-1910): last but one of the Manghit emirs; he was a patron of the arts, and filled his court with scholars and poets. Under Russian supervision he also introduced some social reforms, though in practice these were of limited effect, especially where his revenue was concerned (cf. Chapter 28). Nevertheless he was considered dangerously liberal by the establishment mullahs, and eventually had to move his residence from Bukhara to Karmana, a city about seventy miles to the northeast.

eshon: (Pers. *ishân* "they," honorifically "he, his honor") a title of respect for religious and quasi-religious dignitaries such as doctors of the law (*olim,* pl. *ulamo,* pop. *mullo*), elders of Sufi brotherhoods (*shaykh, pir*)—especially of the Naqshbandi order—and local aristocrats (*khoja, sayid*).

falloq: (cf. Pers. *falak, falaka*) a pole with a rope attached to it at both ends, used for immobilizing the legs while the soles of the feet are beaten; also refers to this punishment, "the bastinado."

faranji (Uz. *paranji,* Russianized as *parandzha*): a tent-like, full-length overcoat for a woman, concealing her features and outline and incorporating, or having attached, a gauze or horse-hair netting (*chashmband*) over the face (cf. the Afghan *burqa'*).

farsakh: a parasang, ideally the distance that a man on foot could travel in one hour; approx. 5–8 km. or $3^1/2$–5 miles, depending on terrain.

Fotiha (Arab. [*surat ul-*]*fâtiha*): the short opening chapter of the Koran, often recited as a prayer of propitiation or thanksgiving, or to treat the sick or "possessed."

ghazal: a poem of between about five and eighteen distichs, with the same rhyme throughout, generally on a lyrical, erotic, or mystical theme.

Hafiz, Shams ud-din Muhammad: (Pers. Hâfez, Taj. Hofiz, from Arab. Hâfiz, "preserver, memorizer [of the Koran]") celebrated Persian lyric poet, lived ca. 1320-1390 in Shiraz, a city of south-west Iran; best known for his mastery of the *ghazal*, he was famous even during his lifetime as far away as India and Central Asia (see Rypka, Chapter VIII).

hookah (Taj. *chilim*): water-pipe (cf. the Persian *qalayân*, Turkish nargileh); the smoke is filtered through water in a flask (the *hoqqa* in Indo-Persian; often beautifully ornamented) and drawn through a long, flexible tube.

imam (Taj. *imom*): leader of public prayers (*namoz*) at a mosque; the office is sometimes held jointly with that of *khatib*.

Isfandiyor (Pers. Esfandyâr): see Rustam.

Jamshid: also known as Jam, a mythological Iranian king and culture hero (cf. the Avestan Yima and Vedic Yama); in Firdawsi's epic he is represented as the fourth king of the first dynasty of Iranian rulers (see Levy's translation, Chapter III).

jinn: supernatural being, usually invisible to humans unless summoned by a spell or talisman. They are said to live in abandoned places, such as ruins, graveyards, or solitary trees, and in the kitchen, stable, or refuse dump of a house; a *jinn* may appear as a black goat or other animal (see also Appendix I, Introduction).

joma: a man's quilted overcoat, generally with a striped pattern, often worn draped over the shoulders with the sleeves hanging loose.

jomacha (diminutive of *joma*): a child's overcoat worn as a head-covering by women, originally as a makeshift veil (*faranji*) in token observance of the prescriptions of public modesty.

kadi (Taj. *qozi*): Muslim judge or magistrate; in the Bukhara emirate, often a district governor and influential landowner.

kedgeree (Taj. *kichri*, from Hindi): porridge-like dish of rice, split lentils, onions, eggs, etc.

khalifa: "caliph, deputy," designation and mode of address of an apprentice or assistant; in the *maktab*, a student monitor appointed by the teacher to keep order and tutor others.

kharmurd [*kardan*]: to gang up on someone and beat him up (school slang, Appendix II; compound of *khar*, an augmentive, and *murd*[*an*] "to die").

khatib: reader of the *khutba* (public bidding to prayer on Friday, followed by a sermon) at a mosque; the office is sometimes held jointly with that of imam.

khoja (cf. Pers. *khwâja*, Turk. hoca): (1) generally, and when used before a name, a term of respect for a man who is socially prominent by reason of education, piety, or prosperity; applied retrospectively to saints, poets, statesmen, etc. (2) specifically, and when used after a name, one of the "aristocracy" of the Bukhara emirate. *Khojas* traced their ancestry to the Arab conquerors of Central Asia, and did not marry their daughters to non-*khojas*; a sub-category were the *sayids*, q.v. (pl. *khojagon*; colloquial variant *khûja*; see Author's Introduction, p. 10).

khonaqoh: a convent or meeting-place for the adherents of a Sufi brotherhood (*tariqat*), in which devotional rituals (*zikr*) and communal meditation are practiced.

khurjin: a pair of saddlebags formed from two square rugs stitched or woven together.

khutba: see *khatib*.

luqata a legal term approximating to escheat; property declared to have been abandoned by its owners and forfeit to the state.

maddoh (Arab. and Pers. *maddâh*; pl. *maddohon*): lit. "panegyrist, encomiast," an itinerant quasi-religious mendicant who praises the virtues and recounts the exploits of cultic heroes such as Ali and Abu Muslim, or of local saints.

madrasa: a Muslim college of higher education, especially in theology and religious law (*shariat*).

makhdum: lit. "served," i.e. "master"; in Central Asia, a conventional epithet of the sons of religious dignitaries such as a kadi or *rais*.

maktab: a primary school for children, generally a single room adjacent to the local mosque and taught by the imam/*khatib* (see also Appendix II, Introduction).

man: maund, a unit of weight varying locally; in Bukhara it was equivalent to about 290 lb. (8 Russian *pud* or one Iranian *kharvâr*).

mehmonkhona: lit. "guest-house," the public section of a Tajik home, where the menfolk live and entertain; a room in a house, or a porch or separate building in the outer yard of a large house (*havli*), where visitors can be received and guests lodged, and where the men of the family can have meals, meetings, etc., with others of the community.

minbar: the stepped dais in a mosque from which the *khatib* addresses the congregation.

Mir[-i] Arab madrasa: the largest of the Bukhara madrasas, built in 1530-34 and named for [A]mir Abdullah Yamini, of Arab descent, who is buried there. Up until the 1980s it housed one of the Soviet Union's only two operating Islamic seminaries (the other was the Imam Isma'il al-Bukhari madrasa in Tashkent).

mirob: lit. "water-lord," the official charged with distributing irrigation water, which is meted out to specific clients at specified times for fixed periods and at fixed rates, by means of sluices along the canal system. Theoretically elected by the local farmers, the Bukharan *mirobs* were appointed by the government.

mir shab: lit. "commander of the night [watch]," the chief of the emir's police.

mirzo: originally "[a]mir's son, prince"; a conventional title (before the name) for government scribes or other educated persons (e.g., poets) in the secular rather than religious sphere.

mufti: a doctor of Islamic law empowered to deliver a written decision (Arab. *fatwa*, Taj. *rivovat)* on a point of jurisprudence.

mullo: (from Arab. *mawlâ[nâ]*, "[our] master") mullah; popular term for a teacher and interpreter of Islamic law of any rank, most often applied to one of the village "clergy" (cf. *eshon*, *imom*, *khatib*); a form of address (preceding the name) for any literate or reputedly literate person.

mutavalli: (1) superintendent or manager of a *vaqf* estate (q.v.); where the *vaqf* comprised arable land, the *mutavalli* was in sole control of the distribution of fields to be worked and the collection and apportioning of revenues, and was in effect a major landowner; (2) specifically (Mutavalli), the name of a rich landowning family of the Mirakoni Khojas of Soktaré, originally from Iran.

nabot: a sweet confection made by dribbling sugar syrup over suspended cotton threads; the syrup cools in the form of clear icicles.

namoz: the statutory prayer of Islam: a prescribed liturgy to be performed, after ritual ablution, at five fixed times each day, and communally once on Friday.

nasta'liq: a flowing Persian calligraphic style much used in manuscripts of poetry and monumental inscriptions.

nimcha: unit of weight, equivalent to a little over a pound; cf. *qabza*.

niyat: in Islam, a conscious decision to undertake a religious duty such as prayer, fasting, or pilgrimage, which obligates one to complete the same.

okhund: title applied to a senior mullah, esp. a teacher at one of the better madrasas of Bukhara.

pari: fairy; a supernatural being often perceived as a beautiful maiden; gregarious and mischievous, *paris* may be either ill- or well-disposed to humans (see also Appendix I, Introduction).

pilau (Taj. [*osh-i*] *pilav*): a dish made with rice and meat, with various other ingredients and seasoning.

pud: (Rus.) a Russian unit of weight, equivalent to 36 lb. (see *man*).

pul: (from Greek *obolos*) a copper coin of Central Asia, exchanged at the rate of four to the kopek; in the Bukhara emirate, 80 *pul* were nominally equivalent to one silver *tanga* (q.v.), but as a result of inflation in the rate of the *tanga* against the kopek, by the 1890s there were in practice only 64 *pul* to the *tanga*.

qabza: (Arab.) lit. "handful," a measure of dry goods weighing one *nimcha*, equivalent to $^1/2$ kg. or $1^1/4$ lb; also called *lûnda*.

qalandar: a wandering or solitary dervish.

Qo-qo Steppe: stretch of land irrigated by the Shofirkom canal from the Zarafshon, lying north of Vobkand, between Ghijduvon and Shofirkom, at the edge of the sand desert.

qori: (Arab. *qâri'*) a "reader," one who recites the Koran from memory, especially on occasions such as the fast of Ramadan or a requiem for the dead. There were special schools (*qorikhona*) in Bukhara where blind children were trained as *qoris*; hence as a personal epithet *qori* may simply mean "blind" (see Becka, "Traditional Schools, I," pp. 319-20 and notes).

Qozibacha, Qozizoda: lit. "kadi's son," a rich landowning family of the Mirakoni Khojas (q.v.) of Soktaré.

Qof, Mount: (Pers. *Kuh-e Qâf*) legendary mountain range at the edge of the known world, the abode of *paris* and *devs*; traditionally identified with the Caucasus.

rais: (Arab. *ra'îs* "chief") an official of the Bukhara emirate, charged with supervising public compliance with Islamic law (*shariat*) and checking the accuracy of weights, measures, and market rates; equivalent to the classical Islamic *muhtasib* (q.v., in *Encyclopedia of Islam*).

raion: (Rus.) administrative division adopted after the Revolution, and applied in Central Asia to the *tuman* (q.v.).

Ramadan: (Taj. *Ramazon*) ninth month of the Muslim lunar calendar, during which all adult believers (except those sick or on a journey) are expected to fast strictly between dawn and dusk. Since the lunar year is ten days shorter than the solar year, Ramadan may occur at any season over a period. The end of the month is celebrated joyfully with fairs and fireworks.

rescript (Taj. *rivoya, rivoyat-i sharif*): a fatwa, a written judicial ruling issued by a religious scholar in response to a question of shari'a law.

ruboi: (Arab. *rubâ'î*) a short Persian verse form comprising a quatrain rhyming AABA.

Rustam, Isfandiyar and **Siyavush:** mythical heroes of the Iranian national epic. Rustam involuntarily slew the shah's son, Isfandiyar, in revenge for which he was later killed by treachery. Siyavush, a son of the shah Kay Kavus and trained by Rustam, quarreled with his father and fled to the rival kingdom of Turan, where he was murdered; this precipitated the final stage of the age-old war between Turan (representing the steppe nomads of Central and Inner Asia) and Iran (the sedentary population of the Iranian plateau and Central Asia), in which Iran was victorious. There was a "grave" of Siyavush near Bukhara, the center of a cult in early Islamic times (Frye, p. 27). The literary repository of these legends is the *Shâhnâma* of Firdawsi (ca. 940-1020): see Levy's translation, Chapters VI, IX, XIV.

Sa'di, (Shaykh) Abu Abdillah Musharrif ud-din): celebrated Persian poet and moralist (ca. 1213-1292), a native of Shiraz. His father died when he was twelve; later he fled the Mongol invasion for Baghdad, and subsequent travels, so it is said, took him to Central Asia. His best-known works are the ten-chapter *Bustan* ("orchard"), in rhyming couplets, and the eight-chapter *Gulistan* ("rose garden"), in a mixture of prose and verse. Aini wrote a study of Sa'di (Stalinabad, 1942) and edited a selection from the *Bustan* (Stalinabad, 1945); see Rypka, Chapter VIII.

Sadr-i Ziyo: see Sharifjon Makhdum.

sahhof: traditional bookseller and stationer, who would also bind and repair books and manuscripts, make papier-maché pen-cases, reed pens, exercise books, etc.

salom: see *assalomu alaykum*.

sandali: a large stool under which a low charcoal brazier may be placed and over which quilts are draped, extending over the adjacent floor, for people to sit or sleep around in winter (called a *korsi* in Iran).

sang: (1) lit. "stone," a unit of weight, ca. 12-18 lb.; (2) same as *farsakh*..

Sari-mazor(-i Ghijduvon): lit. "at the cemetery," a suburb of Ghijduvon.

sayid: (Arab. *sayyid*) one reputed to be a lineal descendant of the Prophet Muhammad; before a personal name, denotes a member of a subcategory of the aristocratic *khoja* class, q.v.

shariat: (Arab. *sharî'a*) Islamic religious law, observance of which is incumbent upon all Muslims from puberty; based on the Koran, on records of the instructions and practice of the Prophet and his Companions ("Tradition"), and on subsequent concensus by doctors of the law. Infractions are punished with prescribed penalties administered by the kadi.

Sharifjon Makhdum: more formally, Muhammad Sharif "Sadr-i Ziyo" Makhdum (1865-1931), was a pupil of Ahmad Donish (q.v.; see also Chapter 29, esp. notes 4 and 5). He became a noted historian, politician, and patron of scholarship and the arts in Bukhara. His anthology of the Persian poetry of his contemporaries (*Tizkor ul-ash'or*, 1910), composed entirely in verse, mentions Aini with approval. Aini devotes the first two chapters of Part Three of his Reminiscences to an account of his benefactor and his literary soirees; see also Allworth, *Central Asia*, pp. 354-6.

shashmaqom: the cycle of six *maqoms* in Turkestan's classical music. The Tajik and Uzbek *maqom*, like the Persian *dastgâh* and the Indian raga, is a melodic framework with its own scale and repertory of traditional melodies (*savt*), serving as a basis for ornamentation and improvisation by individual instrumentalists and/or vocalists. A performance generally starts simply, in the lower register, gradually reaches a climax (*avj*) of emotion and ornamentation in the higher register, and descends again to close in the lower register. Aini was somewhat of an authority on *shashmaqom*, and wrote an article on the art ("San'atkori buzurg," in *Baroyi adabiyoti sotsialisti* [For a Socialist Literature] 1936, No. 2, pp. 9-12). See also in Allworth, *Central Asia*, Chapter 15 (by Johanna Spector), esp. p. 468ff., and Levin, index.

shir-birinj: a rice dish made with milk and butter and sweetened, served as a main course.

Siyavush: see Rustam

sufa, suffa: a raised platform of packed earth in the courtyard or garden of a house or teahouse, covered with rugs and cushions, where one may relax, chat, drink tea, etc. (Arab. *suffa*, whence also English "sofa").

surah: (Arab.) a chapter of the Muslim scripture, the Koran (Taj. *Qur'on*); with the exception of the *Fotiha* (lit. "opening [surah]"), these are conventionally arranged in order of decreasing length, and numbered 1–114. The shorter ones are often learned by heart and used as prayers.

surnay: a strident double-reed woodwind instrument, related to the medieval European shawm and the modern oboe (cf. the Turkish *zurna* and Indian *shahnay*).

tanga: Bukharan silver coin, equivalent in the 1870s to 20 kopeks, falling to about 15 by the 1890s.

tanob: (Arab. tanâb, "rope") a square measure of land equivalent approx. to one quarter hectare or two-thirds of an acre.

tuman, tumon: district; administrative subdivision of a province (*viloyat, beklik*) under the Bukhara emirate, superseded in Soviet times by the term *raion*.. (From the Turco-Mongol term for "ten thousand [men]," the functional equivalent of a modern military division; probably originally the size of a district where the grazing, produce, taxes, etc. would support 10,000 mounted warriors.)

usto: (Pers. *ostâd*) master; designation and title of an established artisan (potter, carpenter, iron-founder, etc.) with his own shop.

vaqf: property, esp. productive land, endowed in perpetuity for charitable purposes, such as poor relief or the upkeep of a mosque or madrasa; such property was taxed at a more favorable rate than land privately owned (see also *mutavalli*).

yertish, yirtish: (Uz.) a gift of cloth distributed to relatives of the deceased, mourners, and officiating clergy at a funeral.

Zarafshon: (Taj. "gold-strewing," Rus. Zeravshan) a major river of Central Asia; rising between the Zarafshon and the Turkestan ranges of western Tajikistan, it waters the oases of Panjikent, Samarkand and Bukhara, and is lost in the "sands of Oxus"—the Kizil Kum desert—before it reaches the Amu Darya.

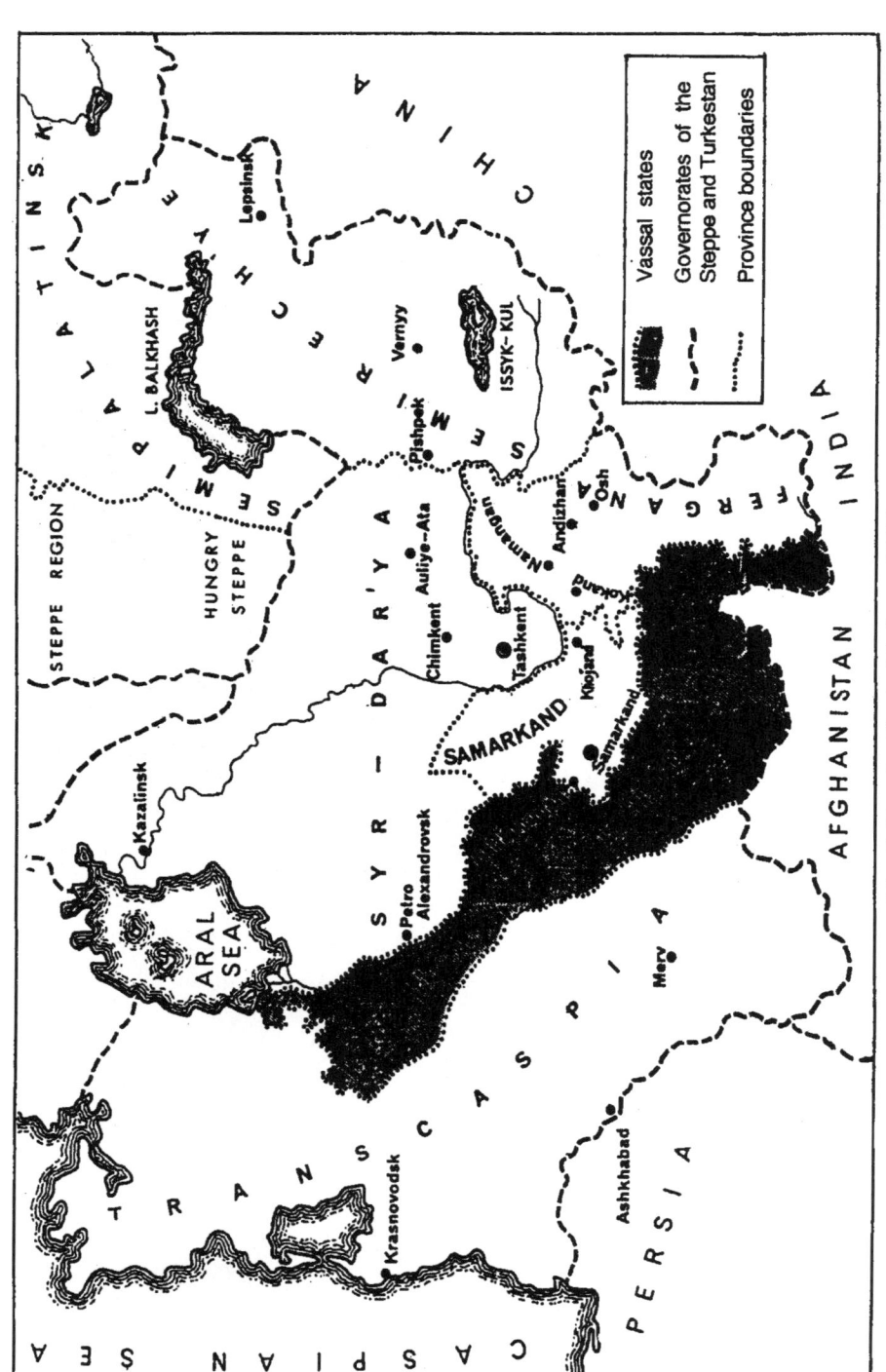

Map 2. Russian Central Asia, ca. 1896

Legend:
- Vassal states
- Governorates of the Steppe and Turkestan
- Province boundaries

SELECTED BIBLIOGRAPHY

This annotated list includes works referred to in the text and apparatus of the translation, with the addition of some books and articles of more general interest. It is divided into three sections: (1) The principal Tajik and Persian editions, Russian translations, and extracts in English, of Aini's *Yoddosht'ho* (Reminiscences); (2) Tajik and Persian editions and extracts in English of *Ahmadi devband* (Appendix I), *Maktabi kūhna* (Appendix II), and other works of Aini mentioned in the text or notes; (3) Works on Aini and the historical and cultural background, chiefly in English.

(1) Editions and Translations of *Reminiscences*

S. Aynī. *Yoddosht'ho* I & II. Stalinabad, 1954. In one volume, Cyrillic script; photographs; 406 pp. Part I (pp. 1-195) is the source of the present translation (checked against the next two editions listed). Also published as Vol. 6 of *Kulliyot* (Collected Works; see below, section 2).

Sadriddin Aynī. *Yoddosht'ho*, 4 parts in 2 vols., Cyrillic. Dushanbe: Adib, 1990.

Sadr al-din 'Ayni. *Yâddâsht'hâ..* Ed. ['Ali Akbar] Sa'idi-Sirjâni. Tehran: Âgâh, 1361/1984. Five volumes (*jeld*) in one, Perso-Arabic script; introduction, Tajik-Persian glossary, notes on Tajik grammar, indexes, photographs; 960 pp. The text comprises the four parts of Aini's Reminiscences plus a 33-page supplement which corresponds to the last half of *Mukhtasari tarjumayi holi khudam* [My Concise Autobiography], as per pp. 59-97 in *Aknun navbati qalamast*, Vol. 1 (see below, section 2).

Sadriddin Aini. *Vospominaniia* [Reminiscences]. Tr. from Tajik [into Russian] by Anna Rozenfel'd; Ed. A. Rozenfel'd, A. A. Semenov, N. A. Kisliakov, A. N. Boldyrev. Moscow, Leningrad: A. N. SSSR, 1960. Four parts in one volume, with an extensive introduction and notes (ca. 140 pp.), photographs; 1088 pp.

—. *Bukhara*: *vospominaniia*. Tr. from Tajik [into Russian] by Sergei Borodin. Moscow: Sovetskii pisatel', 1961. Four parts in one volume, 565 pp. plus 20 pp. afterword and notes by L. Klimovich. Borodin completed the translation of Part One in 1949; Aini did not approve of the cover title "Bukhara," since he had already called the first two books *Dar sahro* ("In the Country"), but he did not live to see the completed work (see Kholida Aini, p. 86).

S. Aini. *Bukhara*. Tr. [from Russian into English] by Robert Daglish. *Soviet Literature* 1953, No. 9, pp. 3-89. A slightly abridged version of Part Two of Reminiscences; this is referred to as *Bukhara* in our footnotes.

Sadriddin Aini. "Bukhara." Tr. [from Russian into English] by Ralph Parker. *Soviet Literature* 1958, No. 8, pp. 100-141. A sequence of eight chapters (16th through 23rd) from Part Four of Reminiscences.

—. *Bukhara*: *Reminiscences*. Tr. [from Russian] into English by Holly Smith. Moscow: Raduga, 1986. An abridged version of Part One titled "In the Village," together with "The Death of the Moneylender" (*Margi Sûdkhûr*), a brief introduction and endnotes.

—. "Kori Nurullo's Suitcase" and "The Prince who was to be a Soothsayer." Tr. by Jiří Bečka and Iris Urwin. *New Orient* (Prague, bimonthly) 1960, No. 4, pp. 18-20; also in Bečka, *Sadriddin Aini*, pp. 57-61 (see section 3). A two-chapter sequence (seventh and eighth) from Part Four of Reminiscences.

"Selections from the Memoirs of Sadriddin Aini." Tr. [from Tajik] by Rachel Lehr and Kim T. Mueser. *Central Asian Survey*, Vol. 3 (1984) No. 4, 89-100. A three-chapter sequence from Part One of Reminiscences (corresponding to Chapters 1-3 above).

(2) Other Works of Aini

S Aynī. *Aknun navbati qalamast*: *osori barguzida dar du jild* (Now it is the Turn of the Pen: anthology in two volumes). Dushanbe: Irfon, 1977 (Vol. 1), 1978 (Vol. 2). Vol. 1 contains Aini's Concise Autobiography (*Mukhtasari tarjumai holi*

khudam, dated 22 April 1949, Samarkand), pp. 11-97, and 114
short articles. Of these, the following are mentioned in the
present work: *Omuzishi man az Maksim Gor'kii* [What I
Learned from Maxim Gorky], p. 308; *Devi haftsar* [The
Seven-Headed Demon], p. 351; *Intikhobot va javonon* [Elec-
tions and Young People], p. 388. Vol. 2 contains the four
novellas *Jallodoni Bukhoro* [The Butchers of Bukhara],
Ahmadi devband (the source of Appendix I), *Maktabi kūhna*
(the source of Appendix II), and *Margi sūdkhūr* [Death of the
Moneylender], and the novel *Yatim* [The Orphan].

Sadriddin Aynī. *Kulliyot* [Collected Works, in Tajik]: 15 volumes,
of which 13 have appeared to date. Stalinabad/Dushanbe,
1958-1981. The following volumes contain works of Aini
cited above. Vol. 1: *Odina*; *Jallodoni Bukhoro*; *Mukhtasari
tarjumai holi khudam*. Vol. 2: the novel *Dokhunda* [The
Highlander]. Vol. 3: the novel *Ghulomon* (Slaves). Vol. 4:
Margi sūdkhūr; Yatim.. Vols. 6-7: *Yoddosht'ho*. Vol. 8: Poems
(with glossary). Vol. 11: *Shaykhurrais Abualī Sino*; *Dar borai
Firdavsī va "shohnoma"-i ū*; *Alisher Navoī*; *Chahor darvesh*.
Vol. 12: *Lughati nimtafsilii tojikī* (Aini's dictionary of literary
Tajik; 535 pp. of entries, compiled 1938). Vol. 13: *Vosifī va
khulosai "Badoye' ul-vaqoye'"* (Vâsefi, with a summary of his
"Marvelous Events").

Sadriddin Aini. "The Death of the Moneylender." See *Bukhara.
Reminiscences* in section (1).

Sadr al-din 'Ayni. *Marg-e sudkhur*. Jahân Book Co., 1995. Text
of the novella in Perso-Arabic script, with notes in Persian and
an English introduction reprinted from Rypka's *History of
Iranian literature* (section 3 below).

S. Aini. "Memoirs of the Past." Tr. [from Russian] by Margaret
Wettlin. *Soviet Literature* 1967, No. 9, pp. 5-20. An abridged
version of *Maktabi kūhna* (see Appendix II).

Sadriddin Aynī. *Namuna-yi adabiyot-i tojik* (Representative
Sample of Tajik Literature). Moscow, 1926. In Arabic script;
almost impossible to find.

—.*Qizbola, yoki Kholida* (The Little Girl, or Kholida). Berlin,
1924. Written in 1922, when Aini was teaching at Samarkand,

this was the first elementary school reader in Uzbek. In thirty lessons it traces the maturing of the heroine (who bears the same name as Aini's daughter) from a spoiled child into a committed and self-confident teacher.

(3) The Historical and Cultural Background

Aini, Kamal S., ed. *The Book of [the] Life of Sadriddin Aini.* General editing by M. S. Asimov. Dushanbe: Irfon, 1978. A lavishly-produced pictorial celebration of the centenary of Aini's birth, compiled by his son; titled also in Russian (*Kniga zhizni S. A.*) and Persian (*Kârnâma-ye S. 'A.*). The main text (26 pp.) is in Russian, with shorter prefaces in English and Persian; 280 illustrations, captioned in Russian. Most of the illustrations in our present volume are taken from this work, by kind permission of Dr. Aini.

Aini, Kholida. *Zhizn' Sadriddina Aini* (*kratkii khronologicheskii ocherk*). Dushanbe: Donish, 1982. A year-by-year account of Aini's life, by his daughter; supplemented by notes to *Yoddosht'ho*, revised from the translation by Rozenfel'd (119 pp.).

Allworth, Edward, Ed. *Central Asia: A Century of Russian Rule.* New York: Columbia University Press, 1967. Reissued as . . . *120 Years of Russian Rule* (1989) and . . . *130 Years of Russian Dominance* (1994) with supplementary chapters. A collection of essays by Allworth and others on the history, society, and culture of Russian and Soviet Central Asia. Maps, illustrations, index; 552 pp. (1994, 650 pp.).

—.*Uzbek Literary Politics.* London: Mouton, 1964. There is no account in English of the evolution of Soviet Tajik literature as such; this carefully-documented study of the sometimes stormy progress of Uzbek literature—in which Aini played a part—fills some of the gap for the earlier period.

Atkin, Muriel. *The Subtlest Battle. Islam in Soviet Tajikistan.* Philadelphia: Foreign Policy Research Institute, 1989. Charts and assesses the course of atheistic education and the campaigns against religion and superstition (not always clearly distinguished by either Muslims or Communists; cf. "Ahmad the Exorcist").

Bacon, Elizabeth E. *Central Asians under Russian Rule: a Study in Culture Change*. Ithaca, London: Cornell University Press, 1980. A cultural anthropological study, with photographs, maps, and—in this, the later (paperback) edition—an introduction by Michael M. J. Fischer. Chapter III, "Traditional Oasis Culture," is the most relevant to this translation.

Bečka, Jiří. *Sadriddin Aini, Father of Modern Tajik Culture*. Naples, 1980 (Istituto Universitario Orientale: Seminario di Studi Asiatici, *Series Minor* V). The only full-length study of Aini in English, with a detailed bibliography and illustrations; 111 pp.

—. "Tajik-Afghan Relations and the Writings of Sadriddin Aini." *Archív Orientální* 46 (1978), pp. 97-111.

—. "Traditional Schools in the Works of Sadriddin Aini and Other Writers of Central Asia." *Archív Orientální* 39 (1971), pp. 284-321 [Part I]; 40 (1972), pp. 130-163 [Part II]. A documented account of the type of *maktab* (Part I) and *madrasa* (Part II) attended by Aini.

Bennigsen, Alexandre, and Chantal Lemercier-quelquejay. *La presse et le mouvement national chez les musulmans de Russie avant 1920*. Paris: Mouton, 1964. A study of many of the newspapers and journals that strongly influenced Aini and other madrasa students around the turn of the century; extensively illustrated; 386pp.

Bennigsen, Alexandre, and S. Enders Wimbush. *Muslim National Communism in the Soviet Union*. University of Chicago Press, 1979 (Publications of the Center for Middle Eastern Studies, No. 11). In the words of a reviewer, "goes far toward explaining the seemingly irrational attraction of many Muslims to Marxism-Leninism, beginning in the old Russian colonial empire in Central Asia." 267 pp.

Christie, Ella R., FRGS. *Through Khiva to Golden Samarkand*. London: Seely, Service & Co., 1925. A woman traveler's account of Central Asia in the 1920s, with a wealth of contemporary photographs.

Ferdowsi [Firdawsi. *The Epic of the Kings: Shah-nama, the National Epic of Persia*. Tr. by R. Levy. University of Chicago Press, 1967 (Persian Heritage Series, No. 2). Reprinted in paperback with a new introduction by Dick Davis, Mazda Publishers, 1996. An abridged one-volume prose translation of the classic verse epic, composed ca. 1000 C.E.; 423 pp.

Frye, Richard N. *Bukhara: The Medieval Achievement.* Norman: University of Oklahoma Press, 1965. Revised edition with photographs (paperback), Mazda Publishers, 1996. A short interpretive history of Central Asian Iranian culture, especially at its zenith under the Samanid dynasty.

Hafiz. *Fifty Poems: Texts and Translations, Collected, Introduced and Annotated by A. J. Arberry.* Cambridge University Press, 1953, 1962.

Hitchins, K. "'Aynī, Sadr-al-dīn." *Encyclopædia Iranica* Vol. III, pp. 144-49. Contains a good annotated bibliography, especially of literary criticism.

Levin, Theodore. *The Hundred Thousand Fools of God. Musical Travels in Central Asia (and Queens, New York).* Indiana University Press, 1996. A wide-ranging field study of the musical (and other) cultures of the Tajiks and their neighbors from pre-Soviet up to modern times; includes a music CD.

Medlin, W. K., W. M. Cave, and F. Carpenter. *Education and Development in Central Asia: A Case Study on Social Change in Uzbekistan.* Leiden: Brill, 1971. Includes a description of the traditional *maktab* and *madrasa* (p. 29ff.) and an account of the Jadid syllabus and methods (p. 48ff.), as well as a detailed study of education in the Soviet period.

Perry, John R. "From Persian to Tajik to Persian: Culture, politics and law reshape a Central Asian language." *NSL.8. Linguistic Studies in the Non-Slavic Languages of the Commonwealth of Independent States and the Baltic Republics,* Ed. Howard I. Aronson. Chicago Linguistics Society, The University of Chicago, 1996. 279-305. A summary of the genesis and evolution of literary Tajik, as engineered by Soviet and post-Soviet planners.

—. "Tajik Literature: Seventy Years is Longer Than the Millennium." *World Literature Today: Literatures of Central Asia* 70/3 (Summer 1996), pp. 571-3. The introductory essay to a presentation of post-independence Tajik prose and poetry in translation (pp. 574-88).

Pourhadi, Ibrahim V. "Soviet Tajik Literature." *Middle East Journal*, Vol. 20, No. 1 (Winter 1966), pp. 104-114. Focuses on the generation of writers after Aini, esp. Ulughzoda and Tursunzoda.

Rakowska-Harmstone, Teresa. *Russia and Nationalism in Central Asia: The Case of Tadzhikistan*. Baltimore and London: Johns Hopkins, 1970. A documented study of the political evolution of the Tajik SSR (a *fait accompli* by the time Aini was involved in Tajik politics).

Rypka, Jan, et al. *History of Iranian Literature*. Ed. Karl Jahn. Dordrecht: Reidel, 1968. A comprehensive reference for all Persian and Tajik literary figures mentioned in this work; there is also a valuable section on Tajik literature by J. Bečka (pp. 483-605).

Sa'di, Abu Abdillah Musharrif ud-din. *The Gulistan or Rose Garden of Sa'di*. Tr. by Edward Rehatsek. London: Allen and Unwin, 1964.

—. *Morals Pointed and Tales Adorned: The Bustan of Sa'di*. Tr. by G. M. Wickens. Toronto: University of Toronto Press, 1974.

Wheeler, Geoffrey. *The Modern History of Soviet Central Asia*. London: Weidenfeld and Nicolson, 1964. Chapter IX, "Culture," is particularly relevant. Maps, illustrations; 272 pp.

Errata

Please correct the following errors before reading:

PAGE	LINE	FOR	READ
2	12 up	*usu`ll-i*	*usūl-i*
11	17	*su`ldkhu`lr*	*sūdkhūr*
	18	*nafuru`lshed*	*nafurūshed*
17	10	Mugal	Mughal
	6, 7 up	*tojikı`l*	*tojikī*
20	10 up	*ku`lhna*	*kūhna*
47	20	Yes	"Yes
141	9 up	*khu`lja*	*khūja*
196	2	sister	daughter
221	1	Appendix I	Appendix II
228	3 up	boys,	boys.
254	9 up	p. 126	p. 115
260	11 up	*khûja*	*khūja*
263	3 up	Becka	Bečka

Bibliotheca Iranica
Literature Series No. 6